Trilogues

The events of the last ten years have shaken the "permissive consensus" that kept the European integration process going for many years. "Output democracy," as based on decisions presumably meeting the needs of the citizens, is no longer enough to obtain public support. Never before has a process-oriented approach to European democracy been more urgent. This book aims to address that urgency by providing an account of the European legislative process that is less conventional and does justice to the democratic potential inherent in trilogues. In particular, this book provides a comprehensive reconstruction of the workings of trilogues, relying on internal documents collected through a series of access-to-documents requests; gives meaning to the legal notion of informality, understood as one of the most defining, although elusive, features of trilogues; and squares the practice of trilogues with the European democratic order of the Treaties, showing that such a practice is compatible with a model of "negotiation democracy."

Giacomo Rugge currently works as Legal Advisor in the Legal Service of the Council of the European Union. He was Senior Research Fellow at the Max Planck Institute in Heidelberg and Contract Agent at the European Parliament's Legal Service. He holds a degree in law from the Catholic University of Milan and a PhD from the Goethe University of Frankfurt am Main. He has published extensively in leading journals on EU law.

Cambridge Studies in European Law and Policy

The focus of this series is European law broadly understood. It aims to publish original monographs in all fields of European law, from work focusing on the institutions of the EU and the Council of Europe to books examining substantive fields of European law as well as examining the relationship between European law and domestic, regional and international legal orders. The series publishes works adopting a wide variety of methods: comparative, doctrinal, theoretical and interdisciplinary approaches to European law are equally welcome, as are works looking at the historical and political facets of the development of European law and policy. The main criterion is excellence, i.e. the publication of innovative work, which will help to shape the legal, political and scholarly debate on the future of European law.

Trilogues

The Democratic Secret of European Legislation

Giacomo Rugge
Council of the European Union

CAMBRIDGE
UNIVERSITY PRESS

CAMBRIDGE
UNIVERSITY PRESS

Shaftesbury Road, Cambridge CB2 8EA, United Kingdom

One Liberty Plaza, 20th Floor, New York, NY 10006, USA

477 Williamstown Road, Port Melbourne, VIC 3207, Australia

314–321, 3rd Floor, Plot 3, Splendor Forum, Jasola District Centre, New Delhi – 110025, India

103 Penang Road, #05-06/07, Visioncrest Commercial, Singapore 238467

Cambridge University Press is part of Cambridge University Press & Assessment, a department of the University of Cambridge.

We share the University's mission to contribute to society through the pursuit of education, learning and research at the highest international levels of excellence.

www.cambridge.org
Information on this title: www.cambridge.org/9781009445207

DOI: 10.1017/9781009445238

When citing this work, please include a reference to the DOI 10.1017/9781009445238
First published 2025

A catalogue record for this publication is available from the British Library.

Library of Congress Cataloging-in-Publication Data
Names: Rugge, Giacomo, author.
Title: Trilogues : the democratic secret of European legislation / Giacomo Rugge, Council of the European Union.
Description: Cambridge, United Kingdom ; New York, NY : Cambridge University Press, 2024. | Series: Cambridge studies in European law and policy | Includes bibliographical references and index.
Identifiers: LCCN 2024007058 (print) | LCCN 2024007059 (ebook) | ISBN 9781009445207 (hardback) | ISBN 9781009445191 (paperback) | ISBN 9781009445238 (ebook)
Subjects: LCSH: Legislation–European Union countries. | Democracy–European Union countries.
Classification: LCC KJE5349 .R84 2024 (print) | LCC KJE5349 (ebook) | DDC 328.4/077–dc23/eng/20240214
LC record available at https://lccn.loc.gov/2024007058
LC ebook record available at https://lccn.loc.gov/2024007059

ISBN 978-1-009-44520-7 Hardback

Contents

Foreword

Giacomo Rugge's book is one of the rare monographs, by both legal and political science scholarship, that is dedicated to trilogues. The book is based upon a dissertation for a PhD in law defended at the Goethe University Frankfurt in April 2021, enriched by the author's first-hand professional experience in the European Parliament's Legal Service.

According to the webpage of the European Parliament dedicated to the Ordinary Legislative Procedure (as in September 2023),

> Trilogues are informal tripartite meetings on legislative proposals between representatives of the Parliament, the Council and the Commission. Their purpose is to reach a provisional agreement on a text acceptable to both the Council and the Parliament. They may be organised at any stage of the legislative procedure and can lead to what are known as "first reading," "early second reading" or "second reading" agreements, or to a "joint text" during conciliation. Trilogue negotiations involve, on the Parliament side, a negotiating team consisting of the Chair or a Vice-Chair of the responsible committee, the rapporteur and at least the shadow rapporteurs from each political group that wishes to participate and, on the Council side, representatives of the Presidency of the Council of Ministers. The Commission is equally present.

Trilogues are a phenomenon of European Union institutional functioning – namely, the legislative procedure – that is rarely discussed in the media and hardly explained in handbooks of EU law. There is some literature about that phenomenon, which is reviewed by Giacomo Rugge in his Introduction, but until now the discussion in legal scholarship was to my view scarce, and jurists do not seem to be much interested in trilogues, probably among others because there is relatively little jurisprudence of the Court of Justice of the European Union on the topic.

Rugge's book fills a number of lacunae in legal and political science scholarship. First, the mapping and description of trilogues is particularly precise, as it is supported and informed by extensive consultations of untapped internal documents, obtained through access-to-document requests. Secondly, Rugge has made an in-depth study of legal and political science literature that helps an understanding of whether the phenomenon is only present in the EU legislative procedure and to what extent it is similar to other practices known in parliamentary systems or in presidential congressional systems. Thirdly, Rugge engages with the discussion about the presumed nondemocratic character of trilogues, due to their lack of transparency.

In his Introduction, Rugge explains the title of his book in reference to Walter Bagehot's *The English Constitution*, originally published in 1867. Unlike Albert Venn Dicey – the most prominent British constitutional lawyer of the end of the nineteenth and beginning of the twentieth century – Bagehot was a journalist (editor of *The Economist*), who had studied law for three years but never liked it. It is to Rugge's credit that he leans on Bagehot, because of the insights of *The English Constitution*, especially in its second edition of 1872. While the legal analysis in Rugge's work is fully accurate, he goes far beyond a black-letter-law presentation and shares with the reader the knowledge he has gained from both his research and his practice. The legal analysis is based on about fifty court cases that are usually known for other reasons – except for the judgment of 29 October 1980, in *Roquette Frères* (C-138/79), where the Court of Justice referred to "the fundamental democratic principle that the people should take part in the exercise of power through the intermediary of a representative assembly." Rugge also presents a clear analysis of the relevant written law instruments, especially of soft law. Those analyses are a particularly useful input for scholarly work on the EU legislative procedure.

Beyond the legal analyses, much of the discussion by Rugge in his book is related to political science, legal theory, and political practice about what a democratic parliamentary system is or should be. In contrast to most publications and comments dedicated to trilogues, the author seeks to demonstrate that the phenomenon not only should not be criticized because of its lack of transparency but, on the contrary, is contributing to the democratic nature of the EU legislative process. Rugge argues convincingly that trilogues are quite similar to negotiations that take place in democratic constitutional regimes in the process of drafting and adopting legislation between the political parties that support the government of the day, or even between the different strands of a political party, such as in Germany or the United States, and that they are particularly fitted to the EU type of executive federalism. He will probably not convince fierce opponents of a practice that is often accused of contributing to the EU's democratic deficit, but his arguments should prompt the reader who has no prejudice to think and adopt a personal position.

For all those reasons I can only recommend a close reading of *Trilogues: The Democratic Secret of European Legislation.*

Jacques Ziller,
Honorary Professor of Comparative Public Law and EU Law
(Paris 1 Panthéon Sorbonne and Università di Pavia)

Series Editors' Preface

This study of trilogues in the process of adoption of legislation by the European Union offers extremely stimulating and valuable insights into a very important and often misunderstood aspect of law-making by the European Union. The great merit of trilogues is that they facilitate speedier decision-making by the European Parliament and the Council while ensuring that the views of a wide range of members of the European Parliament can be heard in the process, and allowing the Commission to act as an honest broker and facilitator.

Giacomo Rugge has considerable practical as well as academic experience of the workings of EU decision-making, and brings this to bear in this extensive discussion. His framing of trilogues as the democratic secret of European legislation whets the appetite for what is to come; this is particularly important given that the European Parliament's powers have increased on every occasion when substantive, non-accession-related, amendments have been made to the treaties governing what is now the European Union.

As Rugge rightly observes, supranational legislation is the product of an intricate cooperation, regulated by law and practice. Each item of legislation is the outcome of a delicate exercise, in which political actors have to reconcile different functions, identities, and interests; compromise and consensus are key elements in this process. The importance of soft law instruments in working out how the political institutions of the Union conduct their interactions is rightly acknowledged by Rugge; the instuitutions are bound to act in accordance with what they have agreed between them as regards trilogues, as well as more generally.

With a sure hand, Rugge guides the reader through the various types of trilogues, pointing out that there is no instrument common to the European Parliament, the Council, and the Commission which actually regulates the internal workings of trilogues: this, he observes, may indicate that the Union's political institutions wish to facilitate the spontaneous emergence of practices and shared actions of logic, and to entrust political actors with a higher level of flexibility in this special context; provided that certain basic conditions are observed, all routes and solutions can be explored, on the basis that searching for compromise inevitably implies some creativity. Allowing time between trilogue meetings ensures that the negotiating teams are accountable to their institutions while protecting other institutions against unpleasant surprises at the end of the negotiations, such as the complete rejection of the provisional agreement reached in the trilogue.

Rugge also pays much attention to the informality of trilogues, arguing that as this produces stability and provides social life with a shared meaning, it is one of the normative phenomena that public lawyers must factor in when studying political institutions. He draws on comparisons with the functioning of the Euro Group and of informal Council meetings, noting the importance of seating arrangements, equal levels of representation, and the political sanctioning of misbehavior. He also makes valuable suggestions for tweaks to improve transparency in the process, which make various types of back-door political spaces less relevant; this would certainly be in line with the intention that trilogues, the Euro Group, and informal Council meetings seek to generate genuine exchanges among the participants, away from the posturing which takes place outside such frameworks. Cooperation generates trust, and trust generates cooperation, while respecting channels of accountability for outcomes in measures finally approved.

Rugge then examines how discussions take place in Germany and in the United States between legislative actors; both are federal states and the European Union has a good number of federal characteristics, without going so far as to be a federation. Seeking consensus and compromise is not limited to EU decision-making. The decreasing importance of formal inter-chamber mechanisms, Rugge argues, is paralleled by the decline in the importance of the conciliation committee mechanism as such in EU lawmaking, as the trilogues become more and more the way of reaching agreement on an acceptable text. He then turns to look at trilogues in the light of European democracy, pointing out the importance of the term "society" and of foundational values of the Union, expressed in Article 2 TEU, and that representational democracy in the EU is not limited to the European Parliament and the Council, but embraces the Commission's function of impartiality for the common weal. Impartiality does not, however, equate to being apolitical. Hence it is unsurprising that the Court of Justice has recognized in numerous judgments the need to accept that the Union's political institutions have a considerable margin of discretion in weighing complex competing interests when deciding how to act. Even bartered compromise may display essential features that make compromise democratically valuable, particularly when reasoning is robust. Rugge's analysis and suggestions offer wise counsel for change, and increase the reader's understanding of European democracy and how decision-making at EU level really works.

Particularly in view of these considerable merits, we are delighted to welcome this book into the Cambridge Studies in European Law and Policy series.

Acknowledgments

This book was developed from my PhD thesis, which I wrote during a year-long, immensely enriching research experience at the Max Planck Institute for Comparative Public Law and International Law in Heidelberg and defended at the Goethe University Frankfurt in April 2021. It is the result of a study that I completed before joining the Council Legal Service in January 2023, and the arguments and opinions expressed are my own. In no case should they be considered or construed as representing an official position of the Council of the European Union or the European Council.

Several people made this book possible. I would like to start by thanking Armin von Bogdandy, director of the Max Planck Institute for Comparative Public Law and International Law and my attentive *Doktorvater*. In addition to guiding my research work on trilogues, he taught me how to integrate a multidisciplinary approach into my everyday intellectual toolkit and to internalize criticism as an essential element of any academic endeavor. To this effect, our regular Tuesday seminars, also known as *Dienstagsrunden*, were a crucial training ground. My growth as a legal scholar owes a huge debt to the discussions that took place in that unique setting, with the active participation of truly inspiring legal minds. As we usually say to highlight its transformative impact, no text before the *Dienstagsrunde* is the same after the *Dienstagsrunde*. I also would like to express my sincerest appreciation to Stefan Kadelbach, professor at the Goethe University, for preparing a second opinion in record time and for participating in my thesis defense.

An important stage in the development of this book was nine months' experience as a member of the Legal Service of the European Parliament in Brussels. Under the expert guidance of María José Martínez Iglesias, then director of that Service, I had the chance to gain first-hand experience of trilogues and to integrate my theoretical understanding with invaluable practical insights. I owe further valuable ideas to the generous and acute suggestions of Francesco Bestagno, professor at the Catholic University of Milan, who has closely followed my professional development since my university years. Any remaining mistakes are my own.

Finally, this book could only become a tangible reality through the support of my friends and family, who stood by me throughout the whole process. Among my friends, I would like to mention Kanad Bagchi, Iris Canor, Federica Cristani, Eugenio Fidelbo, Guillaume Futhazar, Angelo Golia, Juan Camilo Herrera Prieto, Christos Kypraios, Rachele Marconi, José Gustavo Prieto Muñoz, Lucas Sánchez de Miquel, Theodor Shulman, Thomas Sparks, Pedro Alejandro Villareal Lizarraga, Valentina Volpe, and Catharina Ziebritzki. Apart from making my working days more enjoyable, they have been a terrific source of inspiration. With their passion and knowledge, they have crucially contributed to opening my eyes to political, social, and cultural realities that were previously unknown to me. As for my family, I would like to thank my father, Fabio Rugge, as he not only instilled in me a fascination and love for the academic work, but he patiently called me back to scientific rigor whenever I was about to give in to rhetorical complacency or fall prey to oversimplification. I would also like to thank my mother, Sabrina Albano, and my brother, Valerio Rugge, as they have always been a source of constant and unconditional support. My wife, Desirée Schmitt, is the reason for it all. This book is dedicated to her.

Table of Cases

Court of Justice

Case C-57/72 *Westzucker GmbH* v. *Einfuhr- und Vorratsstelle für Zucker* EU:C:1973:30
Case C-138/79 *Roquette* v. *Council* EU:C:1980:249
Case C-136/82 *Klöckner* v. *Commission* EU:C:1983:132
Case C-188/85 *Fediol* v. *Commission* EU:C:1988:400
Case C-34/86 *Council* v. *Parliament* EU:C:1986:291
Case C-204/86 *Greece* v. *Council* EU:C:1988:450
Case C-355/87 *Commission* v. *Council* EU:C:1989:220
Case C-331/88 *The Queen* v. *Ministry of Agriculture, Fisheries and Food, ex parte FEDESA and Others* EU:C:1990:391
Case C-366/88 *France* v. *Commission* EU:C:1990:348
Case C-13/92 *Driessen and Others* v. *Minister van Verkeer en Waterstaat* EU:C:1993:828
Case C-65/93 *Parliament* v. *Council* EU:C:1995:91
Case C-280/93 *Germany* v. *Council* EU:C:1994:367
Case C-417/93 *Parliament* v. *Council* EU:C:1995:127
Case C-25/94 *Commission* v. *Council* EU:C:1996:114
Case C-443/97 *Spain* v. *Commission* EU:C:2000:190
Case C-171/00 P *Libéros* v. *Commission* EU:C:2002:17
Case C-445/00 *Austria* v. *Council* EU:C:2003:445
Case C-344/04 *IATA and ELFAA* EU:C:2006:10
Case C-518/07 *Commission* v. *Germany* EU:C:2010:125
Case C-137/08 *VB Pénzügyi Lízing* EU:C:2010:659
Case C-463/10 P *Deutsche Post and Germany* v. *Commission* EU:C:2011:656
Case C-77/11 *Council* v. *Parliament* EU:C:2013:559
Avis 2/13 *Adhésion de l'Union à la CEDH* EU:C:2014:2454

Case C-409/13 *Council* v. *Commission* EU:C:2015:217
Case C-105/15 P *Mallis and Malli* v. *Commission and ECB* EU:C:2016:702
Case C-394/15 P *Dalli* v. *Commission* EU:C:2016:262
Case C-521/15 *Spain* v. *Council* EU:C:2017:982
Case C-626/15 *Commission* v. *Council (Antarctic MPAs)* EU:C:2018:925
Case C-643/15 *Slovakia* v. *Council* EU:C:2017:631
Case C-16/16 P *Belgium* v. *Commission* EU:C:2018:79
Case C-57/16 P *ClientEarth* v. *Commission* EU:C:2018:660
Case C-73/17 *France* v. *Parliament (Exercice du pouvoir budgétaire)* EU:C:2018:787
Case C-621/18 *Wightman and Others* EU:C:2018:999
Case C-128/17 *Poland* v. *Parliament and Council* EU:C:2019:194
Avis 1/17 *Accord ECG UE-Canada* EU:C:2019:341
Case C-418/18 P *Puppinck and Others* v. *Commission* EU:C:2019:1113
Case C-597/18 P *Council* v. *K. Chrysostomides & Co. and Others* EU:C:2020:1028
Case C-650/18 *Hungary* v. *Parliament* EU:C:2021:426
Case C-24/20 *Commission* v. *Council (Adhésion à l'acte de Genève)* EU:C:2022:911
Case C-157/21 *Poland* v. *Parliament and Council* EU:C:2022:98

Opinions of Advocates General

Case C-27/59 *Campolongo* v. *High Authority* EU:C:1960:21, Opinion of AG Roemer
Case C-34/86 *Council* v. *Parliament* EU:C:1986:221, Opinion of AG Mancini
Case C-439/13 P *Elitaliana* v. *Eulex Kosovo* EU:C:2014:2416, Opinion of AG Jääskinen
Case C-16/16 P *Belgium* v. *Commission* EU:C:2017:959, Opinion of AG Bobek
Case C-73/17 *France* v. *Parliament (Exercice du pouvoir budgétaire)* EU:C:2018:386, Opinion of AG Wathelet
Case C-597/18 P *Council* v. *K. Chrysostomides & Co. and Others* EU:C:2020:390, Opinion of AG Pitruzzella
Case C-551/21 *Commission* v. *Council (Signature d'accords internationaux)* EU:C:2023:579, Opinion of AG Kokott

General Court

Case T-175/96 *Berthu* v. *Commission* EU:T:1997:72
Case T-222/99 *Martinez and Others* v. *Parliament* EU:T:2001:242
Case T-371/03 *Le Voci* v. *Council* EU:T:2005:290

Case T-562/12 *Dalli* v. *Commission* EU:T:2015:270
Case T-17/14 *U4U and Others* v. *Parliament and Council* EU:T:2016:489
Case T-75/14 *USFSPEI* v. *Parliament and Council* EU:T:2017:813
Case T-754/14 *Efler and Others* v. *Commission* EU:T:2017:323
Case T-540/15 *De Capitani* v. *Parliament* EU:T:2018:167
Case T-360/19 *Jalkh* v. *Parliament* EU:T:2019:899
Case T-88/20 *Rivière and Others* v. *Parliament* EU:T:2021:664
Case T-163/21 *De Capitani* v. *Council* EU:T:2023:15
Case T-682/21 *ClientEarth* v. *Council* EU:T:2024:165

German Federal Constitutional

Zustimmungsgesetz (Bundesrat), 25 June 1974, 2 BvF 2, 3/73
Häusliches Arbeitszimmer, 7 December 1999, 2 BvR 301/98
Lippeverband, 5 December 2002, 2 BvL 5/98
Sitzverteilung im Vermittlungsausschuss, 8 December 2004, 2 BvE 3/02
Fünf-Prozent-Sperrklausel EuWG, 9 November 2011, 2 BvC 4/10
Spiegelbildlichkeit von Ausschüssen, 22 September 2015, 2 BvE 1/11
Vermittlungsausschuss (Kompetenzgrenzen), 15 January 2019, 2 BvL 1/09

Italian Constitutional Court

Judgment no. 239/2018, 25 October 2018, IT:COST:2018:239

Supreme Court of the United States

McGrain v. *Daugherty*, 273 U.S. 135 (1927)
INS v. *Chadha*, 462 U.S. 919 (1983)

Introduction

> Perhaps no other field of human knowledge is the source of such abundant and perpetual illusions as the science that deals with political institutions. Political institutions are phenomena the mere description of which is an operation of gigantic proportions. And this not only because the form of the political institutions often disguises and distorts their substance, but also because, being the outcome of a continuous and insurmountable conflict of irreconcilable principles, those institutions always present themselves under multiform and elusive appearances.
>
> Santi Romano[1]

I.1 Framing the Phenomenon

Secret, opaque, messy, stealthy, furtive, clandestine, surreptitious, underhanded. I am not speaking of a private lodge or, worse, of a sinister organization plotting against the prosperity and well-being of a state or a region. I am speaking of the European legislative machinery. These are some of the adjectives that one comes across when reading newspapers and blogs.[2] Academic literature also abounds with fierce criticisms. Many scholars believe that supranational legislation is the outcome of an impenetrable, adrift, detached process, which does not live up to the

[1] Santi Romano, "Lo Stato moderno e la sua crisi," in *Scritti minori* (Giuffrè, 1950), vol. 1, p. 311 (my translation).

[2] Charlemagne, "Giving Faces to 'Faceless Eurocrats,'" *The Economist*, 21 May 2022; Hendrik Wieduwilt, "Viele heimliche Gesetzgeber: Für die Flut der Vorschriften sorgt längst nicht mehr nur der Bundestag," *Frankfurter Allgemeine Zeitung*, 28 November 2018; Jim Yardley, "Has Europe Reached the Breaking Point?," *The New York Times Magazine*, 15 December 2015; Harry Cooper, "Where European Democracy Goes to Die," *Politico*, 12 July 2016.

democratic credentials the European Union supposedly adheres to.[3] And to make matters worse, the legislative process of the EU has also been criticized from inside the European institutional setup. On 12 July 2016, the European Ombudsman, at the end of an own-initiative inquiry into the transparency of the European legislative process, published a decision reproaching the supranational institutions for lacking accessibility and proximity to the citizens and recommending more openness and accountability.[4]

To be sure, one of the main targets of public criticism is an established practice of the European legislature known as "trilogues." By this term, scholars and practitioners refer to informal meetings held behind closed doors by small groups of representatives from the Parliament, the Council, and the Commission. During these meetings, which can take place at different stages of the legislative procedure, participants discuss and negotiate *en petit comité* legislative files, with a view to drawing their political views together. In figurative terms, trilogues have often been likened to a sort of "smoke-filled room," which in US political jargon is a place where a small group of powerful people take secret decisions that do not pay regard to the general interest.

On the face of it, the European legislative process can hardly be imagined without trilogues. These have become standard practice for the adoption of EU legislation. Given the inherent difficulties in attaining policy changes (legislative procedures at EU level have been designed to protect the interests of minorities and to empower veto players),[5] trilogues play the key function of simplifying the legislative environment in which the institutions operate. The diffusion and relevance of these meetings is confirmed by data. The latest activity report of the European Parliament (EP) shows that, during the last parliamentary term (2014–2019), the EP took part in about 1,135 trilogues, which in turn led

[3] See, e.g., Alberto Alemanno and Laurent Pech, "Thinking Justice outside the Docket: A Critical Assessment of the Reform of the EU's Court System" (2017) 54 *Common Market Law Review* 129–175 at 147: "Trilogues are sufficiently problematic from the point of view of transparency and democracy that the [Court of Justice] should have refrained from agreeing to participate in informal negotiations regarding a contentious reform in a format which is hard to reconcile with the democratic requirements flowing from Title II of the TEU."

[4] European Ombudsman, "Decision of the European Ombudsman Setting Out Proposals Following Her Strategic Inquiry OI/8/2015/JAS Concerning the Transparency of Trilogues," OI/8/2015/JAS, 12 July 2016.

[5] George Tsebelis, *Veto Players: How Political Institutions Work* (Sage/Princeton University Press, 2002), p. 248 ff.

to the adoption of 314 legislative files. This is an average of a little under four trilogues per adopted file, similar to the figures of the previous parliamentary term (2009–2014).[6]

Trilogues have also received official recognition outside the supranational institutional milieu. In 2011, for instance, the German Federal Constitutional Court referred to trilogues when striking down a national provision that stipulated a 5 percent threshold in the election of German representatives to the European Parliament. The Court argued that the elimination of the 5 percent threshold was not likely to jeopardize the overall good functioning of the EP, whereas its maintenance was liable to disproportionately violate the rights of the German citizens and political parties to electoral and equal opportunities. As regards trilogues, the Court stated that "[e]ven if parliamentary representatives had to consult with a larger number of political forces in the European Parliament, it is neither explained nor otherwise evident that representation of the European Parliament in the trilogues would no longer be possible, or only at disproportionate expense."[7] In other words, the Court recognized the importance of trilogues for the European legislative process and took the trouble to elucidate that its decision was not liable to place an undue burden on their workings.

Now, trilogues are part and parcel of one of the most influential political systems in the world, which wields power over about 450 million people. After the elections to the Indian Lok Sabha, the elections to the European Parliament are – at least on paper – the "second-biggest democratic show on Earth."[8] They take place in twenty-seven Member States, which in turn participate in the adoption of European legislation through their governmental representatives in the Council and must then implement and enforce such legislation in their respective territories under the shadow of primacy and direct effect. All these circumstances make a rather compelling case for a thorough study of trilogues and their interplay with the democratic order set out in the Treaties. I will shortly explain how this study intends to contribute to the existing literature on the topic. But before that, a brief explanation of the book title is in order.

[6] European Parliament, "Activity Report: Developments and Trends of the Ordinary Legislative Procedure: 1 July 2014–1 July 2019 (8th parliamentary term)," PE 639.611, at 8 f.

[7] German Federal Constitutional Court, Case No. 2 BvC 4/10, 9 November 2011 – *Fünf-Prozent-Sperrklausel EuWG*, para. 114.

[8] "Changing Parliamentary Perspectives," *The Economist*, 18 May 2019.

I.2 Trilogues as the Democratic *Secret* of European Legislation

The most conspicuous word in the title of this book is, probably, "secret." The use of "secret" is readily explained. The word is taken from Walter Bagehot's 1867 book *The English Constitution*. At the very beginning of that book, Bagehot famously argued that "the efficient secret of the English Constitution may be described as the close union, the nearly complete fusion," the "singular approximation" of the executive and legislative powers.[9] I believe this is a suitable description of what happens in trilogues. They indeed realize a singular approximation of the different European legislative institutions. And although this approximation is not as complete as in Bagehot's cabinet, it is strong and structured enough to create "a combining committee," "a *hyphen* which joins, a *buckle* which fastens."[10] It is therefore possible to claim that trilogues are the "efficient secret" of the European constitution: something not expressly regulated in the Treaties, but crucial to the existence and functioning of the European political system. But that is not all.

Next to its most traditional meaning of something "unknown or unrevealed,"[11] the word "secret" as in *The English Constitution* has at least two other meanings. The first meaning captures the nature of the cabinet as "something surprising or extraordinary,"[12] something that commands reverential respect mixed with wonder and that makes the English constitution superior to other constitutions (especially that of the United States).[13] The second meaning encapsulates the successful institutionalization of a constitutional body, a body that has to be kept firmly divided from the Monarchy and from the House of Commons, despite conflating elements of both – "a committee of the legislative body selected to be the executive body."[14] This reading is predicated on the etymology of the

[9] Walter Bagehot, *The English Constitution* (first published 1867, Cambridge University Press, 2004), p. 8 f.

[10] Ibid., p. 10.

[11] Against the notion that Bagehot's *The English Constitution* was unveiling something unknown or unrevealed, Miles Taylor, "Introduction," in Walter Bagehot, *The English Constitution* (Oxford University Press, 2009), p. xxi, arguing that "the idea of cabinet government had already become well-known by the time Bagehot produced his work."

[12] "secret, n., sense I.4.c," in *Oxford English Dictionary* (Oxford University Press, July 2023).

[13] There is no sentence that can better convey this sense of surprise and awe than the following: the cabinet "is a creature, but it has the power of destroying its creators. It is an executive which can annihilate the legislature, as well as an executive which is the nominee of the legislature. It *was* made, but it *can* unmake; it was derivative in its origin, but it is destructive in its action." See Bagehot, *The English Constitution*, p. 11 f.

[14] Ibid., p. 9 f.

word "secret."[15] "Secret" derives from the Latin word "*secretus*," which is the past participle of "*secernere*." By employing this word, Bagehot also indicates a product or device that results from the (inter)action of other elements and grows separate from them. To the extent that the notion of "efficient secret" hints at such a process of individualization, it proves suitable to describe the actual nature of trilogues as separate, autonomous constitutional joint bodies.

Finally, there is another reason why Bagehot's book and his "efficient secret" are so valuable for my work. As Bagehot set about writing his account, he was aware that the existence of a powerful body such as the cabinet might appear at odds with the traditional understanding of the English political system as hinging on the sovereignty of Parliament. In the introduction to the 1872 second edition of the book, he admitted as much by stating: "No doubt it may be beneficial; many seeming anomalies are so, but at first sight it does not look right."[16] As the trajectory of the cabinet in the constitutional history of England teaches us, knowledge and time may indeed turn anomalies into systems. Who would nowadays deny that the "efficient secret" described in *The English Constitution* embodied a key development towards a more accountable constitutional order?

Bagehot argued his case with such prowess, vitality, and authority that, as Kenneth Wheare maintained, what he "said happened soon became accepted as what should happen. His work was descriptive; it became normative."[17] I cannot aspire to such greatness. I will thus content myself with providing some arguments in favor of trilogues and, thereby, a perspective other than the one from which they are usually approached and appraised. At this point the question legitimately arises: why have I not kept the adjective "efficient" in the title? Trilogues are often criticized for epitomizing a typical fixation of the European institutions with efficiency, in defiance of other important legitimacy channels.[18] Since the objective of this book is to argue that trilogues are not just legitimate for

[15] This hypothesis is not unlikely, considering Bagehot's keen interest in physiology. See, e.g., Walter Bagehot, *Physics and Politics* (first published 1873, Cambridge University Press, 2010).

[16] Bagehot, *The English Constitution*, p. 212.

[17] K. C. Wheare, "Walter Bagehot" (1974) 40 *Proceedings of the British Academy* 173–197 at 195.

[18] For an effective presentation of this criticism, Päivi Leino, "The Politics of Efficient Compromise in the Adoption of EU Legal Acts," in Marise Cremona and Claire Kilpatrick (eds.), *EU Legal Acts: Challenges and Transformations* (Oxford University Press, 2018), p. 30.

their (purported) efficiency but also – and above all – for the procedure they instantiate, I have chosen to drop the adjective entirely.

I.3 The State of the Art: A Short Literature Review

There is a significant body of literature concerning the European legislative process and trilogues. Many of those contributions are descriptive in nature and are often written by former or current civil servants with first-hand experience of how legislation comes into existence.[19] Although these contributions may sometimes have limited theoretical and normative ambitions, they serve an important objective: they provide a true-life understanding of how the European legislative process plays out. And such an understanding is a "commodity" that non-insiders might find rather difficult to attain. Other contributions, instead, contain both descriptive and normative parts. After sketching out the relevant legal framework, these works discuss the problematic issues that arise from trilogues and affect the EU legislative process. They often put the emphasis on the lack of transparency and/or on the alteration of the institutional balance in the actual functioning of, and interplay between, the European legislative institutions. This strand of literature

[19] Here is a partial list of contributions written by (former or still in office) EU officials that have enriched my understanding of the European legislative process: Andrea Manzella, "Legislation and Legislative Procedures between the Parliament, the Council and the Commission," in Giuliano Amato, Enzo Moavero-Milanesi, Gianfranco Pasquino, and Lucrezia Reichlin (eds.), *The History of the European Union: Constructing Utopia* (Bloomsbury, 2019), p. 199 ff.; Anita Bultena, "Negotiations in the Ordinary Legislative Procedure: The Perspective of the European Parliament," in Flora A. N. J. Goudappel and Ernst M. H. Hirsch Ballin (eds.), *Democracy and Rule of Law in the European Union: Essays in Honour of Jaap W. de Zwaan* (Asser Press/Springer, 2016), p. 93 ff.; María Gómez-Leal Pérez, "El procedimiento legislativo ordinario en la práctica: los acuerdos en primera lectura" (2015) *Cuadernos Europeos de Deusto* 101–118; Javier Guillem Carrau, "Los trílogos en el procedimiento legislativo de la UE: el *informal law making* en la nueva agenda legislativa europea" (2014) 92–93 *Revista de las Cortes Generales* 45–74; Katrin Huber and Michael Shackleton, "Codecision: A Practitioner's View from Inside the Parliament" (2013) 20 *Journal of European Public Policy* 1040–1055; Enrique Barón Crespo, "El desarrollo de la codecisión como procedimiento legislativo de la UE" (2012) *Cuadernos Europeos de Deusto* 19–47; Una O'Dwyer, "La dynamique historique des relations interinstitutionnelles. Le point de vue d'un praticien sur l'évolution de la procédure de codécision" (2010) *Revue du droit de l'Union européenne* 487–526; Jean-Paul Jacqué, "Une vision réaliste de la procédure de codécision," in Aline De Walsche and Laure Levi (eds.), *Mélanges en hommage à Georges Vandersanden: promenades au sein du droit européen* (Bruylant, 2008), p. 183 ff.; Christian Pennera and Johann Schoo, "La Codécision – Dix ans d'application" (2004) 40 *Cahiers de droit européen* 531–565; Michael Shackleton, "The Politics of Codecision" (2000) 38 *Journal of Common Market Studies* 325–342.

encompasses in-depth doctrinal analyses,[20] including the only two monographs (in German) on the topic to date.[21]

Trilogues have also drawn the attention of political scientists. Their contributions are mainly based on inductive argumentation and hypothesis testing and comprise theoretical and empirical studies, both quantitative and qualitative. Some of these studies focus on the question as to which institution has profited the most from the practice of trilogues;[22] some others provide evidence as regards the impact of trilogues on the interplay and internal organization of the different institutions;[23] and others still investigate the conditions under which trilogues are likely to occur and succeed.[24] Moreover, many studies elaborate on the democratic legitimacy of European legislation;[25] and some have finally begun to use

[20] Jelena von Achenbach, "Transparenz statt Öffentlichkeit und demokratischer Repräsentation: Aktuelle Entwicklungen des Verhandelns in Trilogen im EU-Gesetzgebungsverfahren" (2018) *Die Öffentliche Verwaltung* 1025–1034; Francesca Martines, "I triloghi alla luce dei principi di democrazia, equilibrio istituzionale, efficienza e trasparenza" (2018) *Diritto pubblico comparato ed europeo* 311–348; Deirdre Curtin and Päivi Leino, "In Search of Transparency for EU Law-Making: Trilogues on the Cusp of Dawn" (2017) 54 *Common Market Law Review* 1673–1712; Jelena von Achenbach, "Verfassungswandel durch Selbstorganisation: Triloge im europäischen Gesetzgebungsverfahren" (2016) 55 *Der Staat* 1–39.

[21] Fabian Giersdorf, *Der informelle Trilog. Das Schattengesetzgebungsverfahren der Europäischen Union* (Duncker & Humblot, 2019); Jelena von Achenbach, *Demokratische Gesetzgebung in der Europäischen Union* (Springer, 2014).

[22] Rory Costello and Robert Thomson, "The Distribution of Power among EU Institutions: Who Wins under Codecision and Why?" (2013) 20 *Journal of European Public Policy* 1025–1039; Olivier Costa, Renaud Dehousse, and Aneta Trakalová, "Codecision and 'Early Agreements': An Improvement or a Subversion of the Legislative Procedure?" (2011) *Notre Europe*.

[23] Tom Delreux and Thomas Laloux, "Concluding Early Agreements in the EU: A Double Principal–Agent Analysis of Trilogue Negotiations" (2018) 56 *Journal of Common Market Studies* 300–317; Frank M. Häge and Daniel Naurin, "The Effect of Codecision on Council Decision-Making: Informalization, Politicization and Power" (2013) 20 *Journal of European Public Policy* 953–971; Huber and Shackleton, "Codecision."

[24] Rik de Ruiter and Christine Neuhold, "Why Is Fast Track the Way to Go? Justifications for Early Agreement in the Co-Decision Procedure and Their Effects" (2012) 18 *European Law Journal* 536–554; Christine Reh, Adrienne Héritier, Edoardo Bressanelli, and Christel Koop, "The Informal Politics of Legislation: Explaining Secluded Decision Making in the European Union" (2011) 46 *Comparative Political Studies* 1112–1142; Anne Rasmussen, "Early Conclusion in Bicameral Bargaining: Evidence from the Co-decision Legislative Procedure of the European Union" (2010) 12 *European Union Politics* 41–64.

[25] Santino Lo Bianco, "Informal Decision-Making in the EU: Assessing Trialogues in the Light of Deliberative Democracy," in Jaap de Zwaan, Martijn Lak, Abiola Makinwa, and Piet Willems (eds.), *Governance and Security Issues of the European Union: Challenges Ahead* (Asser Press/Springer, 2016), p. 75 ff.; Christine Reh, "Is Informal Politics Undemocratic?

comparative analysis to offer a "realistic" perspective of the European legislative process.[26] Although not presenting conclusive results, this literature is of crucial importance for those legal scholars who are interested in offering a reliable normative assessment of the complex dynamics at play when the EU institutions legislate. My work has benefitted immensely from these contributions.

As this short review makes clear, though, trilogues are not exactly virgin territory. Hence the question: what is the contribution I intend to make with this book? My contribution is threefold. First, I provide a comprehensive reconstruction of the workings of trilogues, relying on internal documents collected through a series of access-to-documents requests. Secondly, I give a meaning to the legal notion of informality, understood as one of the most defining yet most elusive features of trilogues. Thirdly, I square the practice of trilogues with the European democratic order set out in the Treaties, eventually showing that such a practice is compatible with a model of "negotiation democracy." My work is doctrinal, in that it reconstructs the nature and practice of trilogues by giving systematic meaning to a collection of fragmented legal material. It is theoretical, in that many of the conclusions that I reach have a cognitive dependence on scientific theories.[27] Here, in greater detail, is how I intend to proceed.

I.4 Structure of the Book

This book begins with a chapter devoted to the history of trilogues, tracing their origins and showing why they were created and how they have changed over time. In particular, the chapter highlights that trilogues have characterized the "European way" of adopting legislation since 1975, when the Parliament attained its first competences in budgetary matters and successfully advocated for the establishment of a conciliation procedure. The establishment of this procedure, which bears

Trilogues, Early Agreements and the Selection Model of Representation" (2014) 21 *Journal of European Public Policy* 822–841; Christopher Lord, "The Democratic Legitimacy of codecision" (2013) 20 *Journal of European Public Policy* 1056–1073.

[26] Justin Greenwood and Christilla Roederer-Rynning, "Taming Trilogues: The EU's Law-Making Process in a Comparative Perspective," in Olivier Costa (ed.), *The European Parliament in Times of EU Crisis: Dynamics and Transformations* (Palgrave Macmillan, 2019), p. 121 ff.

[27] Holger Andreas, "Theoretical Terms in Science," in Edward N. Zalta (ed.), *The Stanford Encyclopedia of Philosophy* (2021).

striking similarities to today's trilogues, should be regarded as a "critical juncture." It set a specific trajectory of institutional development and consolidation that has significantly shaped legislative interactions up to the present day, especially in the wake of several Treaty amendments that have increasingly placed the three institutions in a relationship of mutual dependence.

Chapter 2 presents the current institutional framework, with a special focus on the exercise of the legislative function. After a brief presentation of the most relevant institutional principles, notably those of effectiveness, institutional balance, and sincere cooperation, the chapter turns to the Parliament, the Council, and the Commission and explains their prerogatives and internal structures in the light of the concept of "executive federalism." The chapter shows that the legislative institutions of the EU, in line with the principles of autonomy and internal differentiation, allocate important preparatory tasks to different internal bodies – parliamentary committees, Committee of Permanent Representatives (Coreper), and *Groupe des relations interinstitutionnelles* (GRI), and analyzes the role of those bodies in the adoption of legislation.

Chapter 3 reconstructs the functioning of the European legislative process in practice. To this end, it systematizes the main normative instruments that steer and discipline the behavior of European political actors and civil servants, including the (rather bare) Treaty provisions, the relevant interinstitutional agreements, the European Parliament's Rules of Procedure, and the provisions set out in internal documents, especially administrative circulars. This chapter posits that administrative circulars are important for institutional interactions, as they contribute to regularizing the conduct of political actors (regulative component), creating normative expectations (normative component), and generating values, beliefs, and assumptions that actors internalize and accept as part of their "repertoire of unquestioned routines and habits" (cultural-cognitive component).[28] As far as trilogues are concerned, all these provisions testify to the existence of a norms-based, institutionalized environment, congenial to legal analysis.

[28] W. Richard Scott, *Institutions and Organizations: Ideas, Interests, and Identities*, 4th ed. (Sage, 2014), p. 56, who puts forward the following "omnibus conception of institutions: Institutions comprise regulative, normative, and cultural-cognitive elements that, together with associated activities and resources, provide stability and meaning to social life."

Chapter 4 is dedicated to the concept of informality as a crucial legal concept for the understanding of trilogues. It begins from a twofold observation. First, the informal nature of trilogues is stated in black and white in a significant variety of legal instruments. Secondly, the role of legal scholarship is to make sense of that unequivocal characterization. Drawing on institutional theory, this chapter argues that informality is a full-blown concept of EU law, and sets about defining its characteristics. To that end, it compares trilogues with two other informal bodies, namely the Euro Group and the informal Council meetings. The core idea of this chapter is that the codification of informality translates into legal terms the intention of the institutions to protect certain spaces from an excessive penetration of legal normativity. This intention, in turn, is indicative of the desire to preserve those spaces for the emergence of powerful social frameworks where genuine exchanges among actors may occur[29] – exchanges that should be conducive to compromise.

Chapter 5 is comparative in nature and explores the enactment of legislation in two federal polities, namely the United States and Germany. The objective of this chapter is to highlight that while national legislative processes are dominated by party politics, the European legislative process is dominated by trilogues – and, to some extent, trilogues make up for the absence of a genuine party system at EU level. It is within and between political parties and trilogues, respectively, that positions are discussed, coalitions cemented, institutional interdependences managed, political differences solved, and compromises brokered. When legislative files eventually reach the floor of the competent legislative institutions, their fate is – most of the time – already sealed. This chapter aims at highlighting that leaving legislative and inter-chamber coordination to party structures is no more – and possibly less – democratically accountable than entrusting it to trilogues, especially in times of strong partisanship and grand coalitions.

Finally, Chapter 6 examines the main findings about trilogues in light of the democratic principles set out in the Treaties. In particular, the chapter argues that trilogues offer an important democratic contribution because they put compromise at the very heart of the European legislative process. Compromise, through its practice of mutual concessions, is arguably the best means to approximate two constitutional requirements: equality and representation – or, better put, the aspiration to democratic equality in a

[29] Ibid., p. 59.

system of representative institutions. Furthermore, the chapter argues that the existence and prevalence of trilogues reveal the EU's structural closeness to those polities that belong to the model of "negotiation democracy." This model was developed by Gerhard Lehmbruch with special reference to Germany, Austria, and Switzerland. I argue that Lehmbruch's model provides a fruitful basis for comparative research and a solid foundation for understanding the EU.

Three final caveats are in order. First, analyzing trilogues means gaining in-depth insight into how European institutions enact legislation. Following the well-known "inter-supra-infra trichotomy" developed by Joseph Weiler,[30] this book concerns the supranational mode of government. Secondly, and relatedly, the book elaborates neither on the role of national apex courts (be they constitutional or supreme) nor on the role of national parliaments. The main argument for such an exclusion is that although those actors powerfully influence the interpretation and application of EU law, they are not part of the European legislative authority as such and do not directly participate in the adoption of Union legislation. However, national parliaments are key vehicles of democratic legitimacy; the Treaties expressly expect them to hold their governments to account, especially when those governments act as members of the Council (Art. 10 (2)(2) TEU); and the legitimacy of the whole EU is vitally dependent on their active contribution. This analysis therefore considers, whenever relevant, the effects of trilogues on the ability of national parliaments to control their governments. Finally, this book begins from the assumption that the democratic credentials of the European Union are significantly perfectible. However, it also posits that those credentials are not as precarious as is often maintained, and this is also due to the important contribution of trilogues. What follows is an attempt to substantiate that claim and thereby to mitigate the aura of suspicion that lingers around the European legislative machinery.

[30] J. H. H. Weiler, "European Democracy and Its Critics: Polity and System," in *The Constitution of Europe: "Do New Clothes Have an Emperor?" and Other Essays on European Integration* (Cambridge University Press, 1999), p. 274.

1 A Historical Reconstruction

1.1 Introduction

This chapter provides a historical account of when trilogues were conceived and how they have developed and adapted over time. The reason for starting my analysis of trilogues with a historical reconstruction is that *history matters*. History matters because institutions, like other human constructs, do not enjoy unfettered control over their development. As Paul Pierson put it,

> [E]arly steps in a process may fundamentally restrict the range of options available at later ones; identifying the mechanisms that generate such constraints can be a source of powerful insights into the determinants of institutional change; important influences on courses of development may operate only over extended periods of time and are unlikely to be captured by snapshot accounts focused on the choices of particular actors.[1]

Indeed, examining trilogues using this theoretical approach enabled me to appreciate features that I would otherwise have overlooked, dismissed as irrelevant, or not understood.

Unlike many scholarly contributions, which tend to trace the origins of trilogues to the inception of the codecision procedure in 1993,[2] I will show that trilogues have shaped legislative interactions ever since the Parliament gained its first prerogatives in budgetary matters in 1975. This account will lay bare two interdependent and self-reinforcing institutional trends. On the one hand, it will highlight the increasing strengthening of the European

[1] Paul Pierson, *Politics in Time: History, Institutions, and Social Analysis* (Princeton University Press, 2004), p. 133 f.

[2] See, e.g., the widely cited publication by Michael Shackleton, "The Politics of Codecision" (2000) 38 *Journal of Common Market Studies* 325–342.

Parliament as a legislative powerhouse. On the other hand, it will show the concurrent proliferation of trilogues as a tool to ensure legislative cooperation and conflict resolution. In this context, it is not easy to discern if trilogues have been the cause or the effect of these developments – it is something of a chicken-and-egg question. It is, however, safe to maintain that, in terms of power enhancement, the European Parliament has been the ultimate beneficiary of these dynamics.

My reconstruction will take a diachronic approach. It will start with a brief presentation of the state of European institutions at the beginning of the 1970s (Section 1.2). It will then analyze a "critical juncture" of the European constitutional evolution, namely the signing of the 1975 Joint Declaration on Conciliation, which created the first trilogues (Section 1.3). The chapter will then move on to explore the content and meaning of the 1982 Joint Declaration on Budgetary Matters, which transferred the conciliation procedure to the context of budgetary negotiations and gave it the official name of "trilogue" (Section 1.4). It will then show how, under the Single European Act and the cooperation procedure, trilogues came to acquire features and functions of common practice (Section 1.5). It will conclude with an appraisal of the post-Maastricht era (from 1993 until today), which has brought about a veritable revolution in the European legislative culture and has enshrined trilogues as the secret of European legislation (Section 1.6).

1.2 The Starting Point: The Council, the Commission, and a Harmless Assembly

To fully appreciate this historical account, it is important to briefly present the overall political context within which the institutional developments under consideration took place.[3] I would like to begin with an anecdote reported by David Williamson, a long-standing European civil servant and Émile Noël's successor as the Commission's Secretary-General (1987–1997):

> I do recall that soon after I first arrived in the European Commission and was still unversed in the balance of power, we were concerned to move fast on a particular piece of proposed legislation. "Does the European Parliament have to be

[3] Report of the Working Party Examining the Problem of the Enlargement of the Powers of the European Parliament: "Report Vedel," 25 March 1972, at 32 f. On the Vedel Report, Avi Shlaim, "The Vedel Report and the Reform of the European Parliament" (1973) 27 *Parliamentary Affairs* 159–170.

consulted?" I asked my colleagues. "Yes" they said. "Well, what was their opinion?" "I do not know, I shall have to go and see."

After checking, the Parliament's opinion turned out to be negative. As Williamson added, with a hint of sarcasm, this was "consultation differing little from non-consultation."[4]

In the original setup, the Assembly was undeniably weak. It was widely perceived as a fledgling institution, not worthy of being called "Parliament."[5] Margaret Thatcher is even said to have referred to it as a "Mickey-Mouse Parliament."[6] Indeed, the founding Treaties had endowed the Assembly with a mere advisory role. Legislation resulted from an exclusive dialogue between the Commission, as proposer, and the Council, as decider. In the intentions of the Treaties' drafters, however, this was only the starting point for a more ambitious political plan.[7] A window of opportunity for reforming the institutions presented itself at the beginning of the 1970s. Amid a situation of growing international economic instability, due to the end of the Bretton Woods system and the 1973 oil crisis, many key actors began to advocate for a more influential, more assertive, and stronger Europe. These actors maintained that only a united Europe could address the structural problems of an increasingly complex and interdependent world.[8] However, they also believed that the Council, with its "pure, diplomatic style negotiations,"[9] could not provide the supranational power structures with an adequate degree of

[4] David Williamson, "Conciliation Procedure in the European Law-Making Process" (2006) 12 *Journal of Legislative Studies* 1–7 at 2.

[5] It is no coincidence that the Treaty drafters chose to call it "Assembly" rather than "Parliament." The Assembly gave itself the name "European Parliament" through a two-line resolution in 1962. It presented this name change as an innocuous measure to bring clarity to the uncertainties deriving from the fact that "sa dénomination n'[était] pas identique dans les quatre langues officielles de la Communauté" (its name [was] not identical in the four official languages of the Community). See Résolution relative à la dénomination de l'Assemblée, OJ 1962 No. P31/1045.

[6] Charlemagne, "A Powerful Yet Puny Parliament," *The Economist*, 22 October 2020.

[7] See, e.g., Opinion of Advocate General Roemer in Joined Cases C-27/59 and C-39/59 *Campolongo* v. *High Authority* EU:C:1960:21, p. 418, affirming that the "European Treaties . . . constitute no more than the partial achievement of a far-reaching general programme which is characterized by the overriding concept of a more extensive integration of European States."

[8] The Vedel Report stated, in rather dramatic terms, that "[t]he 'crisis of civilization' in the world of today, the protest everywhere against existing societies . . . the emergence of issues, newly discovered or resurrected, which cast doubt on man's very reasons for living – all this would suggest that Europe's mission in the decades ahead is taking on a new dimension." See "Report Vedel," at 21.

[9] Ibid., at 27.

legitimacy, especially with a view to strengthening the stance of the Communities both inside and outside Europe.

In such a context, many turned their attention to the European Parliament. Of course, the EP was following all these developments with keen interest. Since the beginning of the 1960s, it had sought a greater role in the supranational institutional setup. On several occasions, it had justified its claims in the following terms: "[T]he powers of the European Parliament must be extended in order to strengthen the democratic structure of the Community."[10] In other words, the EP was convinced that placing itself at the very heart of the European edifice was crucial to make the supranational polity more democratic. To bolster its case, it structured the discourse about its role around the correspondence between parliamentarization and democratization.[11] This correspondence is ideologically palatable and politically unattackable. It therefore enjoyed great resonance among many prominent politicians and scholars.[12]

In those years, an important thrust towards the parliamentarization of the Communities also came from the "Group Vedel." Created by the Commission in 1971, this working group was composed of fourteen independent experts. Its task was to assess the consequences of strengthening the role of the EP in the Communities' institutional setup. In its final report, the Group affirmed that "[a]s the authors of the Treaties were interested more in the construction than the government of Europe, they did not give the Parliament a very important place among the Community institutions, no doubt thinking that the matter would

10 Résolution sur les compétences et les pouvoirs du Parlement européen, OJ 1963 No. P106/1913 (my translation).

11 By "parliamentarization," EU legal scholarship usually refers to the process by which, since the 1970s, the European Parliament has been progressively expanding its legislative influence. It is worth remembering, however, that the concept pertains to constitutional law history and indicates the process by which, over a span of about 100 years – starting with Great Britain in 1832–1834 and concluding with Germany in 1917 and Spain in 1931 – European constitutional monarchies gradually lost the prerogative to appoint and dismiss ministers at will. See Dieter Nohlen, "Parlamentarisierung," in Dieter Nohlen and Rainer-Olaf Schultze (eds.), *Lexikon der Politikwissenschaft: Theorien, Methoden, Begriffe* (C. H. Beck, 2002), vol. 2, p. 612.

12 See, e.g., David Marquand, *Parliament for Europe* (Jonathan Cape, 1979), p. 87 ff. For a critique of the correspondence between parliamentarization and democratization, Joseph H. H. Weiler, "Parlement européen, integration européenne, démocratie et légitimité," in Jean-Victor Louis and Denis Waelbroeck (eds.), *Le Parlement européen dans l'évolution institutionnelle*, 2nd ed. (Editions de l'Université de Bruxelles, 1989), p. 325 ff.

have to be reviewed when the time came: hence the legal and political ambiguity of the European Parliament's position."[13]

At the time, the report enjoyed a positive reception in the institutions, in the national bureaucracies, and in the academic world.[14] However, as one of its drafters showed, the report had a significant impact beyond the years immediately following its adoption.[15] It not only provided influential guidance for subsequent Treaty reforms,[16] it also contributed in a crucial manner to establishing the principle of parliamentarism as the accepted standard of legitimacy in the supranational political discourse.[17] Following this principle, all the successive amending Treaties expanded the scope of the EP's legislative competences. The parliamentarization of the EU started in the 1970s – with the attribution to the European Parliament of its first prerogatives in budgetary matters and its first direct election in 1979 – and continued in the 1980s, 1990s, and 2000s, through a series of amending Treaties that led to the creation of what now is a full-fledged bicameral system, with the Parliament and the Council as equal branches of the European legislative authority.

It is in that context that the establishment and institutionalization of trilogues took shape. The intensification of the interinstitutional contacts deriving from the growing influence of the EP urged the institutions to devise means to coordinate their interplay. Created shortly after the 1970s Budgetary Treaties, trilogues have been adjusting themselves to the constantly changing institutional environment for almost fifty years. In this sense, they have shown a high adaptive capacity. But before starting with the historical reconstruction of trilogues, a clarification is in order.

[13] "Report Vedel," at 29.

[14] Mary T. W. Robinson, "The Political Implications of the Vedel Report" (1972) 7 *Government and Opposition* 426–433 at 432.

[15] Jochen Abr. Frowein, "Erinnerungen an die 'Groupe Vedel,'" in Ulrich Becker, Armin Hatje, Michael Potacs, and Nina Wunderlich (eds.), *Verfassung und Verwaltung in Europa: Festschrift für Jürgen Schwarze zum 70. Geburtstag* (Nomos, 2014), p. 57 ff.

[16] Julie Garman and Louise Hilditch, "Behind the Scenes: An Examination of the Importance of the Informal Processes at Work in Conciliation" (1998) 5 *Journal of European Public Policy* 271–284 at 272, maintaining that "[c]odecision-making was mooted as early as 1972 in a Parliamentary report entitled 'The Enlargement of the Powers of the European Parliament.'"

[17] Skeptical about the suitability of the parliamentary form of government for the supranational integration process were the two German members of the "Group Vedel," namely Jochen Abr. Frowein and Ulrich Scheuner. See Jochen Abr. Frowein, "Die rechtliche Bedeutung des Verfassungsprinzips der parlamentarischen Demokratie für den europäischen Integrationsprozeß" (1983) 18 *Europarecht* 301–317 at 302.

In what follows, I will speak of a variety of institutional mechanisms and processes that, despite being called by different names ("conciliation," "tripartite dialogue," "tripartite meetings," and so on) and being enshrined in different documents, present the same underlying logic as well as similar and relatively stable features. I will therefore treat those mechanisms as belonging to the same class of phenomena and employ a descriptive paradigm, which I will simply term "trilogue." This paradigm will encompass all mechanisms with a reasonable degree of institutionalization, whereby groups of representatives from the Parliament, the Council, and the Commission gather to discuss legislative matters and reduce the risk of gridlocked political conflicts, with the Commission usually playing the role of mediator. I will thus show that there exists a clear pattern of institutional development, featuring the continuity of this paradigm. In the analysis, all the mechanisms belonging to the trilogue paradigm will be either called by their specific names ("conciliation," "tripartite dialogue," "tripartite meetings," and so on) or generally labeled as "trilogues."

1.3 The 1975 Joint Declaration on Conciliation: The Blueprint of Trilogues

In 1970 and 1975, the Member States signed the so-called Budgetary Treaties, namely the Treaty of Luxembourg and the Treaty of Brussels.[18] These Treaties endowed the European Parliament with competences of budgetary decision-making and oversight.[19] With the former Treaty, the EP acquired the competence to decide on the noncompulsory expenditure of the then European Economic Communities, especially those disbursements not "necessarily resulting from the Treaty or from acts adopted in accordance therewith."[20] With the latter Treaty, the EP was endowed with the competence to reject the draft budget in its entirety.[21]

[18] The Treaty of Luxembourg was signed on 22 April 1970 and became effective on 1 January 1971. See Traité portant modification de certaines dispositions budgétaires des traités instituant les Communautés européennes et du traité instituant un Conseil unique et une Commission unique des Communautés européennes, OJ 1971 No. L2/1. The Treaty of Brussels was signed on 22 July 1975 and became effective on 1 June 1977. See Treaty Amending Certain Financial Provisions of the Treaties Establishing the European Economic Communities and of the Treaty Establishing a Single Council of the European Communities, OJ 1977 No. L359/1.

[19] Richard Crowe, "The European Budgetary Galaxy" (2017) 13 *European Constitutional Law Review* 428–452.

[20] Art. 203(4), (5), and (6) EEC Treaty, as amended by the Treaty of Luxembourg.

[21] Art. 203(8) EEC Treaty, as amended by the Treaty of Brussels.

The European Parliament welcomed these constitutional changes, believing that they embodied an important – albeit long-overdue – step forward in the process of democratizing the European legal order.[22] This new institutional balance was also welcomed by the European Commission, which in those years saw its legislative influence decline, especially due to the 1966 Luxembourg Compromise, and came to consider the European Parliament as a potential ally in its efforts to countervail the overpowering role of the Council in legislative matters. However, the European Parliament was not entirely satisfied. According to a prevalent view among Members of the European Parliament (MEPs), the creation of a new budgetary order not only called for an equal participation of the EP in the adoption of the yearly financial plan,[23] but it also required the EP's contribution to the adoption of any decisions that might impact on the Communities' funds. In particular, the EP felt that the establishment of a real supranational budgetary authority went hand in hand with its involvement not only a posteriori – when deciding the annual budget – but also a priori – when passing legislation with a strong impact on the coffers of the EU.[24] Impeding the European Parliament from having a say over those decisions was tantamount, so the EP's argument went, to "a reduction in parliamentary democracy in the Community and the Member States as a whole."[25]

By employing all political means at its disposal,[26] the EP convinced the Council and the Commission to sit at the negotiating table and discuss how to strengthen its budgetary competences. The three institutions

[22] On various occasions, the EP had claimed the power of the purse for itself. See, e.g., Resolution Embodying the Opinion of the European Parliament on the Communication from the Commission of the European Communities to the Council on the Strengthening of the Budgetary Powers of the European Parliament, OJ 1973 No. C87/8, para. 10, stating that "in all parliamentary democracies, Parliament alone can approve new expenditure, even when the constitution restricts the right to propose such expenditure to the Executive."

[23] Crowe, "The European Budgetary Galaxy," 431.

[24] European Parliament, "Report Drawn Up on Behalf of the Committee on Budgets on the Letter from the Council of the European Communities on the Draft Joint Declaration by Parliament, the Council and the Commission on the Establishment of a Conciliation Procedure," PE 39.488/fin., 17 February 1975, at 10.

[25] Ibid., at 10.

[26] For instance, Georges Spènale, then Chairman of the EP's Committee on Budgets and future President of the EP, tabled a motion of censure against the Commission led by Sicco Mansholt on 16 November 1972 and withdrew it on 12 December 1972, after the Commission committed itself to putting forward, as a matter of priority, proposals relating to the widening of the Parliament's budgetary power. See ibid., at 17.

agreed to find solutions that did not involve amendments to the Treaties.[27] After almost two years of interinstitutional talks, the negotiating teams reached an agreement. Drawing from a short resolution recorded in the minutes of the Council on the date of the signing of the Treaty of Luxembourg (22 April 1970),[28] the institutions decided that the reinforcement of the EP's budgetary competences was to be attained by establishing a conciliation procedure. The details concerning the functioning of this procedure were laid down in an interinstitutional agreement: the Joint Declaration on the Conciliation Procedure of 4 March 1975.[29] The objective of the procedure was to enable the Parliament to participate in the preparation and adoption of decisions "which g[a]ve rise to important expenditure or revenue to be charged or credited to the budget of the European Communities."[30] By so doing, the Joint Declaration acknowledged what many regarded as a "logical connection" between budgetary competences and legislation giving rise to expenditure.[31]

The procedure was to take place in a "'Conciliation Committee' consisting of the Council and representatives of the European Parliament," with the Commission participating in the work and actively assisting the

[27] Ibid., at 19.

[28] Francesco Pasetti-Bombardella, "Le Parlement face au Conseil," in Jean-Victor Louis and Denis Waelbroeck (eds.), *Le Parlement européen dans l'évolution institutionnelle*, 2nd ed. (Editions de l'Université de Bruxelles, 1989), para. 33. For the text of the Council's "Resolution on Community acts having a financial effect and on cooperation between the Council and the Assembly," see European Parliament, "Budgetary Provisions of the Treaties of the European Communities (Derogation Period) – Annexed Documents and Implementing Procedure," December 1972, at 11.

[29] Joint Declaration of the European Parliament, the Council and the Commission, OJ 1975 No. C89/1. For a detailed analysis of the Joint Declaration, John Forman, "The Conciliation Procedure" (1979) 16 *Common Market Law Review* 77–108. This procedure is not to be confused with the conciliation procedure provided for by Art. 294(10) TFEU, within the framework of the Ordinary Legislative Procedure. The English term "conciliation" is somehow misleading because it applies to both procedures. Other European languages employ different terms: *concertation* and *conciliation* (French), *Konzertierung* and *Vermittlung* (German), *concertazione* and *conciliazione* (Italian).

[30] The establishment of the conciliation procedure went well beyond what was strictly required by the Treaties. See Forman, "The Conciliation Procedure," 81. The Council agreed to sign the Joint Declaration because the Parliament had suggested that, should its requests remain unfulfilled, it would have used its newly acquired budgetary prerogatives to prevent the implementation of legislation with budgetary consequences. See Richard Corbett, Francis Jacobs, and Darren Neville, *The European Parliament*, 9th ed. (John Harper, 2016), p. 306.

[31] "Report on European Institutions: Presented by the Committee of Three to the European Council (October 1979)," at 58.

other institutions. The procedure could be started under specific conditions, namely that the draft piece of legislation had general application and appreciable financial implications and that its adoption was not required by acts already in existence. The Conciliation Committee could be convened upon request of either the Parliament or the Council and only to the extent that "the Council intended to depart from the Opinion adopted by the European Parliament." When the positions of the two institutions were "sufficiently close, the European Parliament may give a new Opinion, after which the Council [had to] take definitive action." This meant that the Council remained formally free, when adopting the act in question, to depart from the outcome of the negotiations. As a former President of the European Parliament put it, the procedure was "more like an appeal for clemency in which the MEPs ask[ed] the national Ministers in Council to think again." But, as he also conceded, it occasionally proved effective in enabling the EP to influence specific pieces of legislation.[32]

The conciliation procedure was the first genuine manifestation of the trilogue paradigm.[33] It provided for the creation of a three-party body in charge of facilitating the attainment of agreements between the Parliament and the Council in case of political differences. The Commission participated in the meetings to help the other two institutions settle their divergences. The Council took part in the Conciliation Committee with a delegation led by the incumbent Presidency and comprising all its members.[34] The Parliament participated with a delegation consisting of nine MEPs reflecting the political composition of the Parliament and including the chairs and rapporteurs of the committees concerned.[35]

[32] Lord Plumb, "Building a Democratic Community: The Role of the European Parliament" (1989) 45 *The World Today* 112–117 at 114.

[33] It is worth highlighting that the Joint Declaration on the Conciliation Procedure is still in force. There is at least one case in which a conciliation procedure might be launched, notably when the Council intends to adopt implementing measures of the Act concerning the election of the representatives of Parliament by direct universal suffrage. See Act Concerning the Election of the Representatives of the Assembly by Direct Universal Suffrage, OJ 1976 No. L278/5, Art. 13. See also Forman, "The Conciliation Procedure," 98 f.

[34] Forman, "The Conciliation Procedure," 87 f.

[35] See Art. 22A of the EP Rules of Procedure in force at that time, as modified by Resolution on the addition to the Rules of Procedure of the European Parliament of a new Rule 22A on the conciliation procedure embodied in the Joint Declaration of the European Parliament, the Council and the Commission of 4 March 1975, OJ 1977 No. C6/82.

In its first years of application, the conciliation procedure was launched seldom, despite all the debates and political ferment that had preceded its inception.[36] As affirmed by the "Three Wise Men Report" of 1979,[37] this situation was due to the existence of conflicting opinions among the institutions as to the real purpose and implications of conciliation.[38] The procedure could indeed have a dual effect. On the one hand, it could promote closer and smoother cooperation among institutions. On the other hand, it could serve more dubious purposes, such as the alteration of the institutional balance set out in the Treaties. The Council was especially wary of the possibility that the Parliament might exploit the conciliation procedure to attain more influence in the legislative realm. Many specialists of European institutional affairs believed that "in the eyes of the EP, the broad aim of [conciliation] was to gradually place Parliament on an equal footing with the Council not only in budgetary matters, but also in the legislative process as a whole."[39]

At the end of 1981, interested in strengthening the legislative influence of the EP and in finding a common solution to the poor implementation of the conciliation procedure, the Commission presented its fellow institutions with a new draft Joint Declaration. The Commission's draft envisaged an important novelty: the extension of the conciliation procedure to *all important* Community acts.[40] In response to this initiative, the EP adopted an amended text of the Commission's draft, in which it expressed its interest in devising a real legislative cooperation with the Council by means of a new Joint Declaration.[41] Even the European Council, in the

[36] At the end of 1978, the institutions had initiated only four conciliations, although the Commission had identified more than twenty other cases where the procedure might have applied. See Forman, "The Conciliation Procedure," 90.

[37] On the initiative of Giscard d'Estaing, then President of the French Republic, the European Council, in the Brussels Summit of 4 and 5 December 1978, decided to set up a working party, also known as Committee of the Three Wise Men, and gave it the task to formulate suggestions as to how to ameliorate the working of the institutions. Part of the "Three Wise Men Report" was dedicated to the conciliation procedure. See "Report on European Institutions," at 84 ff. For an insider perspective on the report, Edmund Dell, "The Report of the Three Wise Men" (1993) 2 *Contemporary European History* 35–68.

[38] "Report on European Institutions," at 84.

[39] Emilio Wille, "The Conciliation Procedure and the European Parliament's Pursuit of Legislation Power" (1984) 49 *Il Politico* 489–500.

[40] European Commission, "Communication to the Council and the European Parliament on the Conciliation Procedure," COM(81)816 final, at 2.

[41] Resolution on the Draft Second Joint Declaration of the European Parliament, the Council and the Commission on the Conciliation Procedure, OJ 1984 No. C10/31. See also Wille, "The Conciliation Procedure," 491.

famous Stuttgart "Solemn Declaration on European Union" of June 1983, declared itself willing to "enter into talks with the European Parliament and the Commission with the aim, within the framework of a new agreement, of improving and extending the scope of the conciliation procedure."[42] Political will across the institutions seemed to converge.

As it turned out, a formal amendment of the Joint Declaration proved impossible. Despite various attempts to reach an agreement in the Council, the Danish delegation stubbornly opposed any changes to the status quo. As a stopgap solution, the Council agreed to apply the 1975 Joint Declaration in a more flexible way. In practical terms, the Council acceded to applying conciliation to cases that, strictly speaking, did not fall within the concept of legislation with "appreciable financial implications."[43] Such a solution prevented interinstitutional conflicts from coming to a head, but it clearly fell short of placating the Parliament's quest for a greater role in the adoption of European legislation. More confrontations were to come.

That said, it is possible to affirm that the signing of the 1975 Joint Declaration marked the genesis of trilogues.[44] In fact, the success of the conciliation procedure was conditional upon its ability to create a genuine trilogue among the legislative institutions. Such a belief was stated in unequivocal terms by the Commission in a 1981 communication: "[I]f the conciliation procedure is to achieve its objective, a genuine 'trialogue' must be established during which the Commission will have to make every effort to foster political understanding between the three institutions."[45] In other words, the establishment of the conciliation procedure should be regarded as a "critical juncture" in the development of the supranational legislative authority. It gave birth to a paradigm that, as will emerge in the remainder of this chapter, has had a long-lasting institutional legacy, becoming the secret of the European legislative process.[46] For instance, the conciliation procedure – and the trilogue embodied therein – represented the blueprint for the negotiation and

[42] European Commission, "Solemn Declaration on European Union," Bulletin of the European Communities No. 6/1983, at 26.

[43] Corbett, Jacobs, and Neville, *The European Parliament*, p. 307.

[44] Fiona Hayes-Renshaw and Helen Wallace, *The Council of Ministers*, 2nd ed. (Palgrave Macmillan, 2006), p. 216.

[45] European Commission, "Les relations entre les institutions de la Communauté," COM(81) 581 final, 7 October 1981, at 12 (my translation).

[46] Pierson, *Politics in Time*, p. 135: "Junctures are 'critical' because they place institutional arrangements on paths or trajectories, which are then very difficult to alter."

drafting of the 1982 Joint Declaration on the Budgetary Procedure.[47] And it is not by chance that the term "trilogue" made its first official appearance in the French version of that declaration. Let us take a closer look.

1.4 The 1982 Joint Declaration on Budgetary Matters: Let's Call It "Trilogue"

As already mentioned, the budgetary Treaties of 1970 and 1975 introduced into EU primary law the distinction between compulsory and noncompulsory expenditure. Under those Treaties, the Council gained final say over the compulsory expenditure, whereas the Parliament gained final say over the noncompulsory expenditure. However, this soon proved to be a poor choice in terms of constitutional design.[48] By establishing a two-pronged budgetary authority – with Parliament and Council exclusively responsible for specific types of expenditure – the Budgetary Treaties did nothing but render the adoption of the annual budget a battlefield for power struggles between the two institutions.[49] Especially after 1975, these struggles occurred almost yearly and "each year with similar, if not identical, features."[50] They essentially concerned the distinction between noncompulsory and compulsory expenditure and therefore the delimitation between the Parliament's and the Council's budgetary competences.

Indeed, the adoption of the EEC's budget was – and still is – fraught with problems,[51] such as finding common ground between the Commission and the required majorities in the Council and in the EP; reaching a compromise within an extremely tight time limit of about three months; and to do all this while complying with a highly intricate and technical body of EU law – the Financial Regulation and the Multiannual Financial Framework, among others.[52] Advocate General Mancini went as far as to maintain that "the machinery established by

47 Joint Declaration by the European Parliament, the Council and the Commission on Various Measures to Improve the Budgetary Procedure, OJ 1982 No. C194/1.

48 Pieter Dankert, "The Joint Declaration by the Community Institutions of 30 June 1982 on the Community Budgetary Procedure" (1983) 20 *Common Market Law Review* 701–712.

49 William Nicoll, "EEC Budgetary Strains and Constraints" (1987) 64 *International Affairs* 27–42 at 28.

50 Opinion of Advocate General Mancini in Case C-34/86 *Council* v. *Parliament* EU:C:1986:221, para. 2.

51 See, e.g., Case C-77/11 *Council* v. *Parliament* EU:C:2013:559.

52 Nicoll, "EEC Budgetary Strains and Constraints," 30.

the Treaty for preparing and adopting the budget was virtually impossible to operate."[53] It is against this backdrop that the 1982 Joint Declaration on Budgetary Procedure and the "Tripartite Dialogue" came into being. Here are the facts.

In 1981, the Parliament and the Council proved unable, despite all efforts, to strike a compromise on the noncompulsory expenditure. This inability left the Communities without a financial plan for 1982. Feeling that such an impasse was primarily due to the noncooperative attitude of its fellow institutions, the Council initiated legal proceedings before the Court of Justice.[54] In a last bid to reach an agreement, the Presidents of the Parliament and the Council began joint discussions and, as from the beginning of March 1982, they were joined by the President of the Commission. The negotiations eventually led, in June 1982, to the signing of the Joint Declaration on the Community Budgetary Procedure and the withdrawal of the Council's lawsuits against the Parliament and the Commission.[55]

The 1982 Joint Declaration established an interinstitutional coordination mechanism called "Tripartite Dialogue."[56] The French version of that declaration employed the term "trilogue."[57] This was the first time that the term was used in a legal instrument. The "Tripartite Dialogue" or "trilogue" provided that whenever either the Parliament or the Council could not accept the expenditure classification put forward by the Commission in its draft budget, the matter had to be referred to a meeting of the Presidents of the Parliament, the Council, and the Commission. After this meeting, the President of the Commission, in its

[53] Opinion of Advocate General Mancini in Case C-34/86 *Council* v. *Parliament*, para. 2. See also Jean-Paul Jacqué, "La pratique des institutions communautaires et le développement de la structure institutionnelle communautaire," in Roland Bieber and Georg Ress (eds.), *Die Dynamik des Europäischen Gemeinschaftsrechts* (Nomos, 1987), p. 378.

[54] Case C-72/82 *Council* v. *Parliament* and Case C-73/82 *Council* v. *Commission*.

[55] Jean-Louis Dewost and Marc Lepoivre, "La déclaration commune du Parlement européen, du Conseil et de la Commission relative à différentes mesures visant à assurer un meilleur déroulement de la procédure budgétaire, signée le 30 juin 1982" (1982) 25 *Revue du Marché Commun* 514–525 at 515.

[56] Florian von Alemann, *Die Handlungsform der interinstitutionellen Vereinbarung* (Springer, 2006), p. 328.

[57] The German version used the term *Dreiseitendialog*, whereas the Italian version used the term *dialogo a tre* (see para. II.5. of the 1982 Joint Declaration). However, many actors preferred to use the French term *trilogue* also when writing or speaking in other languages. See, e.g., the then Council's Director-General Nicoll, "EEC Budgetary Strains and Constraints," 32.

capacity as chair of the "Tripartite Dialogue," had to report to the Parliament and the Council. Following the political priorities laid out by the three Presidents, the budgetary authority was called upon to work out the details of the draft budget, thus ensuring its timely adoption.

As shown by this description, there exists an evident resemblance – if not a seamless continuity – between the 1975 Joint Declaration on Conciliation and the 1982 Joint Declaration on Budgetary Matters, in that they both envisaged trilogues among representatives from the three institutions to facilitate legislative coordination and political disputes resolution. This resemblance was so readily apparent that, after the adoption of the 1982 Joint Declaration, political and judicial actors kept on using the term "conciliation" to refer to the recently established "Tripartite Dialogue."[58] These circumstances are evidence of an incipient consolidation of the trilogue paradigm. Such consolidation was further bolstered by the Court of Justice a few years later, in its 1986 landmark judgment in *Council* v. *Parliament*.

In that judgment, which arose from an action for annulment against the 1986 budget and concerned the interplay between the disputing institutions in the exercise of the budgetary power, the Court affirmed that "it may not intervene in the process of negotiation between the Council and the Parliament which must result ... in the establishment of the general budget of the Communities." It also added that "it [did] not have to consider to what extent the Council's or the Parliament's attitude during the entire negotiations on the budget prevented them from arriving at an agreement," concluding that "problems regarding the delimitation of ... expenditure ... [were] the subject of an interinstitutional conciliation procedure set up by the [1982] Joint declaration ... and that they [were] capable of being resolved in that context."[59]

These excerpts not only show that the Court acknowledged the legal relevance of the "Tripartite Dialogue" set out in the 1982 Joint

[58] See, e.g., European Parliament, "Report Drawn Up on Behalf of the Committee on Budgets on the Joint Declaration by the European Parliament, the Council and the Commission on Various Measures to Improve the Budgetary Procedure," PE 79.445/fin., 6 July 1982, at 7. In legal scholarship, Nigel G. Foster, "The New Conciliation Committee under Article 189b EC" (1994) 19 *European Law Review* 185–194 at 189, who, while predicting little relevance of conciliation after the establishment of the codecision procedure by the Treaty of Maastricht, added: "with the exception of use in the budgetary procedure." This provides further evidence of the fact that, in the eyes of political actors and legal scholars, "conciliation" and "Tripartite Dialogue" were practically the same thing.

[59] Case C-34/86 *Council* v. *Parliament*, paras. 42, 45, and 50, respectively.

Declaration.[60] They also indicate that the Court saw the "Tripartite Dialogue" as the most appropriate context to sort out budgetary conflicts and as a stage beyond the reach of its scrutiny.[61] Arguably, such case law further motivated the institutions to stick to the "Tripartite Dialogue," improving, refining, and crystallizing its functioning.[62] So much so that they concluded four other interinstitutional agreements on budgetary matters in 1999,[63] 2006,[64] 2013,[65] and 2020[66] – all of them based on the trilogue paradigm. But these events had an impact beyond the field of budgetary cooperation as well. In the second half of the 1980s, the Parliament, the Council, and the Commission employed the trilogue paradigm with increasing regularity and consistency, to the point that, at the beginning of the 1990s, it was officially labeled a "general practice." In this regard, a crucial intersection was the adoption of the Single European Act and the introduction of a new legislative procedure: the cooperation procedure.

[60] Jacqué, "La pratique des institutions communautaires," p. 396.

[61] The judgment eventually pushed the institutions to resume trilogues and led to the adoption of the budget only one week after its delivery. See European Commission, "Resumption of 1986 Budget Procedure," Bulletin of the European Communities No. 7–8/1986, at 10. On this judgment, Roland Bieber, "Rechtswirkung und gerichtliche Kontrolle des EG-Haushalts. Zugleich Anmerkung zur Entscheidung des EuGH vom 3. Juli 1986, Rs. 34/86 (Rat gegen Europäisches Parlament)" (1986) 101 *Deutsches Verwaltungsblatt* 961–968 at 966. For a critical appraisal, Francesco Pasetti-Bombardella, "La controversia fra il Consiglio e il Parlamento europeo sul bilancio generale 1986" (1986) *Rivista di diritto europeo* 207–216.

[62] About two years after the 1986 judgment, the ECJ, in another case relating to the Communities budget, brought about a partial *revirement* of its case law. After confirming its findings in *Council* v. *Parliament*, the Court added that the Treaties empowered it to verify whether "in the context of inter-institutional cooperation the institutions . . . ignore the rules of law [or] exercise their discretionary power in a manifestly wrong or arbitrary way." See Case C-204/86 *Greece* v. *Council* EU:C:1988:450, para. 17.

[63] Interinstitutional Agreement of 6 May 1999 between the European Parliament, the Council, and the Commission on Budgetary Discipline and Improvement of the Budgetary Procedure, OJ 1999 No. C172/1.

[64] Interinstitutional Agreement between the European Parliament, the Council and the Commission on Budgetary Discipline and Sound Financial Management, OJ 2006 No. C139/1.

[65] Interinstitutional Agreement of 2 December 2013 between the European Parliament, the Council, and the Commission on Budgetary Discipline, on Cooperation in Budgetary Matters and on Sound Financial Management, OJ 2013 No. C373/1.

[66] Interinstitutional Agreement of 16 December 2020 between the European Parliament, the Council of the European Union, and the European Commission on Budgetary Discipline, on Cooperation in Budgetary Matters and on Sound Financial Management, as well as on New Own Resources, including a Roadmap towards the Introduction of New Own Resources, OJ 2020 No. L433I/28.

1.5 The Single European Act: Trilogues Become a General Practice

The Single European Act (SEA) was signed in February 1986 and became effective in July 1987. Among its objectives was the extension of the EP's legislative prerogatives. To this end, the Treaty envisaged the following innovations: the establishment of two new legislative procedures called "cooperation procedure" and "assent procedure," respectively, as well as the extension of the already existing consultation procedure to other policy fields.[67] As the name suggests, the assent procedure required the Council to obtain the Parliament's "yea" before certain legislation could be passed – the assent required an absolute majority of MEPs' votes. The cooperation procedure, instead, provided for two readings of the Commission's draft legislative act and entitled the EP to reject the Council's first reading common position; such an objection by the EP could then be overruled only by a unanimous vote in the Council.[68]

These changes gave relevant political leverage to the Parliament, which could make it arduous for the Council to pass unwelcome legislation. However, these new procedures, especially the cooperation procedure, were often criticized for being too messy and for putting at risk the ability of the institutions to decide. In some remarks made in March 1986 during a conference on the Single European Act in Brussels, Pierre Pescatore, former judge at the Court of Justice of the European Communities, gave his pointed appraisal of the cooperation procedure:

> [T]he implementation of the [cooperation procedure], with its numerous hitches and time limits, will considerably slow down the already difficult and excessively long decision-making process; ... it is clear that if there are divergences between the different parties taking part in the procedure, the result will be non-decision i.e. a blocking of the system. This is obvious from article 149, par. 2, lett. f.[69]

In the light of this widely held concern, and since the Intergovernmental Conference had decided not to codify "conciliation" into the Treaties,[70]

67 For a detailed account of the Single European Act's negotiating history, Jean De Ruyt, *L'Acte unique européen: commentaire* (Editions de l'Université de Bruxelles, 1987), p. 67 ff.

68 The cooperation procedure applied primarily to the establishment of the internal market, but also in the fields of social policy, economic and social cohesion as well as research and technological development.

69 Agence Europe, "Europe documents n. 1397," 27 March 1986. See also Pierre Pescatore, "Some Critical Remarks on the 'Single European Act'" (1987) 24 *Common Market Law Review* 9–18.

70 De Ruyt, *L'Acte unique européen*, p. 121. See also Claus-Dieter Ehlermann, "Die Einheitliche Europäische Akte: Die Reform der Organe" (1986) 9 *Integration* 101–107 at 106. Ehlermann,

EU institutions and legal scholars began to discuss the appropriateness of applying the trilogue paradigm to the newly established procedures.[71] Especially the European Parliament, which had declared itself unhappy with the outcome of the SEA's negotiations,[72] stated that after the entry into force of the amending Treaty on 1 July 1987, it would have "exploit[ed] to the very limit the possibilities offered by [it]," including the application of conciliation in all the new policy areas within the purview of the Communities. It is indeed in this period that the EP, regardless of the procedure to be applied, began to introduce in its legislative resolutions the following standard formula: "[T]he European Parliament ... reserves the right to open the conciliation procedure should the Council propose to depart from this opinion."

In the following years, the EP adopted other resolutions concerning the application and workings of conciliation. For instance, it reiterated "its request that the conciliation procedure be extended to all major areas of legislation in order to allow a dialogue in the search for compromises between the two arms of the legislative authority."[73] Furthermore, it called upon the Council and the Commission to "reach agreement with Parliament on a second Joint Declaration on the conciliation procedure," with a view to extending its scope to "all major Community legislation including those areas subject to the cooperation procedure."[74] In its relentless pursuit of legislative influence, the EP finally claimed the prerogative "to demand the opening of the conciliation procedure with the Council if the Council wishe[d] to provide for a committee procedure [that is, comitology] in a legal act."[75]

The Council and the Commission never took a conclusive position about these requests.[76] After the adoption of the SEA, they were probably

who acted as the Commission's legal advisor in the negotiations on the Single European Act, reported that the Parliament, too, showed little interest in formalizing the trilateral meetings in the Treaties.

71 Roland Bieber, "Das Gesetzgebungsverfahren der Zusammenarbeit gemäß Art. 149 EWGV" (1989) 22 *Neue Juristische Wochenschrift* 1395–1402 at 1400.

72 Resolution on the Position of the European Parliament on the Single Act Approved by the Intergovernmental Conference on 16 and 17 December 1985, OJ 1986 No. C36/144.

73 Resolution on the Results Obtained from Implementation of the Single Act, OJ 1988 No. C309/93.

74 Resolution on the Conciliation Procedure, OJ 1989 No. C69/151. See also Kieran St. Clair Bradley, "Legal Developments in the European Parliament" (1989) 9 *Yearbook of European Law* 235–270 at 247.

75 Resolution Closing the Procedure for Consultation of the European Parliament on the Proposal for a Regulation Laying Down the Procedures for the Exercise of Implementing Powers Conferred on the Commission, OJ 1986 No. C297/94.

76 Foster, "The New Conciliation Committee," 190.

reluctant to conclude new interinstitutional agreements with the EP or to endorse its requests officially, lest the Parliament might gain further legislative influence. They preferred, instead, to involve the EP on a case-by-case basis, when reasons of political expediency so suggested. But the Parliament was not happy with such an arrangement. Eager to convey its sense of frustration and disappointment, it voted on a resolution to complain that conciliation had "so far proved of limited value." But it also affirmed that the procedure retained "the potential for developing into a valuable means of reconciling divergences of view." The Council and the Commission were therefore asked to cooperate "to make [conciliation] more effective and also to ensure its smooth combination with the cooperation procedure."[77]

Although I do not doubt that the resolution was motivated by a genuine perception of being excluded from legislative matters, I would take the Parliament's complaints with a pinch of salt. Different sources reveal that, in those years, European legislative institutions were making fair use of trilogues, and that the Parliament was involved in a fruitful dialogue with its counterparts, sometimes even beyond what the Treaties allowed.[78] For instance, the Parliament, the Council, and the Commission launched conciliation when discussing the adoption of a regulation amending the European Regional Development Fund.[79] They also relied on the procedure when drafting the Community Charter of the Fundamental Social Rights of Workers, adopted on 9 December 1989 by a declaration of all Member States (except for the United Kingdom).[80] Moreover, in April 1989, a parliamentary delegation led by its Vice-President gathered with the Council and the Commission to reach a compromise on two regulations concerning own resources collection.[81] Finally, trilogues played a pivotal role when, after the German reunification on 3 October 1990, the European institutions were to ensure the "rapid passage" of emergency interim measures to

[77] Resolution on the Conciliation Procedure.

[78] Lord Plumb, "Building a Democratic Community," 114.

[79] Resolution on the Results of the Conciliation with the Council on the Proposal for a Regulation Amending Regulation (EEC) No 724/75 Establishing a European Regional Development Fund, OJ 1985 No. C72/56.

[80] Bradley, "Legal Developments in the European Parliament," fn. 72. As pointed out by Bradley, resorting to conciliation for negotiating the Social Charter clearly went "beyond the terms of the Joint Declaration of 4 March 1975 on the conciliation procedure" (fn. 167).

[81] Statement by the President, OJ 1989 No. C158/14.

allow a seamless incorporation of the former Democratic Republic into the Communities.[82]

Besides, only a few years after the EP's abovementioned complaints, the institutions adopted an interinstitutional agreement, with the title Arrangements for the Proceedings of the Conciliation Committee under Article 189b, which was preceded by the following joint statement:

> Current practice under the cooperation procedure generally, particularly in the most sensitive cases, involves talks between the Council Presidency, the Commission and the Chairmen or/and the rapporteurs of the relevant committees of the European Parliament. The Institutions confirm that this practice should continue and could be developed under the procedure provided for in Article 189b of the Treaty establishing the European Community [codecision procedure].[83]

And so they did. After the Treaty of Maastricht became effective, the "talks" between the Parliament, the Council, and the Commission acquired the features of an entrenched institutional practice. So much so that in 2000 a keen observer of institutional affairs could maintain that it had become almost impossible to imagine the legislative process without those talks.[84] As I will show in the next section, the complexity and *lourdeur* of the newly established codecision procedure prompted the Parliament, the Council, and the Commission to give more structure and stability to the trilogue paradigm. The idea of codeciding, instead, made the institutions feel part of a joint enterprise that encouraged them to modify their self-understandings and their mutual behaviors.

1.6 From Maastricht to Lisbon: The Flourishing of Trilogues

On 1 November 1993, the Treaty of Maastricht entered into force.[85] It introduced important constitutional changes, including the codecision procedure.[86] Established alongside the consultation, the assent, and the

[82] Martin Westlake, "The Community Express Service: The Rapid Passage of Emergency Legislation on German Unification" (1991) 28 *Common Market Law Review* 599–614.

[83] Art. 189b: Phase preceding the adoption of a common position by the Council, OJ 1993 No. C329/141.

[84] Shackleton, "The Politics of Codecision," 336.

[85] Treaty on European Union, together with the Complete Text of the Treaty Establishing the European Community, OJ 1992 No. C224/1.

[86] For one of the most famous critical reviews of the negotiation process of the Treaty of Maastricht, see Deirdre Curtin, "The Constitutional Structure of the Union: A Europe of Bits and Pieces" (1993) 30 *Common Market Law Review* 17–69.

cooperation procedures, codecision provided for the equal participation of the Council and the Parliament in the adoption of European legislation. At the beginning, it applied to fifteen legal bases. The following amending Treaties – the Treaty of Amsterdam in 1999, the Treaty of Nice in 2003, and the Treaty of Lisbon in 2009 – extended its scope of application, so that the codecision now applies to eighty-five legal bases. The Treaty of Lisbon also changed its official name into "Ordinary Legislative Procedure" (OLP).[87]

In its Maastricht version, the codecision procedure envisaged up to three readings, with the possibility for the Parliament and the Council to convene a Conciliation Committee in case of outstanding political differences. The Committee could be established during the second reading and consisted of members of the Council (or their representatives) and an equal number of representatives of the European Parliament. Its task was to facilitate an agreement between the co-legislators on a draft text, with the Commission taking all the necessary initiatives for reconciling the EP's and the Council's positions. The procedure has essentially remained unaltered ever since, except for some innovations introduced by the Treaty of Amsterdam.[88]

[87] Apart from further extending the scope of application of the codecision procedure, the Treaty of Lisbon introduced in primary law the distinction between "Ordinary Legislative Procedure" (OLP) and "Special Legislative Procedures" (SLPs). The OLP "shall consist in the joint adoption by the European Parliament and the Council of a regulation, directive or decision on a proposal from the Commission." The SLPs, instead, shall consist in "the adoption of a regulation, directive or decision by the European Parliament with the participation of the Council, or by the latter with the participation of the European Parliament" (Art. 289 TFEU). In the case of SLPs, the "participating" institution can be required either to give its consent (formerly known as "assent procedure") or to draw a nonbinding opinion (consultation procedure) on draft legislation. The Treaty of Lisbon also eliminated the cooperation procedure.

[88] These were indeed not insignificant changes. First, whereas the Treaty of Maastricht obliged the co-legislators to always start the second reading, the Treaty of Amsterdam gave the possibility to the Council and the Parliament to conclude the procedure at the end of the first reading, with the Council adopting the first-reading opinion of the Parliament. Secondly, the Treaty of Maastricht provided that, after the unsuccessful convening of the Conciliation Committee, the Council could reinstate its second-reading common position, obliging the Parliament to reject it with an absolute majority, if necessary. The Treaty of Amsterdam eliminated the right of the Council to reinstate its second-reading common position. This meant that if there had been no agreement between the Parliament and the Council after the Conciliation Committee, the draft act fell. In essence, the changes introduced by the Treaty of Amsterdam are still in force today.

In this new institutional context, trilogues played a key role. They are widely credited with having supplied a set of arrangements by which legislative interactions and conflicts could be adequately managed, channeled, and framed. They not only inspired the creation of the Conciliation Committee,[89] whose workings have been further regulated in a series of interinstitutional agreements concluded in 1993,[90] 1999,[91] and 2007.[92] They also provided the practitioners of codecision with a hands-on scheme to structure institutional interactions *before* conciliation. These interactions came to resemble those "talks" that, according to the 1993 Resolution on Article 189b, the institutions used to carry out under the cooperation procedure, and that they pledged to continue and develop under the codecision procedure. In this respect, it is worth considering the opening passage of a short report prepared by the European Parliament a few months ahead of the 1996 Intergovernmental Conference that led to the adoption of the Treaty of Amsterdam:

> The codecision procedure introduced by Article 189b of the Treaty on European Union confirms the trend, which was heralded by the conciliation procedure introduced in 1975, and subsequently by the cooperation procedure set up by the Single European Act, towards basing legislative decision-making processes on dialogue and negotiation between Parliament/the Council and the Commission.[93]

At the same time, the prospect of conciliation led the practitioners of codecision to believe that "conciliation should not be seen as the automatic and sole mechanism for resolving conflicts of opinion."[94] As the cited report put it, codecision implies "a cumbersome procedure which may go as far as four readings. There is no requirement to go through all the stages of the procedure; on the contrary: the aim should be to reach

[89] The features of the Conciliation Committee make it akin to domestic inter-chamber coordination mechanisms, especially the German *Vermittlungsausschuss*, as provided for by Art. 77 of the German Basic Law. On these similarities, Dana Burchardt and Max Putzer, "Kompetenzgrenzen im deutschen und europäischen Vermittlungsverfahren" (2011) 26 *Zeitschrift für Gesetzgebung* 68–91; Foster, "The New Conciliation Committee," 191 ff. On the functioning of the German *Vermittlungsausschuss*, see Chapter 5, Section 5.3.2.

[90] Arrangements for the Proceedings of the Conciliation Committee under Article 189b, OJ 1993 No. C329/141.

[91] Joint Declaration on Practical Arrangements for the New Co-decision Procedure (Art. 251 of the Treaty Establishing the European Community), OJ 1999 No. C148/1.

[92] Joint Declaration on Practical Arrangements for the Codecision Procedure of 13 June 2007 (Article 251 of the EC Treaty), OJ 2007 No. C145/5.

[93] European Parliament, "Task-Force on the 'Intergovernmental Conference': Briefing No. 8 on the Codecision Procedure," JF/bo/146/95, 20 July 1995, at 1.

[94] Shackleton, "The Politics of Codecision," 330.

agreement in the early stages of the procedure so as to avoid, if possible, entrenched positions which would make it excessively lengthy."[95] So, as soon as codecision came into force, the institutions began to organize trilogues to make the legislative process more cooperative and effective. Although in an initial phase these trilogues served only as preparatory meetings for the Conciliation Committee,[96] soon enough the institutions began to move them further upstream, in first and second reading.

With their proliferation also came their first official acknowledgment. The 1999 Joint Declaration referred to them as "appropriate contacts" and, more importantly, as a "practice" worth preserving and expanding. Shortly thereafter, in a report to the European Council, the Council affirmed that those contacts were "essential" to the success of codecision, adding that they were "needed throughout the procedure."[97] The Parliament and the Commission certainly shared this belief, as they agreed to adopt the 2007 Joint Declaration on Codecision, which includes the following clauses: the "practice involving talks between [the institutions] has proved its worth"; "the institutions confirm that this practice ... must continue to be encouraged."

What is also worth highlighting is that the European legislative institutions have essentially agreed to limit the degree of formalization of trilogues. For instance, in the above-cited report, the Council stated that there was "no need for these instruments to be formalized," insisting on preserving their "vitality and flexibility."[98] A similar view was expressed at the end of 2002 by the Working Group IX on Simplification during the drafting of the Treaty establishing a Constitution for Europe. In its final report to the Convention, the Working Group specified that, after holding a hearing of two experts,[99] the majority of its members

[95] European Parliament, "Task-Force on the 'Intergovernmental Conference,'" at 1.

[96] Shackleton, "The Politics of Codecision," 334, where the author affirms that it was during the Spanish Presidency, in the second half of 1995, that the institutions "agreed on the general principle of holding preparatory trilogues." See also Sophie Boyron, "Maastricht and the Codecision Procedure: A Success Story" (1996) 45 *International and Comparative Law Quarterly* 293–318 at fn. 62.

[97] Council of the European Union, "Report by the Presidency and the General Secretariat of the Council to the European Council on Making the Co-decision Procedure More Effective," 13316/1/00 REV 1, 28 November 2000, paras. 8 and 32.

[98] Ibid., para. 36.

[99] The two experts were Giorgos Dimitrakopoulos, then Vice-President of the European Parliament with responsibility for conciliation, and Jean-Paul Jacqué, then Director of the Codecision Unit in the Council. See European Convention, "Final Report of Working Group IX on Simplification," CONV 424/02, 29 November 2002, at 24.

declared themselves against making a reference to trilogues in the Constitutional Treaty because the "effectiveness of the institutional 'tria-logues' lay in their flexibility and informal nature."[100] Again, on the occasion of a conference for the twentieth birthday of the codecision procedure, Jean-Paul Jacqué affirmed that the set of common rules and principles governing the operation of that procedure – in particular, the Treaties and the 2007 Joint Declaration on Codecision – had been purposely conceived in vague terms, so that practitioners could enjoy "the necessary degree of flexibility and discretion when dealing with the 'hidden part of the iceberg.'"[101]

What is more, the inception of codecision and the thriving of trilogues came with another important – although less evident – development. They entrained a deep change in the legislative culture of the EU, especially as regards the hitherto prevalent style of communication and interaction. A shift from a confrontational to a more cooperative interplay occurred. As an observer put it, codecision and trilogues ushered in "a new dynamic within the legislative arena of the European Union"; they "created a virtuous circle in which co-operation and trust were mutually reinforcing" and favored "the growth of shared norms of behavior encouraging the search for consensus."[102] In other words, they contributed in a decisive way to generating social capital among political actors.

When it was only consulted, the EP used to have an "*attitude tribunicienne*."[103] In its resolutions, instead of proactively contributing to the making of EU legislation, it usually adopted impressive-sounding phrases and fascinating oratory and later complained about not being taken seriously by the Commission and the Council, which favored a more pragmatic, to-the-point approach. After codecision, the EP saw its role and responsibilities change significantly. It was now involved on equal terms with the Council in the adoption of many legislative acts; it had to justify its policy preferences vis-à-vis its electorate and its legislative partners; it had to ensure the quality of European legislation. In other words, the Parliament was no longer a fledgling institution and had to act accordingly.

[100] Ibid., at 25.
[101] European Parliament, "20 Years of Codecision: Conference Report," 5 November 2013, at 4.
[102] Shackleton, "The Politics of Codecision," 326 f. and 333.
[103] Jean-Paul Jacqué, "Une vision réaliste de la procédure de codécision," in Aline De Walsche and Laure Levi (eds.), *Mélanges en hommage à Georges Vandersanden: promenades au sein du droit européen* (Bruylant, 2008), p. 197.

For its part, the Council had been the undisputed master of the supranational legislative authority for about forty years. Its working culture featured discreet diplomatic negotiations and the persistent search for compromise.[104] Not surprisingly, the Council considered the EP unsuited to its newly acquired position. It deemed it almost "vexing" to share its legislative power with such an unpragmatic and clamorous institution. In the first years of codecision, the Council saw the Parliament as a *parvenu* that lacked the required institutional experience and gravitas. Yet the new procedure had put the Parliament and the Council on an equal footing. It had made them interdependent, thereby imposing goal-oriented cooperation. This situation impelled both institutions to set aside old prejudices and change perspectives.

The Commission had to adapt to the changed institutional setting as well. After Maastricht, it was no longer in a tandem relationship with the Council. It was now part of a genuine legislative triangle. Exploiting its near monopoly over the legislative initiative, its mastery of technical information, and its presence throughout all legislative stages (Council meetings, Coreper meetings, EP committee meetings, and so on), the Commission further established itself as a connecting link between the two co-legislators. The legislative dialogue was now the prerogative of the Parliament and the Council; the Commission participated in it with a view to assisting the two co-legislators in reaching viable compromises, while promoting the general interest of the Union.

That said, the Conciliation Committee and the "appropriate contacts" have enjoyed two opposite fates. The former has steadily lost importance, whereas the latter have increasingly established themselves as part and parcel of the supranational legislative process. In the fifth legislative term (1999–2004), the proportion of codecision files that reached the conciliation stage amounted to 22 percent. In the sixth (2004–2009), seventh (2009–2014), and eighth (2014–2019) legislative terms, this fell dramatically to 5 percent, 2 percent, and 0 percent, respectively, thereby rendering the Conciliation Committee all but obsolete.[105] Other data also needs to be factored in, namely that in the fifth legislative term the percentage of

[104] Jacqué, "Une vision réaliste," p. 192.

[105] European Parliament, "Activity Report: Developments and Trends of the Ordinary Legislative Procedure: 1 July 2014–1 July 2019 (8th Parliamentary Term)," PE 639.611, at 3. In the fourth legislative term (1994–1999), the proportion of codecision files that reached the conciliation stage amounted to 33.5 percent. See Andreas Maurer, "(Co-)Governing after Maastricht: The European Parliament's Institutional Performance 1994–1999," POLI 104/rev., October 1999, at 20. It is worth remembering, though, that

codecision files that were adopted either at the end of the first reading (with the Council adopting the Parliament's first reading position) or at the beginning of the second reading (with the Parliament adopting the Council's first reading position) accounted for 54 percent of all enacted legislation. In the sixth, seventh, and eighth legislative terms, this increased to 82 percent, 93 percent, and 97 percent respectively, thereby rendering second and third legislative readings practically redundant.[106]

These developments substantiate the claim that since codecision became effective, the legislative culture of the EU has undergone profound changes. A consensus among the institutions has emerged as to the necessity of endorsing trilogues as the secret of European legislation.[107] Such a consensus is reflected in the above figures, which testify to the near obsolescence of the Conciliation Committee and the dramatic increase of legislative acts adopted at first reading. These developments also confirm that trilogues are so ingrained in the constitutional fiber of the EU that analyzing the European legislative process without considering them would be like separating the bones of the law from the flesh of real constitutional life. To avoid such a "painful" separation, the next two chapters will be devoted to reconstructing the operation of the supranational legislative process in the light of trilogues. But before that, I will close this historical reconstruction with some concluding remarks.

1.7 Conclusions

The entry into force of the Budgetary Treaties marked an important moment in the history of European legislative relations. It set in motion a process whereby the Parliament, exploiting the power of the purse, could effectively "blackmail" the Council into sharing an ever-increasing portion of legislative powers. For its part, the Council could not always oppose outright a greater involvement of the representatives of the peoples of Europe in the supranational legislative process without jeopardizing its own legitimacy. It was therefore cyclically forced to make concessions.

during the fourth legislative term it was not yet possible to conclude codecision files at first reading (see fn. 88).

106 European Parliament, "Activity Report," at 3.

107 On the existence of such a consensus, Christilla Roederer-Rynning and Justin Greenwood, "Black Boxes and Open Secrets: Trilogues as 'Politicised Diplomacy'" (2021) 44 *West European Politics* 485–509 at 493 ff.

A first crucial concession, which I regard as a "critical juncture," was the signing of the 1975 Joint Declaration on Conciliation. With it, the institutions introduced a trilogue paradigm whereby three small delegations from the Parliament, the Council, and the Commission met to discuss and negotiate the content of relevant pieces of European legislation, with the Commission participating as mediator. Despite having taken different forms ("conciliation," "tripartite dialogue," "tripartite meetings," and so on) and having undergone some inevitable adjustments, that paradigm generated positive feedback and led to political actors preserving and improving it over the years, especially after the inception of the codecision procedure. These circumstances not only bespeak the high adaptive capacity and resilience of the trilogue paradigm, but they also reveal its essentiality for the European legislative process.

A key role in this evolutionary process has been played by the interinstitutional agreements and the EP's Rules of Procedure. The former have been used, time and again, as means to supplement and better structure the European constitutional framework,[108] thereby giving birth to a sort of *Inter-Organ-Geschäftsordnungsrecht* (interinstitutional rules of procedure).[109] The latter have often been employed by the Parliament to crystallize institutional practices, especially when these entailed power gains for itself vis-à-vis the other institutions. To be fair, the EP has also contributed to making trilogues more open to public scrutiny. With the "Manzella Report" in 1998,[110] the Parliament launched a phase characterized by regular amendments to its Rules of Procedure to improve the transparency of the legislative process. With this in mind, I can now turn to analyzing in greater detail the current role and internal functioning of each of the three institutions that make up the European legislative triangle.

[108] Roberto Baratta, "Notes sur les fonctions et limites des accords interinstitutionnels," in Antonio Tizzano (ed.), *Verso i 60 anni dai Trattati di Roma: stato e prospettive dell'Unione europea* (Giappichelli, 2016), p. 37 ff.

[109] Roland Bieber, "Artikel 232 (ex-Artikel 199 EGV) [Geschäftsordnung; Verhandlungsniederschriften]," in Hans von der Groeben, Jürgen Schwarze, and Armin Hatje (eds.), *Europäisches Unionsrecht*, 7th ed. (Nomos, 2015), vol. 4, p. 679.

[110] Resolution on the New Codecision Procedure after Amsterdam, OJ 1998 No. C292/140.

2 Setting the Stage

The European Institutional Triangle

2.1 Introduction

In the previous chapter, I carried out a historical reconstruction of trilogues. I showed that the origins of trilogues hearken back to the 1975 Joint Declaration on the Conciliation Procedure and that they have been an increasingly consolidating feature of the European legislative process, to the point that they now permeate the day-to-day life of EU politics. With this chapter, I aim to set out the background and context for the analysis of the law and practice of trilogues, which I will undertake in the next chapter. To this end, I will consider each legislative institution separately, with a special focus on prerogatives, internal structures, and working methods (Sections 2.4, 2.5, and 2.6). Accurate knowledge of these aspects can help shed light on the meaning and importance of trilogues for the functioning of the European legislative process. As an explanatory framework, I will use the concept of executive federalism (Section 2.3). Other works have already chosen this path, yielding insightful results.[1]

According to the Treaties, the European legislative authority consists of the Parliament and the Council.[2] This implies that EU legislative acts enjoy a dual legitimacy,[3] the one stemming from the European Parliament, which represents the European citizens, and the other stemming from the Council, which represents the Member States.[4] The

[1] Philipp Dann, "The Political Institutions," in Armin von Bogdandy and Jürgen Bast (eds.), *Principles of European Constitutional Law*, 2nd ed. (Hart/C. H. Beck/Nomos, 2011), p. 243 ff.

[2] Arts. 14(1) and 16(1) TEU.

[3] Armin von Bogdandy, "Founding Principles," in Armin von Bogdandy and Jürgen Bast (eds.), *Principles of European Constitutional Law*, 2nd ed. (Hart/C. H. Beck/Nomos, 2011), pp. 27, 39, 49 f., 53.

[4] Art. 10(2) TEU.

Treaties, however, also acknowledge an important role for the Commission. This institution enjoys a near monopoly over the legislative initiative with a view to promoting the general interest of the Union.[5] The workings of, and relations between, the Parliament, the Council, and the Commission are shaped by three important institutional principles, those of effectiveness, institutional balance, and loyal cooperation. It is therefore around these principles that I will organize my analysis of trilogues. Let us take a closer look.

2.2 The European Institutional System as a Unity of Decision and Purpose

The EU legislative authority results from the combined effect of three different yet interlocked acts of will. However, this is easier said than done. When regulating the Ordinary Legislative Procedure, the Treaties provide for "a series of discrete stages"[6] between three completely autonomous institutions, whose different legislative roles, different sources of legitimacy, and different self-understandings receive legal recognition and protection through the principle of institutional balance ("[e]ach institution shall act . . . in conformity with the procedures, conditions and objectives set out in [the Treaties]"). In effect, EU primary law does not say much about how legislation is to be enacted. And yet without some form of cooperation, it would be hard to imagine how the Parliament and the Council, with the participation of the Commission, could ever agree on the substance of the simplest political matters, let alone identical legislative language. Thus, to make legislation a tangible reality, EU primary law prompts the institutions to seek close cooperation. To this end, it establishes a general principle, which stipulates that "[t]he institutions shall practice mutual sincere cooperation."[7] The fact that the legislative activity of the EU "requires there to be a *close* . . . collaboration between the institutions concerned," if not a genuine "inter-institutional dialogue," has been acknowledged by the Court of Justice of the European Union (CJEU) on various occasions.[8]

[5] Art. 17(2) TEU.

[6] European Commission, "Ordinary Legislative Procedure (Article 294 TFEU): Guide to Internal Procedure," SPI(2011)25, at 9.

[7] Art. 13(2) TEU.

[8] The first citation is taken from Case T-540/15 *De Capitani* v. *Parliament* EU:T:2018:167, para. 103 (emphasis added); the second is taken from Case C-65/93 *Parliament* v. *Council* EU:C:1995:91, para. 23. For similar considerations, Case C-643/15 *Slovakia* v. *Council* EU:C:2017:631, para. 179; Case C-280/93 *Germany* v. *Council* EU:C:1994:367, para. 36.

The foregoing considerations throw a key feature of the European constitutional framework into sharp relief, namely the existence of a separation of functions – whose normativity rests on the principle of institutional balance – together with a constitutional commitment to cooperating – whose normativity rests on the principle of mutual sincere cooperation. The Treaties thus project a clear, although somewhat oxymoronic, understanding of political authority: "a government of separated institutions *sharing* powers."[9] Article 13(2) TEU encapsulates this understanding by bringing the principles of institutional balance and mutual sincere cooperation together in the same provision: "Each institution shall act within the limits of the powers conferred on it by the Treaties … The institutions shall practice mutual sincere cooperation." To ensure the positive coexistence of both principles, the Court has sometimes intervened to condemn the instrumental use of one principle against the other.[10]

But Article 13 TEU has a richer scope and provides for a third – often neglected – organizational provision, whose goal is to give a teleological compass to the other two. Its paragraph 1 stipulates that "[t]he Union shall have an institutional framework which shall aim to promote its values, advance its objectives, serve its interests, those of its citizens and those of the Member States, and ensure the consistency, effectiveness and continuity of its policies and actions."[11] This provision reflects the desire of the High Contracting Parties, as also expressed in the Preamble to the TEU, to create "a single institutional framework" and can be said to envisage the principle of effectiveness. To be precise, the provision implies that the exercise of public authority at the supranational level postulates the existence of institutions apt to create what Hermann Heller in his *Staatslehre* called "*organisierte Entscheidungs- und Wirkungseinheit*," which could be loosely translated as "unity of decision

[9] This sentence is taken from Richard E. Neustadt, *Presidential Power and the Modern Presidents: The Politics of Leadership from Roosevelt to Reagan* (The Free Press, 1991), p. 29, who employed it to describe the actual nature and functioning of the US system of checks and balances. For the interplay of these principles in bicameral systems, Damiano Nocilla, "Autonomia, coordinamento e leale collaborazione tra i due rami di un parlamento bicamerale" (1998) 48 *Rivista trimestrale di diritto pubblico* 935–983.

[10] Case C-65/93 *Parliament* v. *Council*, para. 17.

[11] Martin Nettesheim, "Art. 13 EUV [Organe der Union]," in Eberhard Grabitz, Meinhard Hilf, and Martin Nettesheim (eds.), *Das Recht der Europäischen Union* (C. H. Beck, 2015) vol. 1, para. 4.

and purpose."[12] As the provision prescribes, this unity takes shape through institutional efforts and political actions for the realization of joint objectives, integrating and reconciling the aspirations of the EU with those of its citizens and Member States.[13] In the case of legislation, only if the institutions manage to synthesize their interests into effective and continuous acts of political will can they establish a unified legislative authority, capable of attaining objectives of common interest.

In operative terms, the provision of Article 13(1) TEU gives flexibility to the institutional balance set out in the Treaties, while putting the institutions' duty of sincere cooperation within a more pragmatic, goal-oriented horizon. In fact, no political system, even those that place significant roadblocks on their institutions' ability to act, can afford to render decision-making entirely impossible.[14] Maintaining the status quo – with all its political, economic, and social implications – should always be the result of a deliberate decision rather than the consequence of too fragmented a political system.[15] Representative institutions serve the purpose of connecting the subjects with the object of democracy, namely the citizens with the exercise of public authority. A representative system incapable of deciding would therefore default on its democratic obligations and ultimately betray its *raison d'être*. It would be the last frontier of human inconsistency, if not wholly diabolical. Article 13(1) TEU may therefore be regarded as a suitable legitimacy basis for those activities and arrangements through which the institutions seek to ensure their effective functioning.[16] In this spirit, I can now start to analyze the

[12] Hermann Heller, *Staatslehre* (A. W. Sijthoff's Uitgeversmij N.V., 1934), p. 228 ff. The expression has been translated into English as "organized efficacious, decision unit." Cf. Hermann Heller, "The Nature and Structure of the State" (1996) 18 *Cardozo Law Review* 1139–1216 at 1164.

[13] Christian Calliess, *Die neue Europäische Union nach dem Vertrag von Lissabon* (Mohr Siebeck, 2010), p. 118.

[14] Daniel Innerarity, *Democracy in Europe: A Political Philosophy of the EU* (Palgrave Macmillan, 2018), pp. 35 and 265 f. See also Opinion of Advocate General Wathelet in Case C-73/17 *France* v. *Parliament (Exercice du pouvoir budgétaire)* EU:C:2018:386, para. 38.

[15] Amy Gutmann and Dennis Thompson, *The Spirit of Compromise: Why Governing Demands It and Campaigning Undermines It* (Princeton University Press, 2012), p. 2, arguing that "[p]rivileging the status quo does not mean that nothing changes. It just means that politicians let other forces control the change. The status quo includes not only a current state of affairs but also the state that results from political inaction."

[16] Case C-136/82 *Klöckner* v. *Commission* EU:C:1983:132, para. 10, where the ECJ affirmed that, when the Treaties do not provide detailed arrangements as regards the concrete functioning of the legislative procedures, "it is a matter for the . . . institutions to provide, by common consent and in accordance with their respective powers, for the form which their cooperation shall take."

Parliament, the Council, and the Commission, respectively. As previously mentioned, to make sense of the complicated institutional structure of the EU, I will use the concept of executive federalism as privileged heuristic prism. This choice, however, calls for a justification.

2.3 Executive Federalism as Heuristic Prism

Various reasons militate in favor of choosing the concept of executive federalism as a heuristic prism. I believe that, as compared to other approaches, executive federalism is better suited to explain and make sense of different key aspects of the European institutional setting. "Executive federalism" refers to a specific constitutional organization whereby the implementation of federal legislation is entrusted to the constituent units' administrations. Noncentralized implementation "allows for a common framework and tailor-made implementation at the same time, taking into account local peculiarities."[17] Of course, the effective functioning of executive federalism depends, to a large extent, on the existence of efficient cooperation instruments that connect the two levels. As it is, executive federalism can explain and make sense of the multi-level nature of the EU – with two levels of government, in which the supranational level is responsible for adopting legislation and the national for implementing it – and the ensuing need for extensive cooperation that has always characterized the relationship between supranational and national levels of government.

But that is not all. The explanatory power of the concept of executive federalism goes well beyond the multi-level nature of European governance, up to and including the arrangements that characterize the horizontal relations among supranational institutions. In this sense, executive federalism can explain, first, the presence and influence of the Council within the European constitutional framework as an institution that combines both legislative and executive functions. Secondly, it can rationalize the role of the Commission as an executive institution largely independent from the legislative authority, despite several attempts at its parliamentarization – with the last in order of time being the (perhaps defunct) *Spitzenkandidaten* process. Thirdly, it can make sense of the prevalence of informal bodies, such as trilogues, as means to build compromises to gather the widest possible support among the actors involved.

[17] Francesco Palermo and Karl Kössler, *Comparative Federalism: Constitutional Arrangements and Case Law* (Hart, 2017), p. 156 f.

Furthermore, executive federalism helps explain the accountability issues that affect European policy-making.[18] Responsibility is not easy to attribute in a system of executive federalism – the accountability concerns that inspired the two important German federalism reforms of 2006 and 2009, with their focus on the so-called *Entflechtung* (disentangling), are certainly instructive.[19] European decisions are adopted in Brussels, but they become a tangible reality through the implementing activity of the Member States' administrations (Art. 291(1) TFEU).[20] Member States' civil servants are those who "give a face," so to speak, to European decisions. The European policy cycle thus encompasses and cuts across supranational, national, and subnational strata, inevitably diffusing (and confusing) political responsibility. This is also why the EU, as distinguished from systems of dual federalism, lends itself more easily to blame-shifting dynamics.[21]

Finally, while explaining and making sense of the idiosyncrasies of such a framework, executive federalism does not project the EU towards a specific *telos* (such as federal state, confederation, regulatory entity, and so on), as it leaves it open to different developments and possible outcomes. In other words, executive federalism, as here understood, is effectively descriptive but not normatively laden.[22] It does not, for instance, have the polemic connotation that Jürgen Habermas attributes to it.[23] Against this background, I can now turn to analyze the single institutions that constitute the interinstitutional triangle. I will do so by highlighting

[18] See the analysis of the German system of executive federalism by Florian Meinel, *Vertrauensfrage. Zur Krise des heutigen Parlamentarismus* (C. H. Beck, 2019), p. 25, arguing that those pathologies that affect the German system of executive federalism are like those that affect the EU, to the point that "what is today frequently lamented as the EU's democratic deficit, has been known in Germany all along" (my translation).

[19] This problem has been prominently studied by political scientist Fritz W. Scharpf under the broader concept of "joint decision-making" (*Politikverflechtung*). Originally used with specific regard to German federalism, the concept was later employed to study the European integration process. See Fritz W. Scharpf, "The Joint-Decision Trap: Lessons from German Federalism and European Integration" (1988) 66 *Public Administration* 239–278. More recently, Jacques Ziller, "Sdoppiamento funzionale e trappola della decisione congiunta nell'Unione europea," in Elisabetta Colombo (ed.), *Le istituzioni e le idee. Studi indisciplinati offerti a Fabio Rugge per il suo settantesimo compleanno* (Giuffrè, 2022), p. 803 ff.

[20] Case C-521/15 *Spain* v. *Council* EU:C:2017:982, para. 47 f.

[21] Innerarity, *Democracy in Europe*, p. 49 f.; Armin Hatje and Jürgen Schwarze, "Der Zusammenhalt der Europäischen Union" (2019) 54 *Europarecht* 153–189 at 164 ff.

[22] Daniel J. Elazar, *Exploring Federalism* (University of Alabama Press, 1987).

[23] Jürgen Habermas, *Zur Verfassung Europas: Ein Essay*, 5th ed. (Suhrkamp, 2014), p. 48 ff.

some of their characteristics, which will also be useful in the following parts of this book.

2.4 The European Parliament: "The Only Parliament in the World Where Everyone Belongs to the Opposition"

As famously stated by the ECJ in *Roquette Frères*, the participation of the European Parliament in the legislative process of the EU reflects "the fundamental democratic principle that the people should take part in the exercise of power through the intermediary of a representative assembly."[24] More than forty years have passed since the Court delivered that judgment, and the Parliament has evolved from a "harmless" consultative assembly into a full-blown legislative chamber, which participates on an equal footing with the Council in the adoption of more than 80 percent of European legislation, bearing witness to an emerging general legislative function at supranational level. However, despite its growing influence in legislative matters and its transformation into a genuine political powerhouse, the EP presents some peculiarities that distinguish it from many national counterparts, especially from those embedded in a system of parliamentary government.

Among these peculiarities, foremost is the absence of an exclusive political link with the Commission.[25] In line with the general notion of executive federalism, the Commission's appointment procedure attributes important prerogatives not only to the EP but also to the (European) Council.[26] The Commission's "source of authority remains twofold, with administrative appointments by the Member States and political election by the Parliament: a balancing act."[27] In addition to ensuring the independence of the Commission vis-à-vis its fellow institutions, the Treaties forbid it to "seek or take instructions from any Government or other institution, body, office or entity."[28] They also demand that the Member States respect the independence of the Commission's Members and not seek to influence them in the performance of their duties.[29] As a result, the motion of censure, whereby a two-thirds majority of the votes cast in the EP can force the Commission to

[24] Case C-138/79 *Roquette* v. *Council* EU:C:1980:249, para. 33.

[25] Dann, "The Political Institutions," p. 252. [26] Art. 17(7) TEU.

[27] Luuk van Middelaar, *Alarums & Excursions: Improvising Politics on the European Stage* (Agenda Publishing, 2019), p. 203.

[28] Art. 17(3)(3) TEU. [29] Art. 245(1) TFEU.

resign,[30] is considered more akin to a procedure of impeachment than to a vote of no confidence.[31]

Be that as it may, in the absence of a stronger political link between the Parliament and the Commission, the former frequently works as a counterweight rather than a supporter of the latter. The hearings that the Parliament carries out prior to approving the Commission are a case in point. During those hearings, MEPs from the entire political spectrum "grill" the candidate commissioners with long and wearing Q&A sessions, thereby confirming the absence of a "majority [within the EP] which perceives itself as a loyal parliamentary base of the Commission."[32] These considerations apply, a fortiori, to the relationship between the EP and the Council, which has always been the Parliament's main rival in the field of legislation. Indeed, the EP's current position in the European institutional framework is the result of more than sixty years of political and judicial conflicts that profoundly shaped the self-perceptions of the co-legislators. They not only embody competing interests, but they also stand for different understandings of the European integration process. At any rate, this competition has never resulted in insurmountable gridlocks, except for the 1980s budgetary crises. Rather, the Parliament and the Council have repeatedly proved willing to set aside their rivalry to pursue common goals, revealing a great deal of mutual tolerance and institutional forbearance. These are the makings of a true "frenemy" relationship.

While the General Court (GC) recently affirmed that the Rules of Procedure of the EP "are inspired by the parliamentary traditions common to the Member States,"[33] it is safe to say that MEPs operate in an environment with specific structures and working methods that, taken together, differentiate the European Parliament from many other parliamentary assemblies. Among those features that make the European Parliament almost unique are the near-absence of a disciplined and systematic majority–opposition division; the presence of a "double filtrage system," which revolves around the parliamentary committees as the true loci of decision-making; and the importance of compromise as the chosen means to determine the content of supranational legislation.

[30] Arts. 17(8) TEU and 234 TFEU.

[31] Frank Decker, "Das Scheitern des Spitzenkandidatensystems und andere populäre Irrtümer über die Demokratisierung der Europäischen Union" (2019) 50 *Zeitschrift für Parlamentsfragen* 870–879 at 871.

[32] Dann, "The Political Institutions," p. 252.

[33] Case T-88/20 *Rivière and Others* v. *Parliament* EU:T:2021:664, para. 42.

First, the institutional system of the EU is not fertile ground for the establishment and thriving of a disciplined and systematic majority–opposition division.[34] This situation results, to a great extent, from the fact that the EU is not a parliamentary system of government and does not have a system of truly transnational parties,[35] due to the persisting inability of the institutions to adopt a uniform electoral procedure. Therefore, the current 705 MEPs come from 209 different national political parties, and the resulting seven European groups encompass very different political trends.[36] Moreover, MEPs belong to 143 different national delegations, with their own political advisors and their own forms of political coordination.[37] Of course, it would be imprecise to maintain that majority–opposition dynamics within the EP never materialize.[38] Seen from the perspective of the opposition, the European Parliament is occasionally home to what Winfried Steffani called "ad-hoc opposition."[39] As the name suggests, this type of opposition "is formed … on the basis of the questions pending for discussion and decision. Both

[34] Andreas Voßkuhle, "Opposition im Europäischen Parlament," in Ulrich Becker, Armin Hatje, Michael Potacs, and Nina Wunderlich (eds.), *Verfassung und Verwaltung in Europa: Festschrift für Jürgen Schwarze zum 70. Geburtstag* (Nomos, 2014), p. 292 ff. See also Case T-222/99 *Martinez and Others* v. *Parliament* EU:T:2001:242, para. 146.

[35] It is worth noting that in 2018 the Italian Constitutional Court took an interesting and, to some extent, unorthodox position about the EU system of government. Concerned with responding to a set of questions on the constitutionality of the 4 percent electoral threshold set out in the Italian voting law for elections to the European Parliament, the Court made reference to "the undoubted transformation of the form of government of the European Union towards parliamentary government" as well as the "enhanced dialectical relationship between the European Parliament and the Commission, which gives rise to the need to promote the formation of a political majority within the assembly." See Italian Constitutional Court, judgment No. 239/2018, 25 October 2018, IT:COST:2018:239, para. 6.5.

[36] European Parliament, "European Parliament: Facts and Figures," PE 747.102, May 2023, at 5.

[37] For a convincing argument against a full-fledged development of party politics at European level, Renaud Dehousse, "Constitutional Reform in the European Community: Are There Alternatives to the Majoritarian Avenue?" (1995) 18 *West European Politics* 118–136 at 134, who submitted that such a development could be problematic for center–periphery relations, which he viewed as crucial for the stability of the Union ("[s]een in this light, the current weakness of European parties, lamented by some, may appear as a disguised blessing").

[38] A recent example of such a dynamic might be the tight vote count on the Commission's Proposal for a Regulation on Nature Restoration (COM(2022) 304 final). In the plenary of 12 July 2023, the EP first rejected the draft legislation by 312 votes to 324, with 12 abstentions. It then adopted a set of amendments by 336 votes to 300, with 13 abstentions.

[39] Winfried Steffani, "Funktionen und Wirkungsmöglichkeiten von Opposition (1968)," in *Parlamentarische und präsidentielle Demokratie: Strukturelle Aspekte westlicher Demokratien*

the majority and the opposition change in their composition depending on the problem at hand. The majority and the opposition are not permanently opposed to each other as relatively closed collectives, but rather as relatively loosely formed ad-hoc groups."[40] However, even the examples of ad hoc opposition are rare, certainly more the exception than the rule.[41]

Secondly, the decision-making process in the European Parliament relies on a "double filtrage system."[42] Positions are initially discussed and negotiated within the various political groups and then within the responsible parliamentary committees, as the true loci of decision-making. Debates in the parliamentary committees are "structured for the explicit purpose of decision-making," whereas debates in the plenary "are highly formalized and not interactive."[43] In fact, in most cases the plenary serves to rubberstamp pre-cooked decisions and to provide public justification for the adopted legislation. It is not by chance that 90 percent of the amendments tabled by the parliamentary committees are eventually adopted in the plenary.[44] The centrality of the committees in parliamentary day-to-day work is typical of those constitutional systems that feature a strong separation between the different branches of government, such as the United States. In those systems, parliaments do not have to create and maintain a majority that supports the Executive. They can therefore invest time and resources on other functions, notably that of enacting legislation.[45] For this reason, the EP is often seen as a "working parliament."[46]

All these considerations bring me to the last element that characterizes the functioning of the EP, namely openness to compromise as an established

(Springer, 1979), p. 239 ff. Similarly, Enrique Barón Crespo, "El desarrollo de la codecisión como procedimiento legislativo de la UE" (2012) *Cuadernos Europeos de Deusto* 19–47 at 33.

40 Steffani, "Funktionen und Wirkungsmöglichkeiten von Opposition," p. 241 (my translation).

41 More broadly on this topic, but still fundamental: Karlheinz Neunreither, "Governance without Opposition: The Case of the European Union" (1998) 33 *Government and Opposition* 419–441.

42 Ibid., 433.

43 Léa Roger, *Voice(s) in the European Parliament: Deliberation and Negotiation in EP Committees* (Nomos, 2016), p. 267.

44 Ibid., p. 36.

45 Christoph Schönberger, "Das Parlament: Geschichte einer europäischen Erfindung," in Martin Morlok, Ute Schliesky, and Dieter Wiefelspütz (eds.), *Parlamentsrecht: Handbuch* (Nomos, 2016) p. 88 ff. See also Innerarity, *Democracy in Europe*, p. 133.

46 Dann, "The Political Institutions," p. 250 f.

political practice.[47] As acknowledged by the General Court, the EP's ability to reach compromises is "particularly necessary owing to the very high number of Members ... the exceptional diversity of cultures, nationalities, languages and national political movements represented in it, the great diversity of the Parliament's activities and the fact that, unlike national parliaments, the Parliament does not have the traditional dichotomy between majority and opposition."[48] In a highly fragmented political environment, such as that of the EP, openness to compromise is not only a very effective way to influence the content of legislation but also an essential means to forge a coherent whole out of all the cultural, national, linguistic, and political diversity that comes together in the EP. In this spirit, openness to compromise ensures the fruitful coexistence of a broad group of individuals with multiple identities and safeguards the decentralized political system resulting from that coexistence. These structural features find expression in the EP's Rules of Procedure, which reflect the idea of a legislative chamber that embraces minorities and seeks to accommodate their interests as far as possible.

As a result, the EP has traditionally cultivated a Janus-like strategy: "unity and centralized strength to the outside, decentralization to the inside."[49] All its internal diversity, which also stems from an electoral system based on purely proportional representation,[50] has always found a superior unifying factor in the desire to appear assertive vis-à-vis the Council and the Commission. And this creates a situation that the former President of the European Council, Herman Van Rompuy, captured in the following terms: "This is the only parliament in the world where everyone belongs to the opposition."[51] Such a situation can be justified by considering the heuristic prism chosen here. In a system of executive federalism, the Parliament is an independently operating actor, whose chief purpose is to represent a counterweight and to offer a strong political alternative to the other branches of government. Given the

[47] Roger, *Voice(s) in the European Parliament*, p. 141. In these terms, see also German Federal Constitutional Court, Case No. 2 BvC 4/10, 9 November 2011 – *Fünf-Prozent-Sperrklausel EuWG*, para. 103.

[48] Case T-222/99 *Martinez and Others* v. *Parliament*, para. 146.

[49] This situation, however, is by no means peculiar to the European Parliament. It was typical, at least until the 1980s, of the US Congress as well. See Winfried Steffani, "Grundzüge des amerikanischen Regierungssystems," in *Parlamentarische und präsidentielle Demokratie: Strukturelle Aspekte westlicher Demokratien* (Springer, 1979), p. 317.

[50] Act Concerning the Election of the Representatives of the Assembly by Direct Universal Suffrage, OJ 1976 No. L278/5, Art. 1(1) (in the version currently in force).

[51] van Middelaar, *Alarums & Excursions*, p. 245.

circumstances, I would argue that structural grounds oppose the development of a "new European opposition culture" in the style of a disciplined and systematic opposition, as advocated by some authors.[52]

2.5 The Council: A Legislative Institution with a Governmental-Bureaucratic Structure

What about the EP's legislative counterpart? How does executive federalism explain and make sense of the Council's role within the European institutional landscape? A good starting point for our analysis is Philipp Dann's observation that "[t]he Council of the European Union is the institutional counterpart to the structure of interwoven competences that characterizes executive federalism." Accordingly, the Council is a meeting point for actors coming from both levels of government, national and supranational; "a meeting point for politicians and bureaucrats, a place to negotiate, to coordinate, and to legislate."[53] As its members are representatives of the national governments at ministerial level and must divide their time between Brussels and their own capitals, the Council avails itself of the support of several committees and working parties (more than 150) and of its rotating Presidency. Generally, the former carry out legislative and other preparatory work; the latter, together with the General Secretariat, ensures that the Council's intricate organizational structure hangs together. The Council, as the decision-making body of ministerial representatives of each Member State, is "only the top of a complex system, best described as a pyramid of groups."[54]

This pyramid consists of three levels. At the top is the Council as the meeting place of ministerial representatives of the Member States. At the intermediate level are the Committee of Permanent Representatives (Coreper) and other specialized committees (for example, the Special Committee for Agriculture) as permanent meeting places of national diplomats in Brussels. And at the bottom level are the working parties as meeting places of national experts. Executive federalism offers a convincing explanation for why the Council features such a presence of

[52] E.g., Voßkuhle, "Opposition im Europäischen Parlament," p. 299 ff.

[53] Both citations are taken from Philipp Dann, "The Council," in Robert Schütze and Takis Tridimas (eds.), *Oxford Principles of European Union Law: The European Union Legal Order* (Oxford University Press, 2018), vol. 1, p. 521.

[54] Ibid., p. 523.

actors from national administrations. Since EU law must eventually be implemented by national administrations, it makes sense to provide those administrations with a say over its content.[55]

Starting from the bottom of this three-tier pyramid, the working parties are composed of officials of the Member States and focus on discussions around a specific subject area. They are chaired by a delegate of the Member State holding the six-month Council Presidency and are entrusted with examining the legislative files assigned to them, discussing the draft text article by article, and evaluating compromise options.[56] Their work is supervised and coordinated by Coreper, which convenes every week in two different configurations, Coreper I and Coreper II.[57] To be precise, the Treaties entrust Coreper with "preparing the work of the Council,"[58] notably with examining all those matters that ultimately reach the Council's agenda.[59] This makes Coreper the main link in the Council's legislative chain.

55 Ibid., p. 520.

56 Committees and working parties are established either by the Treaties (e.g., the Economic and Financial Committee, the Employment Committee, the Trade Policy Committee) or by Council decision (e.g., the Economic Policy Committee, the Financial Services Committee, the Security Committee) or by Coreper pursuant to Art. 19(3) Council RoP.

57 See Arts. 16(7) TEU, 240(1) TFEU and 19 Council RoP. Coreper is the acronym for the French *Comité des représentants permanents*. Coreper I consists of the Member States' deputy permanent representatives and is responsible for preparing the work of six Council configurations, namely (i) agriculture and fisheries, (ii) competitiveness, (iii) education, youth, culture, and sport, (iv) employment, social policy, health, and consumer affairs, (v) environment, (vi) transport, telecommunications, and energy. Coreper II consists of the Member States' permanent representatives and is responsible for preparing the work of the four remaining Council configurations, namely (i) economic and financial affairs, (ii) foreign affairs, (iii) general affairs, (iv) justice and home affairs. The meetings of Coreper I and Corper II are prepared the day before by the "Mertens Group" and the "Antici Group," respectively. These two groups consist of the closest collaborators of Coreper's members. Whereas Coreper I/II usually meet on Wednesdays, Antici/Mertens meet on Tuesdays.

58 Arts. 16(7) TEU and 240(1) TFEU.

59 The ECJ has clarified that Coreper is not an institution of the EU but an auxiliary body of the Council, "for which it carries out preparation and implementation work" (Case C-25/94 *Commission* v. *Council* EU:C:1996:114, para. 26 f.). However, it must be highlighted that Coreper also is a body capable of taking legally binding decisions. Coreper may, for example, adopt "procedural decisions in cases provided for in the Council's Rules of Procedure" (Arts. 240(1) TFEU and 19(7) Council RoP). Accordingly, the ECJ acknowledged that "as the European Union is a union based on the rule of law, a measure adopted by Coreper must be amenable to judicial review where it is intended, as such, to produce legal effects and therefore falls outside the framework of that preparation and implementation function" (Joined Cases C-626/15 and C-659/16 *Commission* v. *Council (Antarctic MPAs)* EU:C:2018:925, para. 61).

Coreper works under the chairmanship of the Member State holding the six-month Presidency and operates, in most cases, on the basis of the reports written by the working parties.[60] However, unlike the working parties, which confine themselves to technical scrutiny of the legislative dossiers, Coreper combines technical expertise and political responsibility. It not only ensures that Member States' interests are properly represented in the legislative cycle but also verifies that those interests are compatible with the protection and further development of the Union.[61] Coreper is fairly successful in striking such a balance because it has a stable presence in Brussels and a developed sensitivity to European institutional culture – at least as compared to the ministers of the Member States, who travel to Brussels only for the Council's meetings. In this respect, it bears noting that the Council, according to Article 237 TFEU, "shall meet when convened by its President on his own initiative or at the request of one of its Members or of the Commission."

As regards the Presidency, its tasks are wide-ranging and include the planning and coordination of the Council's activities, the chairmanship of nearly all Council formations and preparatory bodies, the brokering of compromises among Member States, and the negotiation of legislative files with the Parliament and the Commission.[62] But this short summary does not do justice to the crucial role that the Presidency has come to play in the legislative domain. Invigorated by its representative role in trilogues, the six-monthly rotating Presidency, as embodied by the Member State in office, is essential in determining the content of legislation and its successful adoption. To that end, it can resort to an extensive toolkit, which includes a reasonable degree of negotiating autonomy and the possibility to steer the discussion in the Council through the presentation of compromise texts. Far from being a neutral actor, the Council's Presidency has a powerful political position, which offers each Member State a distinct possibility of leaving a mark.[63]

[60] Art. 21 Council RoP.

[61] Jean-Paul Jacqué, "Lost in Transition: The European Commission between Intergovernmentalism and Integration," in Dominique Ritleng (ed.), *Independence and Legitimacy in the Institutional System of the European Union* (Oxford University Press, 2016).

[62] Council Presidencies organize bilateral meetings with the Member States to clarify specific issues or garner support for compromise amendments. This practice is also recalled in Case C-128/17 *Poland* v. *Parliament and Council* EU:C:2019:194, paras. 14 and 69.

[63] Emanuele Rebasti, "The Legal Regime Applicable to the Council Presidency: Competing Conceptual Approaches and Pragmatic Solutions," in Ramona Coman and Vivien Sierens (eds.), *EU Council Presidencies in Times of Crises* (Palgrave Macmillan, 2024); Dann, "The Council," p. 526; Jeffrey Lewis, "Council of Ministers and European Council," in Erik

In principle, the interaction between the different levels of the pyramid should be based on the notion that the higher level steps in only after the lower level has completed its technical work or exhausted its political capital.[64] This notion, however, does not entail hard-and-fast hierarchies in the internal structures of the Council.[65] As pointed out by Jeffrey Lewis, "legislative dossiers shuttle through the Council between the ministers, preparatory committees, and working parties," making it sometimes difficult to discern where the substance of legislative agreements is attained.[66] Once again, executive federalism provides a powerful key to illuminating this seemingly fuzzy structure. The feebleness of hierarchical dynamics is indeed a common feature in systems of executive federalism, the functioning of which relies heavily on cooperation.[67] As regards the Council, such feebleness has at least two reasons. First, the members of the Council are representatives of sovereign subjects, whose equality before the Treaties is expressly recognized in Article 4(2) TEU.[68] Secondly, since party coherence among the Member States is rather weak, it is difficult to build coalitions and, in turn, predominance of some Member States over others. These reasons also contribute to engendering and reinforcing an element of resistance towards leadership – as the political flipside of hierarchy.[69]

Lastly, some brief observations on the voting requirements in the Council are in order. The Treaties provide that, when applying the Ordinary Legislative Procedure, the Council shall act by qualified majority.[70] This implies a double majority, with at least 55 percent (and

Jones, Anand Menon, and Stephen Weatherill (eds.), *The Oxford Handbook of the European Union* (Oxford University Press, 2012), p. 327 f.; Jean-Paul Jacqué, "Une vision réaliste de la procédure de codécision," in Aline De Walsche and Laure Levi (eds.), *Mélanges en hommage à Georges Vandersanden: promenades au sein du droit européen* (Bruylant, 2008), p. 199.

64 This clearly emerges in Annex V Council RoP, which sets out the Council's working methods.

65 Opinion of Advocate General Kokott in Case C-551/21 *Commission* v. *Council (Signature d'accords internationaux)* EU:C:2023:579, para. 76.

66 Lewis, "Council of Ministers and European Council," p. 325 f., affirming that Council deliberations operate "by networked, 'clan-like' relations of power and authority (rather than a straightforward corporate hierarchy)."

67 Thomas O. Hueglin and Alan Fenna, *Comparative Federalism: A Systematic Inquiry*, 2nd ed. (University of Toronto Press, 2015), p. 238 ff.

68 On the meaning of Art. 4(2) TEU, Lucia Serena Rossi, "The Principle of Equality Among Member States of the European Union," in Lucia Serena Rossi and Federico Casolari (eds.), *The Principle of Equality in EU Law* (Springer, 2017), p. 10 ff.

69 Dann, "The Political Institutions," p. 257.

70 Unless the Commission declares its opposition to the proposed amendments. In that case, the Council shall act unanimously.

fifteen) of the Member States representing at least 65 percent of the EU population voting in favor of a specific piece of legislation.[71] Most of the time, though, the Council decides on ordinary legislation with all Member States voting in favor, revealing the existence of a "consensus culture."[72] This culture finds further expression in what Henry Farrel and Adrienne Héritier called a "principle of diffuse reciprocity over time ... meaning that no Member State or group of Member States ever finds itself as part of a permanent structural minority."[73] The rationale behind this principle is to avoid the creation of a systematic correspondence between "outvoted minorities and national borders,"[74] which would make European legislation politically more vulnerable in the implementation stage. The Council should therefore be viewed as a formally super-majoritarian but substantially consensual institution.

Besides the legitimacy problems it seems to cause, this "consensus culture" enjoys a rather seamless application due to several factors, four of which stand out. First, reaching the requested double majority (while avoiding the blocking minority of at least four Member States representing more than 35 percent of the EU population) leads per se to "large, in fact highly sophisticated super-majorities, which could also be qualified as a form of consensus."[75] Secondly, being aware that during the legislative process a small group of Member States may invoke the "Ioannina-bis" device, thus forcing an extension of the discussions (and producing a sort of softened filibuster),[76] the Council's institutional actors are urged

[71] Art. 16(4) TEU.

[72] Dann, "The Council," p. 540 ff.; Lewis, "Council of Ministers and European Council," p. 322 ff.

[73] Henry Farrel and Adrienne Héritier, "The Invisible Transformation of Codecision: Problems of Democratic Legitimacy" (2003) *Swedish Institute for European Policy Studies* 1–33 at 14.

[74] Christine Reh, "European Integration as Compromise: Recognition, Concessions and the Limits of Cooperation" (2012) 47 *Government and Opposition* 414–440 at 429.

[75] Dann, "The Council," p. 542. The ECJ has recently stated that the blocking minority set out in Art. 16(4) TEU is "relatively easy to achieve." See Case C-157/21 *Poland* v. *Parliament and Council* EU:C:2022:98, para. 309.

[76] See Council Decision of 13 December 2007 Relating to the Implementation of Article 9C(4) of the Treaty on European Union and Article 205(2) of the Treaty on the Functioning of the European Union between 1 November 2014 and 31 March 2017, and from 1 April 2017 (2009/857/EC), OJ 2009 No. L314/73. To be triggered, this device must be invoked by members of the Council representing at least 55 percent of the population or at least 55 percent of the number of Member States necessary to constitute a blocking minority. However, Art. 6 of the 2007 Council Decision stipulates that the "Ioannina-bis" device must be applied "in compliance with the Council's Rules of Procedure." A simple majority of Member States may therefore force a vote on any proposal at any time, thus bringing

to seek the broadest possible support from the earliest stages of the procedure. Thirdly, unless fiercely opposed to a specific piece of legislation, national delegations in the Council refrain from abstaining or voting against it,[77] lest this engender the impression of political defeat. In the public eye, they probably prefer to be on the winning side rather than to come across as isolated opponents.[78]

Fourthly, consensus is so prevalent because the Council's preparatory bodies operate in the shadow of qualified majority voting. The "shadow of the vote" operates as "a threat, an inducement to achieve a consensus, it disciplines participants to play by the rules and show cooperative behavior and it contributes to stabilizing the consensus rule."[79] In all the stages that lead to the adoption of a legislative act, the Member States can share their concerns and expect their fellow members to take those concerns seriously. In return, they are expected to assume an accommodating attitude, especially when group coherence is materializing. A few expressions of disagreement cannot impede the adoption of a decision. What can happen, instead, is the marginalization of the most relentless, uncompromising opponents.[80]

This "culture" also has far-reaching repercussions on how the working parties, Coreper, and the Council reach their decisions. As regards working parties and Coreper, they adopt decisions *by consensus* – understood as the lack of a formal vote.[81] As for the Council, when it comes to deciding on a legislative dossier in public session, the Presidency uses the following standard formula: "The Council should now be in a position to

procrastination to an end (Art. 11(1) Council RoP). The adoption of the "Ioannina-bis" device was Poland's price for accepting the Lisbon Treaty at the June 2007 European Council meeting in Brussels. See Paolo Ponzano, "Il voto nel Consiglio: il compromesso di Ioannina alla luce del Trattato di Lisbona" (2009) *Il Diritto dell'Unione Europea* 77–89.

77 It is worth remembering that, for the purposes of qualified majority, abstentions are substantially equal to negative votes.

78 Stéphanie Novak, "The Silence of Ministers: Consensus and Blame Avoidance in the Council of the European Union" (2013) 51 *Journal of Common Market Studies* 1091–1107 at 1100 ff. The reason why national delegations choose to abstain rather than to vote against a legislative dossier can therefore be explained as follows: "When ministers consider that they have an interest in publicly dissenting, they register a negative vote. When they want to express public dissatisfaction with a measure but also maintain good relations with the Presidency and the Commission, they abstain."

79 Eva Krick, "The Myth of Effective Veto Power under the Rule of Consensus. Dynamics and Democratic Legitimacy of Collective Decision-Making by 'Tacit Consent'" (2017) *Négociations* 109–128 at 115 f.

80 Ibid., 120.

81 As regards the features of this decision-making method, see Chapter 4, Section 4.4.3.

approve the European Parliament's position as set out in [document no.]. I note that the required qualified majority has been reached and that, therefore, the act is adopted."[82] The Presidency then specifies the vote result, mentioning abstentions and negative votes, and draws the attention of possible onlookers to the vote summary as displayed on the screens in the Europa building and video streamed by the Council. However, it is worth highlighting that there exists an administrative practice according to which, before finalizing the Council agenda, the Legislation Programming, Support and Coordination Team "sends a standard e-mail message to delegations ... requesting them to inform the [Team] of any intention to vote against the proposal or to abstain."[83] This practice allows the Council to have a general – though not conclusive – idea of the chances of a legislative file being adopted before the vote is actually held. The dominant "consensus culture" also explains why the Council, as distinct from the EP, votes on draft legislative acts in their entirety and not article by article.

At this point, the question might arise as to whether a more majoritarian understanding of politics within the Council could develop – let us put aside for the moment the question of whether it should. In this respect, I believe that the quest for consensus will remain a deeply entrenched feature of the decision-making practices of the Council, at least in the near future.[84] These practices are the direct consequence of

[82] The standard formula is slightly different when the Council is adopting its first-reading position, instead of approving the legislative act at first reading.

[83] Council of the European Union, "Ordinary Legislative Procedure: Guide for GSC Officials," 11 October 2016, at 18.

[84] The Council's entrenched consensus culture can be exemplified by the controversy that surrounded the adoption of Directive (EU) 2016/2284 on reduction of national emissions of certain atmospheric pollutants. When the file was eventually put to a vote in the Council, Poland and five other Member States (Denmark, Lithuania, Hungary, Austria, and Romania) voted against and Croatia abstained. That was not enough, though, to impede the adoption of the file, as those seven Member States totaled only 17.51 percent of the EU population, well below the required 35 percent threshold for establishing a blocking minority. Therefore, Poland, supported by Hungary and Romania, launched an action for annulment, lamenting, among other things, that the Council had not considered its reservations, thus violating Poland's right to participate fully in the legislative procedure. The ECJ dismissed the action, reminding the applicant that "the adoption of a legislative act in compliance with the relevant provisions of the TFEU, despite the opposition of a minority of Member States, cannot amount to a violation of the principle of loyal cooperation which is incumbent upon the ... Council." See Case C-128/17 *Poland* v. *Parliament and Council*, para. 48 ff.

the heterogeneity of the EU, which calls for the permanent inclusion of all relevant social forces; they are fostered by the socio-cultural similarities of national and supranational civil servants meeting in the Council; and they are politically expedient, for if European legislation flows from consensual support of the Member States, it is more likely to be promptly implemented by national administrations.[85] True, recent studies show that, as a result of Brexit and the growing Euroscepticism at national level, the amount of oppositional voting in the Council is on the rise.[86] It would be a mistake, however, to take these data as conclusive evidence of a growing dissatisfaction of the Member States with the traditional consensus culture of the Council. Oppositional voting can well intervene after the sincere attempts to pursue and attain consensus. In this spirit, the rise of oppositional voting is perfectly compatible with the persistence of the consensus culture that many studies still acknowledge as a predominant trait of the Council's decision-making.[87]

I can now draw together the strands of my observations and offer a general definition of what the Council is. Indeed, the nature and position of the Council within the institutional triangle of the EU is not easy to construe, unless one observes it through the lens of executive federalism. A typical characteristic of the system of executive federalism is to have a parliamentary chamber which brings together the representatives of the people, and an executive council which brings together the executives of the constituent units. From a functional perspective, an executive council is part of the legislature – it is "organized for specifically political, and to some degree legislative, purposes."[88] From an organizational perspective, however, it has a governmental-bureaucratic structure – it is not only an institution of elected politicians, but it also consists of civil servants of the constituent units. Its peculiarity therefore resides in a tension between function (legislative) and structure (governmental-bureaucratic).[89] All these elements can be found in the Council of the EU as well.

[85] See Dann, "The Council," p. 543.

[86] Brigitte Pircher and Mike Farjam, "Oppositional Voting in the Council of the EU between 2010 and 2019: Evidence for Differentiated Politicisation" (2021) 22 *European Union Politics* 472–494.

[87] Stéphanie Novak, Olivier Rozenberg, and Selma Bendjaballah, "Enduring Consensus: Why the EU Legislative Process Stays the Same" (2021) 43 *Journal of European Integration* 475–493.

[88] Amie Kreppel, "Typologies and Classifications," in Shane Martin, Thomas Saalfeld, and Kaare W. Strøm (eds.), *The Oxford Handbook of Legislative Studies* (Oxford University Press, 2014), p. 83.

[89] Dann, "The Council," p. 544.

Therefore, following Philipp Dann's insightful works on this institution, I propose to view the Council as a legislative institution with a governmental-bureaucratic structure.[90]

2.6 The Commission: Between Independent Authority and Classical-Style Government

We now turn to the missing piece of the institutional triangle: the Commission. As stated by the ECJ, "EU legislation is adopted by the EU legislature following the democratic process defined in the EU and FEU Treaties."[91] Since the EU legislature consists of the Parliament and the Council, the question arises: what about the Commission? Why does the Court not even bother to mention it? What is its precise role in the adoption of European legislation? How influential is it vis-à-vis the co-legislators? Well, the constitutional setup is known. Whereas the Treaties attribute the legislative function to the Parliament and the Council only,[92] they also entrust the Commission with a near monopoly over the legislative initiative. This means that the effective exercise of the legislative authority by the Parliament and the Council is conditional upon the Commission presenting a legislative proposal. For want of a better definition, the Court recently affirmed that the Commission is "a key player in the legislative process."[93] This statement, however, does not say much. To get a satisfactory answer, it is necessary to look more systematically at powers and resources, both formal and informal, that the Commission can deploy in the legislative domain, and at how it makes use of them. To this end, it is worth starting with the power of legislative initiative, which is undoubtedly the Commission's long-term "identity badge."

The Commission's near monopoly over the legislative initiative has always been one of the most salient features of the Union system.[94] It is

[90] For a study affirming that the Council is "in between the parliamentary and non-parliamentary form" and advocating for its soft (as opposed to its hard) parliamentarization, Olivier Rozenberg, "The Council of the EU: From the Congress of Ambassadors to a Genuine Parliamentary Chamber?," PE 608.855, January 2019.

[91] Avis 1/17 *Accord ECG UE–Canada* EU:C:2019:341, para. 151.

[92] Arts. 14(1) and 16(1) TEU.

[93] Case C-57/16 P *ClientEarth* v. *Commission* EU:C:2018:660, para. 88.

[94] Nicola Lupo, "The Commission's Power to Withdraw Legislative Proposals and Its 'Parliamentarisation,' between Technical and Political Grounds" (2018) 14 *European Constitutional Law Review* 311–331.

a multifaceted prerogative, which not only entails the Commission's power to decide whether to submit a legislative proposal and the ensuing power to determine the subject matter, objective, and content of that proposal, but also includes two main safeguards. As affirmed by the Court of Justice in a 2015 landmark case, the Treaties stipulate that "where … the Council acts on a proposal from the Commission, it may amend that proposal only by acting unanimously." In addition, the Treaties entrust the Commission, as long as the Council has not acted, with the power "to alter its proposal or even, if need be, withdraw it."[95] As for this second safeguard, the Court made clear that the power of withdrawal does not confer upon the Commission the right to block the adoption of legislation on a whim.[96] Whenever the Commission is bent on withdrawing a legislative proposal, it must comply with some procedural obligations, namely the obligation to state reason and to have due regard to the concerns of the co-legislators.[97]

As a result, the prerogative of legislative initiative, together with its two safeguards, not only enables the Commission to feed into the legislative cycle "the general interest of the Union" (as possibly different from the interests represented by the Parliament and the Council) but also to exert some pressure on the conduct of the legislative work, provided that this pressure does not amount to arbitrarily impeding the Parliament and the Council from exercising their own legislative role. Experts of legislative procedures point out that, in exerting this pressure, the

[95] Art. 293 TFEU as interpreted in Case C-409/13 *Council* v. *Commission* EU:C:2015:217, para. 71 ff. For a negative appraisal of this judgment, Dominique Ritleng, "Does the European Court of Justice Take Democracy Seriously? Some Thoughts about the *Macro-Financial Assistance* Case" (2016) 53 *Common Market Law Review* 11–33 at 19 and 25, who argues that, by protecting the Commission's agenda-setting power and its responsibility for promoting the general interest of the Union, the ECJ has in fact upheld "an out of date functionalist view of the European integration process that overlooks the promotion of the principle of democracy within the EU institutional system"; conceptually, the Commission's power of initiative "should be [better] seen as an 'executive prerogative', which does not imply the power to prevent the adoption of an act by the legislature." For a positive appraisal of this judgment, defined as "legally sound and practically workable," Merijn Chamon, "Upholding the 'Community Method': Limits to the Commission's Power to Withdraw Legislative Proposals – *Council v Commission* (C-409/13)" (2015) 40 *European Law Review* 895–909 at 908.

[96] Case C-409/13 *Council* v. *Commission*, para. 75.

[97] Following the judgment in Case C-409/13 *Council* v. *Commission*, the institutions sought to proceduralize and parliamentarize the exercise of the Commission's power of withdrawal by introducing a set of specific provisions in the 2016 Interinstitutional Agreement on Better Law-Making and in the EP RoP. See Lupo, "The Commission's Power to Withdraw Legislative Proposals," 319 ff.

Commission has generally shown a certain degree of self-restraint and prudence. Despite the legal authority it derives from its "power of the pen," it lacks the necessary political legitimacy to overtly oppose the agreements reached by the co-legislators.[98] In its ambiguous position of "eternal not-yet government,"[99] the Commission cannot behave as a full-fledged counterweight to its fellow institutions, which enjoy stronger democratic mandates.[100] It is not by chance that, especially after the inception of the codecision procedure at the end of 1993, the number of political withdrawals by the Commission, as distinguished from technical ones, can be counted on one hand.

Yet this does not mean that the Commission has no influence over the legislative choices of the Parliament and the Council. In fact, the Commission has a rich palette of resources at its disposal to assert and preserve its preferences and interests throughout the legislative process.[101] For instance, it is the only institution to be present in almost all preparatory and decision-making bodies of both the Parliament and the Council. Through its representatives, it attends parliamentary committee meetings and the EP's plenary sessions as well as the Council's working party meetings, Coreper meetings, and the Council's sittings. Moreover, the Commission can rely on its technical expertise – and the information asymmetry that comes with it – to formulate compromise options for the co-legislators, thereby gaining substantial influence over the outcome.[102] This is especially true when considering that the basis for European decision-making is, first and foremost, expertise.[103] Hence, the Commission's strength "remains formidable, at both initiation and decision-taking stages."[104]

98 Jacqué, "Une vision réaliste," p. 187; Neill Nugent and Mark Rhinard, "The 'Political' Roles of the European Commission" (2019) 41 *Journal of European Integration* 203–220 at 212 f.

99 van Middelaar, *Alarums & Excursions*, p. 248.

100 Jacqué, "Lost in Transition," p. 36 f.

101 For an overview, Jens Blom-Hansen and Roman Senninger, "The Commission in EU Policy Preparation" (2021) 59 *Journal of Common Market Studies* 625–642.

102 María Gómez-Leal Pérez, "El procedimiento legislativo ordinario en la práctica: los acuerdos en primera lectura" (2015) *Cuadernos Europeos de Deusto* 101–118 at 114.

103 van Middelaar, *Alarums & Excursions*, p. 240.

104 Neill Nugent and Mark Rhinard, "Is the European Commission *Really* in Decline?" (2016) 54 *Journal of Common Market Studies* 1199–1215 at 1205 and 1207 f. For another convincing analysis rebutting the "decline of the Commission" thesis, Alexander Bürgin, "Intra- and Inter-Institutional Leadership of the European Commission President: An Assessment of Juncker's Organizational Reforms" (2018) 56 *Journal of Common Market Studies* 837–853.

Behind the ability to influence the legislative process stands a large bureaucratic apparatus – considerably bigger than those of the Parliament and the Council.[105] This is the Commission's breeding ground for knowledge and ideas. It is from here that the Commission draws its extensive expertise. Broadly speaking, the Commission's most relevant organizational units are the College of Commissioners, as a political leadership body, and the Directorates-General, as the bureaucratic structures responsible for specific policy areas (for example, DG International Partnerships, DG Health and Food Safety, DG Agriculture and Rural Development).[106] Each Directorate-General is headed by a senior civil servant, the Director-General, who reports to the Commissioner responsible for that specific policy area. As regards interinstitutional issues, the coordination between political leadership and bureaucratic services hinges on a preparatory body, known as *Groupe des relations interinstitutionnelles* (GRI). The GRI was created by the Commission in 2004 through the merger of two other internal bodies and could loosely be regarded as a functional equivalent of Coreper.[107] Surprisingly, not many systematic descriptions or empirical studies exist as regards the functioning and impact of this most important body; there are just a few exceptions.[108]

As the Commission's preparatory body, the GRI has various tasks.[109] As far as legislative matters are concerned, the GRI examines all the dossiers and prepares the positions to be adopted by the College of Commissioners within the framework of the Ordinary Legislative Procedure.[110] It usually meets on Friday; it consists of the Commission's cabinet members with responsibility for interinstitutional affairs; and it

105 Art. 19 Commission RoP.

106 For a detailed presentation of the bureaucratic structure of the Commission, Neill Nugent and Mark Rhinard, *The European Commission*, 2nd ed. (Palgrave Macmillan, 2015), chs. 4 and 6. See also European Commission, "Communication to the Commission: Governance in the European Commission," C(2020) 4240 final, 24 June 2020.

107 European Commission, "Constitution du Groupe des relations interinstitutionnelles ('GRI') en remplacement du Groupe des affaires parlementaires ('GAP') et du Groupe de suivi pour les affaires du Conseil ('GrAC')," SEC(2004) 1477, 22 November 2004.

108 In particular, Lara Panning, "Building and Managing the European Commission's Position for Trilogue Negotiations" (2021) 28 *Journal of European Public Policy* 32–52.

109 For a description of the role and tasks of the GRI, European Commission, "Interinstitutional Relations Group (GRI): Revised Working Methods of the GRI," SPI (2021) 7, 29 January 2021.

110 European Commission, "Annex to the Commission Decision Amending Its Rules of Procedure: Rules Giving Effect to the Rules of Procedure," C(2010) 1200, 24 February 2010, Rule 6-5.

is chaired by a member of the President's cabinet.[111] Before reaching the College on Wednesday (or on Tuesday during plenary sittings in Strasbourg), the GRI's preparatory work passes through HEBDO – an internal body of the Commission whose name derives from the French *hebdomadaire*, which means "weekly." HEBDO usually meets on Monday and consists of the Commission's heads of cabinet. Its main task is to put the finishing touches to the draft agenda ahead of a meeting of the College and to address those questions that the GRI could not settle, as the Commission follows the general rule that "any question closed during one of the stages of preparation of meetings of the College must not be re-opened during the next stage."[112]

To carry out its tasks, the GRI avails itself of information sheets that, in institutional jargon, are called *fiches*. Prepared by the responsible Directorate-General under the supervision of the relevant Commission cabinet, these information sheets summarize the background, status, and outlook of the legislative files at stake and include suggestions to the College as well as requests for authorization (for example, authorization to withdraw or modify a legislative proposal or to change a political approach). Most issues on which the GRI reaches a common understanding pass on to the College as "point A," meaning that they can be approved without discussion. In brief, the GRI is a key coordination body that aims at making two dimensions meet: that of political goal setting, which rests mainly with the College, and that of administrative expertise, which rests almost exclusively with the Directorates-General. It aims at channeling the policy-making strands pursued by the different DGs into a collegial approach, coherent with the Commission's political guidelines, thus ensuring vertical and horizontal coordination as well as collective responsibility.

That said, to put its expertise to effective use, the Commission needs finesse. If the Parliament and the Council perceive that the Commission is exploiting its expertise to pursue a partisan agenda, they will be less inclined to resort to its help. This in turn will affect the Commission's ability to steer the legislative work to its advantage. Only if it presents itself as a genuine mediator can the Commission gain the attention of its

[111] GRI meetings are prepared by the pre-GRI, which usually meets on Thursday. The pre-GRI consists of the Parliament/Council coordinators who work in the different Directorates-General and is chaired by the Secretariat-General.

[112] European Commission, "Annex to the Commission Decision Amending Its Rules of Procedure: Rules Giving Effect to the Rules of Procedure," Rule 6-5.2.

fellow institutions.[113] To this end, it usually cloaks its interventions and suggestions in a veil of objectivity, following a method that some authors define as "technical depoliticization."[114] This method is extremely effective in bringing the conflicting positions of the co-legislators closer together, as it deprives those positions of their emotional overtones and paves the way for a more matter-of-fact discussion.[115] The Commission is rather successful in applying this method, because it has always cultivated a self-image of an institution that "wants to be political, but above partisan cleavages."[116]

Again, the concept of executive federalism offers a powerful heuristic prism to appreciate the role of the Commission within the supranational institutional framework. Since executive federalism restrains the creation of leadership, effective interactions among separated yet interdependent institutions – such as the Parliament and the Council – become extremely reliant on the intervention of a neutral third party. And this is precisely what the Commission is meant to be.[117] By drawing on its functions of agenda setter, mediator, and guardian, it must ensure that the legislative institutions, especially the Council, do not sacrifice supranational interests in favor of immediate political gains. Owing to its presence at all stages of the legislative process and its ability to access all preparatory bodies, the Commission is extremely well placed to compel the co-legislators to "introduce into their functioning a thoughtful consideration toward common issues."[118] With this in mind, I take sides with those authors that, in different terms and from different perspectives, highlight the risks of a further parliamentarization of the Union through the *Spitzenkandidaten* process.[119] According to those

[113] Jacqué, "Une vision réaliste," p. 200 f.

[114] van Middelaar, *Alarums & Excursions*, p. 240: "A decision appears not as a political choice or the result of deliberations but as a 'solution' to a 'technical' problem"; Dann, "The Political Institutions," p. 261. This method is at the heart of what Renaud Dehousse called "political deficit." See Dehousse, "Constitutional Reform in the European Community," 122 and 124 f.

[115] On objectivity as a very effective dispute resolution technique, see the classic work by Georg Simmel, *Soziologie* (Duncker & Humblot, 1908), p. 104 ff.

[116] Neunreither, "Governance without Opposition," 430.

[117] Dann, "The Political Institutions," p. 259 f.

[118] Innerarity, *Democracy in Europe*, p. 139 f.

[119] François-Vivien Guiot, "La 'Commission politique', une 'commission impossible'? Construction d'un paradoxe" (2021) 57 *Cahiers de droit européen* 419–470; JHR and LB, "Editorial: *Spitzenkandidaten* and the European Union's System of Government" (2019) 15 *European Constitutional Law Review* 609–618 at 618; María José Martínez Iglesias, "The Accidental Democracy: A European Model," in Sacha Garben, Inge Govaere, and Paul

authors, such a parliamentarization would divest the Commission of its independence and – in the absence of a structural revision of the Treaties – of its legitimacy.

Upon considering all the elements hitherto analyzed, the picture of an influential legislative player emerges. Next to the Commission's constitutionally entrenched prerogatives, its expertise, and its internal organization, two other elements complete the picture. First, the Commission takes part in almost all judicial proceedings before the CJEU and, in so doing, promotes its own understanding of disputed provisions of EU law. This is especially true with regard to preliminary rulings of interpretation, where the Parliament and the Council rarely submit observations.[120] Secondly, due to the application of the *Spitzenkandidaten* process, Jean-Claude Juncker, the President of the Commission between 2014 and 2019, could implement an array of impactful changes to the Commission's internal configuration, with the purpose of establishing a more centralized leadership and thereby strengthening its political standing and assertiveness vis-à-vis the Parliament and the Council.[121] Given that Ursula von der Leyen has been even more consistent than her predecessor in pursuing such a reform agenda,[122] the Commission is on what appears to be an irreversible path towards lessening its oft-decried internal fragmentation and specialization.[123]

Nemitz (eds.), *Critical Reflections on Constitutional Democracy in the European Union* (Hart, 2019), p. 205.

120 The EP's Committee on Legal Affairs, which is responsible for advising the EP's President whether to submit observations or intervene in judicial proceedings on behalf of the Parliament, follows a set of guidelines according to which, "[w]here only the interpretation of a provision is at stake, Parliament should not submit observations." See European Parliament, "Notice to Members (10/2015): Guidelines for the Application of Rule 149 of the Rules of Procedure," PE549.409v03-00, 26 May 2021, para. 17.

121 Hansen and Senninger, "The Commission in EU Policy Preparation," 628 f.; Bürgin, "Intra- and Inter-Institutional Leadership."

122 Suzanne Lynch and Ilya Gridneff, "Europe's American President: The Paradox of Ursula von der Leyen," *Politico*, 6 October 2022.

123 Another interesting example of the increased centralization of power in the hands of the Commission's President can be seen in Art. 17(6) TEU, which provides that a "member of the Commission shall resign if the President so requests." Introduced by the Lisbon Treaty, the scope of this prerogative was discussed in detail in Case T-562/12 *Dalli v. Commission* EU:T:2015:270, and the following Case C-394/15 P *Dalli* v. *Commission* EU:C:2016:262. These cases arose from the infamous *Dalligate* and the resignation of John Dalli, then Commissioner for Health and Consumer Policy, accused of seeking to obtain a large sum of money from a Swedish enterprise in exchange for favorable provisions in the drafting of what later became the 2014 Tobacco Products Directive.

That said, the legitimacy of the Commission suffers from a structural tension. The fact that its authority stems from a procedure that dovetails the will of the European Parliament with that of the (European) Council puts it in a situation of ambiguous political allegiance. At the same time, any attempt at fully parliamentarizing the Commission is at odds with EU primary law, which requires the Commission to be independent and forbids its members from seeking or taking instructions from any other institution, national or European. Therefore, the Commission seems to be stuck in limbo: a hybrid between an independent authority and a genuine government.[124] The Commission's hybrid nature emerges, with great clarity, in the tasks that the Treaties assign to it. Like an independent authority, it has sanctioning powers, especially in the field of competition law and state aid; like a government, it plays an indispensable role in the adoption of legislation. However, despite its independence, the Commission is not apolitical – and it is not expected to be so.[125] EU primary law entrusts it with a clear mandate, which the Commission has always interpreted politically. At a later stage, I will conceptualize the role of the Commission in the light of the Treaties' stipulation that "[t]he functioning of the Union shall be founded on representative democracy."[126] For the time being, it suffices to highlight that the Commission's legislative influence depends on a skillful exploitation of its authority (that is, independence coupled with expertise), rather than on a stubborn application of its legal prerogatives. It requires a confident style of negotiating at a dignified remove.

2.7 Conclusions

I have dealt with the role and internal structures of the three legislative institutions at some length because only the accurate knowledge of both allows the true meaning and importance of trilogues in the workings of the European legislative process to be captured. To be sure, other actors could appear on the stage, such as national apex courts and national parliaments. Although those actors will not be the subject of a specific analysis, as explained in the introduction to this book, their presence should influence both the institutional profile of trilogues and their internal functioning.

Supranational legislation is the product of intricate cooperation, regulated by law and practice. Each piece of legislation is the outcome of a

[124] Dann, "The Political Institutions," p. 261.

[125] Case T-562/12 *Dalli* v. *Commission*, para. 133.

[126] See Chapter 4, Section 4.2.4.

delicate exercise, which requires political actors to reconcile different functions, identities, and interests. Neither a hierarchical order nor a quest for supremacy makes sense in such a context. Essential traits are instead a prevailing consensus culture and an unyielding search for compromise. Those traits are the makings of a political process that genuinely reflects federal principles.[127] Furthermore, their combination has the potential for reducing the risk that minorities fall victim to the abuse of those mechanisms that were originally devised to protect them. The instrumental use of the filibuster within the US Senate is a case in point, as it often ends up protecting the interests of small states, which "tend to be significantly less racially and ethnically diverse than the nation as a whole," to the detriment of the minority points of view of the African American, Latino, and Asian populations.[128]

In this spirit, I have argued that the model of executive federalism accounts for much of these complex and delicate arrangements. In no other perspective can the institutional balance and complementing contributions of the three institutions be understood. In a well-received article published shortly after the entry into force of the Maastricht Treaty, Renaud Dehousse presented a series of cogent reasons to oppose a further parliamentarization of the Commission and a strengthening of the majoritarian features of the European political system. In particular, he thought that those developments were likely to accentuate tensions between the Union and its Member States and that "the lack of a body charged with reconciling the various interests [was] liable to be keenly felt."[129] At the time, trilogues were looming on the horizon, with the aim to realize a balance between supranational (European Parliament) and national (Council) interests, through the active influence of the Commission. A reconstruction and a better understanding of how trilogues work will therefore be the subject of the next chapter.

[127] Daniel J. Elazar, "Federalism and Consociational Regimes" (1985) 15 *Publius: The Journal of Federalism* 17–34 at 22, who affirms that federalism "is as much a matter of process as of structure, particularly if process is broadly defined to include a political cultural dimension as well. Elements of a federal process include a sense of partnership on the part of the parties to the federal compact, manifested through negotiated cooperation on issues and programs and based on a commitment to open bargaining between all parties to an issue in such a way as to strive for consensus or, failing that, an accommodation which protects the fundamental integrity of all the partners."

[128] On this problem, Frances E. Lee, "Bicameral Representation," in George C. Edwards III, Frances E. Lee, and Eric Schickler (eds.), *The Oxford Handbook of the American Congress* (Oxford University Press, 2011), p. 282 f.

[129] Dehousse, "Constitutional Reform in the European Community," 130.

3 Unpacking the Law and Practice of Trilogues

3.1 Introduction

As shown in the previous chapter, the European legislative function rests on the contributions of three autonomous institutions, which enjoy far-reaching powers of self-organization. Through those powers, these institutions allocate tasks to different internal bodies according to the notion of "internal differentiation" – institutions decentralize a certain amount of decision-making power, "so that decisions do not overburden the hierarchy and can be made at the point of knowledge."[1] At the same time, EU primary law requires institutions to cooperate in such a manner as to ensure task-oriented relations among political actors. This requirement, which derives from a joint reading of Article 13(1) and (2) TEU, aims at preventing autonomy becoming an impediment to the effective functioning of the European institutional framework.[2]

Arguably, the legislative function creates the most conflict between autonomy and cooperation. Co-legislation is therefore highly coordinated, despite the occasionally vague nature of the provisions of EU primary law that regulate the Ordinary Legislative Procedure (OLP). As evidence of this, one can take the sheer number of interinstitutional agreements, rules of procedure, as well as other (often neglected) sources of law: the administrative circulars. All these sources hint at the existence

[1] Mary Jo Hatch, *Organization Theory: Modern, Symbolic, and Postmodern Perspectives*, 3rd ed. (Oxford University Press, 2013), p. 121.

[2] B. Guy Peters, "Coordination in the EU," in Erik Jones, Anand Menon, and Stephen Weatherill (eds.), *The Oxford Handbook of the European Union* (Oxford University Press, 2012), pp. 796 and 800, arguing that the EU "constitutes a very special challenge to would-be coordinators" and further adding that "[c]oordination is more difficult in the EU than in most national governments."

of articulate structures that seek to create intra- and interinstitutional coordination. Against this backdrop, trilogues showcase these coordination efforts. They contribute to ensuring the consistency, effectiveness, and continuity requested by Article 13(1) TEU; they are in fact an "algorithm" for the realization of those requirements and, as such, enjoy a strong functional justification.

The awareness of the articulate nature of the European legislative function comes with another important insight. Trilogues are part and parcel of a broader *process* that guides actors' intersubjective behaviors. This process consists of "an unbroken gradation of passages, which lead from spontaneous assent and voluntary performance through the intersubjective arrangement which comes to pass by dint of the 'compulsion of social relations' until the arrangement of order by force" – a continuum that stretches from consent to coercion.[3] The richness of instruments whereby the institutions coordinate their legislative action is expressly acknowledged in Article 295 TFEU.[4] Apart from allowing the adoption of a typical instrument (the interinstitutional agreement), Article 295 TFEU also states that "[t]he European Parliament, the Council and the Commission shall consult each other and by common agreement make arrangements for their cooperation." By using the broad term "arrangement," this provision offers legal grounding for a wider set of instruments and structures, including practices and conventions, which exist next to – and together with – legally binding provisions.[5]

My reconstruction begins from here. To better understand the workings of the European legislative process, I cannot limit myself to the scattered legal provisions of the Treaties, the 2007 Joint Declaration on Codecision, and the European Parliament's Rules of Procedure – this would convey only a partial picture of the whole phenomenon. I have therefore chosen to complement those legal provisions with a set of administrative circulars that I was able to examine through a number of access-to-documents requests. Following the pyramid of legal sources,

[3] Hermann Heller, "The Nature and Structure of the State" (1996) 18 *Cardozo Law Review* 1139–1216 at 1171 f. See also W. Richard Scott, *Institutions and Organizations: Ideas, Interests, and Identities*, 4th ed. (Sage, 2014), p. 59 ff.

[4] This provision is a concretization of the duty of sincere cooperation in the legislative domain. See Johann Schoo and Niklas Görlitz, "Artikel 295 AEUV [Interinstitutionelle Vereinbarungen]," in Jürgen Schwarze (ed.), *EU-Kommentar*, 3rd ed. (Nomos, 2012), para. 2.

[5] For a similar interpretation, Olivier Costa, Renaud Dehousse, and Aneta Trakalová, "Codecision and 'Early Agreements': An Improvement or a Subversion of the Legislative Procedure?" (2011) *Notre Europe* 10.

I will reconstruct the European legislative process in a top-down fashion. After offering a brief introduction to the relevant Treaty provisions (Section 3.2.1), I will analyze the 2007 Joint Declaration on Codecision (Section 3.2.2) and clarify the nature of administrative circulars (Section 3.2.3). Finally, I will unite all the above legal material in a coherent whole, describing diachronically how the European legislative process works, including some considerations about the inner workings of trilogues (Sections 3.3, 3.4, 3.5, and 3.6). By so doing, I aim to provide a more systematic and sharper picture of the European legislative machinery.

3.2 The Law and Practice of European Law-Making

3.2.1 The Treaties

According to Article 294 TFEU, the OLP consists of three readings and requires that the Parliament and the Council agree on precisely the same measure in precisely the same form (including punctuation!) before this can become legislation. The procedure may come to an end at any of these readings if the Parliament and the Council reach an agreement. The OLP begins as soon as the Commission submits a legislative proposal to the co-legislators (including the European Economic and Social Committee and the Committee of the Regions, when EU primary law so provides),[6] and these start to analyze it and to establish interinstitutional contacts. At this stage, unlike for the second and third readings, the Treaties do not provide for a defined maximum time limit within which the institutions must decide. The co-legislators may therefore work on a draft legislative act taking as much time they see fit.

Formally, the first reading is initiated by the Parliament, meaning the EP is the first "chamber" to act on a legislative proposal, with the Council then deciding on the EP's position. If the two branches of the European legislative authority cannot reach an agreement by the end of the third reading, the draft proposal is not adopted. To facilitate the successful completion of the procedure, Article 294 TFEU provides for different types of mechanisms, notably time limits, special majority requirements for the adoption of amendments, and a Conciliation Committee. So, in the second reading, the Parliament has up to three months to approve, even by tacit consent, the Council's first-reading position (in which case the act is adopted), to reject it (in which case the procedure is closed), or

[6] Case C-57/16 P *ClientEarth* v. *Commission* EU:C:2018:660, para. 86.

to amend it. To make the rejection or approval of new amendments more difficult, the Treaties oblige the EP to decide by a majority of its component members. At this point, the Council has three months to approve all the amendments (in which case the act is adopted) or, failing that, to convene the Conciliation Committee within six weeks. In other words, the Treaties do not allow the Council to propose further amendments but only to deliberate and vote on the amendments put forward by the Parliament in its second-reading position.

The Conciliation Committee is a body composed of all the members of the Council and an equal number of MEPs (in conformity with the relative size of each political group in the Parliament), for a total number of fifty-four representatives. The Commission also participates, and it has the task of helping the co-legislators reconcile their differences. The Committee has six weeks to reach an agreement on a joint text and, to this effect, it enjoys great latitude. As stated by the ECJ, the wording of Article 294 TFEU "does not ... itself include any restriction as to the content of the measures chosen that enable agreement to be reached on a joint text."[7] At this stage, the main concern is to ensure the successful conclusion of the procedure, avoiding a waste of time and resources. If the Committee fails to approve a joint text, the procedure is closed. If it succeeds, the text is submitted to the Parliament and the Council, which have six weeks to either adopt it or reject it – no amendments are possible at this stage. Only if both branches of the European legislative authority vote in favor of the joint text can the draft piece of legislation finally reach the "statute book."

According to Article 294 TFEU, the role of the Commission changes throughout the procedure. The scope of its powers gradually diminishes as the co-legislators proceed through the readings. At first reading, the Commission holds almost complete sway over its proposal. EU primary law stipulates that if the Council intends to amend the proposal of the Commission, it may do so only by acting unanimously. Furthermore, it stipulates that "[a]s long as the Council has not acted, the Commission may alter its proposal at any time,"[8] without it being obliged to draw up a new proposal or perform any other written formality.[9] As already mentioned, the Court has construed this power in such a manner as to

[7] Case C-344/04 *IATA and ELFAA* EU:C:2006:10, para. 57 ff. [8] Art. 293(2) TFEU.

[9] Case C-643/15 *Slovakia* v. *Council* EU:C:2017:631, para. 179; Case C-280/93 *Germany* v. *Council* EU:C:1994:367, para. 36.

include the most extreme form of alteration: its withdrawal.[10] At second reading, the Commission can no longer alter or withdraw its proposal. The Treaties, however, demand that it issue an opinion on all the amendments adopted by the Parliament; and this opinion will determine the type of vote required in the Council – the Council will have to "act unanimously on the amendments on which the Commission has delivered a negative opinion."[11] Finally, when the co-legislators go to conciliation, the Commission loses any formal power over the legislative proposal. But, owing to its full involvement in the conciliation proceedings, it can still use its expertise to steer the negotiations in a direction favorable to its position.[12]

It is against this complex backdrop that the Parliament, the Council, and the Commission adopted the 2007 Joint Declaration on Codecision, with the aim of filling some of the "silences" left by the drafters in the Treaties. This Declaration is a binding interinstitutional agreement, which – as acknowledged by the General Court – "governs [trilogue] meetings."[13] The choice of the verb "govern" appears entirely appropriate, as this Declaration has become such an important part of the European rules of collective political engagement that institutional actors no longer differentiate between those procedural practices that have a basis in EU primary law and those that have their basis in the 2007 Joint Declaration on Codecision.[14] Let us therefore have a look at its content.

[10] The Court referred to the Commission's power to amend or withdraw a legislative proposal on several occasions. See, e.g., Case C-643/15 *Slovakia* v. *Council*, para. 177 ff.; Case C-445/00 *Austria* v. *Council* EU:C:2003:445, para. 45; C-280/93 *Germany* v. *Council*, para. 36; Case C-13/92 *Driessen and Others* v. *Minister van Verkeer en Waterstaat* EU:C:1993:828, para. 33; Case C-331/88 *The Queen* v. *Ministry of Agriculture, Fisheries and Food, ex parte FEDESA and Others* EU:C:1990:391, para. 37; Case C-355/87 *Commission* v. *Council* EU:C:1989:220, para. 44; Case C-188/85 *Fediol* v. *Commission* EU:C:1988:400, para. 37. However, the uncertainties about the general limits of such power were addressed by the ECJ for the first time in Case C-409/13 *Council* v. *Commission*; and again in Case C-24/20 *Commission* v. *Council (Adhésion à l'acte de Genève)* EU:C:2022:911, para. 76 ff.

[11] Arts. 294(7)(c) and 294(9) TFEU.

[12] On the Ordinary Legislative Procedure and its institutional balance, Jacques Ziller, *Advanced Introduction to European Union Law* (Edward Elgar, 2020), chs. 10 and 11.

[13] Case T-75/14 *USFSPEI* v. *Parliament and Council* EU:T:2017:813, para. 103 ff.; Case T-17/14 *U4U and Others* v. *Parliament and Council* EU:T:2016:489, para. 137 ff. In those cases, the General Court relied on the 2007 Joint Declaration on Codecision to conclude that a compromise reached in trilogues "cannot be regarded as constituting an amendment of that proposal by the Commission itself."

[14] Jeffrey Stacey, *Integrating Europe: Informal Politics and Institutional Change* (Oxford University Press, 2010), p. 202 f.

3.2.2 *The 2007 Joint Declaration on Codecision: Filling (Some) "Constitutional Silences"*

Under the 2007 Joint Declaration on Codecision,[15] the institutions have agreed on "clearing the way, where appropriate, for the adoption of the act concerned at an early stage of the procedure."[16] This provision reflects a desideratum laid down in the Declaration on Respect for Time Limits under the Co-decision Procedure, appended to the Treaty of Amsterdam. With that Declaration, the High Contracting Parties call on the European Parliament, the Council, and the Commission "to make every effort to ensure that the co-decision procedure operates as expeditiously as possible."[17] To that effect, the legislative institutions have committed themselves, on the basis of the Joint Declaration, to "cooperat[ing] through appropriate interinstitutional contacts."

The expression "appropriate contacts" refers to that thick web of interaction channels that the Parliament, the Council, and the Commission have established among themselves "to exchange information ... on the progress of codecision files" and to coordinate their works.[18] The coordination of legislative works occurs, for instance, through information exchange in official venues, such as the EP's committee meetings.[19] Or it can be realized by the Presidents of the three institutions – in the last parliamentary term, for instance, they agreed to meet two or three times a year "in order to raise and discuss issues at the highest level."[20] Moreover, coordination is ensured by the officials working in the General Secretariats, which comprise administrative units expressly entrusted

[15] On the notion of "constitutional silences," Martin Loughlin, "The Silences of Constitutions" (2018) 16 *International Journal of Constitutional Law* 922–935 at 928.

[16] Joint Declaration on Practical Arrangements for the Codecision Procedure (Article 251 of the EC Treaty), OJ 2007 No. C145/5, para. 4 f. See also Interinstitutional Agreement between the European Parliament, the Council of the European Union and the European Commission on Better Law-Making, OJ 2016 No. L123/1, para. 32 ff. With a special focus on this second agreement, María José Martínez Iglesias, "Better Law-Making and the Interinstitutional (Dis)agreements: Some Comments" (2020) 26 *European Law Journal* 108–113.

[17] Treaty of Amsterdam Amending the Treaty on European Union, the Treaties Establishing the European Communities and Certain Related Acts, OJ 1997 No. C340/01.

[18] Joint Declaration on Practical Arrangements for the Codecision Procedure (Article 251 of the EC Treaty), para. 6.

[19] See, e.g., Rule 44(2) EP RoP: "During the examination of a proposal for a legislative act, the committee responsible shall ask the Commission and the Council to keep it informed of the progress of that proposal in the Council and its working parties."

[20] European Parliament, "Activity Report: Developments and Trends of the Ordinary Legislative Procedure: 1 July 2014–1 July 2019 (8th Parliamentary Term)," PE 639.611, at 17.

with that task. Finally, legislative coordination relies on joint administrative bodies. One example is the monthly Interinstitutional Coordination Group (formerly known as Neunreither Group), which brings together high-ranking officials from the Parliament, the Council, and the Commission.[21] The task of this body is to devise possible working arrangements to improve interinstitutional interactions and to solve outstanding differences arising from day-to-day legislative practice.[22]

However, by "appropriate contacts" the 2007 Joint Declaration on Codecision refers, above all, to "tripartite meetings ('trilogues')." With them, the legislative institutions aim at reaching a political "agreement at first and second reading stages, as well as contributing to the preparation of the work of the Conciliation Committee."[23] To take part and negotiate in trilogues, the Joint Declaration requires each "institution, in accordance with its own rules of procedure, [to] designate its participants for each meeting, define its mandate for the negotiations and inform the other institutions of arrangements for the meetings in good time." The Parliament, the Council, and the Commission have complied with this requirement in different ways. While the Parliament has adopted a rather detailed set of provisions in its Rules of Procedure, the Council and the Commission have essentially relied on administrative circulars. Both these approaches seem legitimate, as the Joint Declaration requires the institutions to regulate the matter "in accordance with" – and not "by means of" – their Rules of Procedure. This choice of words leaves the institutions free to pick the instrument(s) they consider most appropriate.

In addition, the 2007 Joint Declaration on Codecision provides a series of provisions expressly dedicated to the workings of trilogues. For instance, it stipulates that the attainment of a trilogue agreement must

[21] The *Neunreither Group* was established in 1987 at the initiative of Karlheinz Neunreither, then EP's Director-General for Committees and Inter-Parliamentary Delegations, with the support and active contribution of Sir William Nicoll, then Council's Director-General for the Relations with the European Parliament, as well as Jean-Claude Eeckhout, then Commission's Director for the Relations with the European Parliament. See Una O'Dwyer, "La dynamique historique des relations interinstitutionnelles. Le point de vue d'un praticien sur l'évolution de la procédure de codécision" (2010) *Revue du droit de l'Union européenne* 487–526 at 493.

[22] For instance, the Interinstitutional Coordination Group is responsible for monitoring at technical level the implementation of the Interinstitutional Agreement on Better Law-Making. See Interinstitutional Agreement between the European Parliament, the Council of the European Union and the European Commission on Better Law-Making, para. 50.

[23] Joint Declaration on Practical Arrangements for the Codecision Procedure (Article 251 of the EC Treaty, para. 7.

always be confirmed by letter. This letter must be sent by the Council to the Parliament or vice versa, depending on when the agreement is reached. Furthermore, the Joint Declaration provides that a deal cannot be changed "without the explicit agreement, at the appropriate level, of both the European Parliament and the Council." Finally, it defines the role to be played by the Commission throughout the negotiations, stating that the Commission "shall facilitate contacts and shall exercise its right of initiative in a constructive manner with a view to reconciling the positions of the European Parliament and the Council, with due regard for the balance between the institutions and the role conferred on it by the Treaty." But there are three further elements of the 2007 Joint Declaration on Codecision that are especially worth analyzing.

A Taxonomy of Trilogues

The 2007 Joint Declaration on Codecision specifies that trilogues "may be held at all stages of the procedure."[24] Officials therefore distinguish among trilogues depending on the legislative reading in which the agreement occurs. Hence, the following four categories:

- First-reading agreements: these flow from trilogue negotiations that take place *ahead of the adoption of the EP's first-reading position*, with the expectation that the EP will then incorporate the result of those negotiations into its first-reading position and that the Council will approve it;
- Early-second-reading agreements: these flow from trilogue negotiations that take place *ahead of the Council's first-reading position*, with the expectation that the Council will then incorporate the result of those negotiations into its first-reading position and that the EP will approve it at the beginning of the second reading;
- Second-reading agreements: these flow from trilogue negotiations that take place *ahead of the EP's second-reading position*, with the expectation that the EP will then incorporate the result of those negotiations into its second-reading position and the Council will approve it;
- Agreements ahead of the Conciliation Committee: these flow from trilogue negotiations that take place *ahead of the formal convening of the Conciliation Committee*, with the expectation that such committee will then incorporate the result of those

[24] Ibid., para. 8.

negotiations into a joint text to be adopted by the Parliament and the Council in third reading.

In addition, the Declaration states that trilogues may be held "at different levels of representation, depending on the nature of the expected discussion."[25] Therefore, institutional actors distinguish between "political trilogues" and "technical trilogues." The former focus on contentious issues and are attended by key political figures. The latter deal with "secondary issues of a technical and non-contentious nature"[26] and are usually attended by officials that rank lower in the political and administrative hierarchy. By employing such a distinction, the institutions want to ensure a good use of the time of the most senior actors, preventing lengthy discussions of detailed technical issues from taking place during political trilogues – this is another example of internal differentiation. Of course, since defining what is "political" and what is "technical" is often a matter of expediency, this distinction results from the co-legislators' joint agreement on a case-by-case basis.

A Two-Level Game

Furthermore, the Declaration stipulates that each institution "will designate its participants for each meeting [and] define its mandate for the negotiations." By so doing, the Declaration establishes a two-level game.[27] To meet in trilogues, negotiators must first obtain a mandate from their respective principals. Once trilogues begin, negotiators operate under the constraint that any agreement must eventually be adopted separately by the co-legislators. Any (even minor) amendment to a final agreement by either institution is considered a rejection of the entire deal. This understanding finds reflection in the EP's Rules of Procedure, which stipulate that "[a]ny provisional agreement . . . shall be given priority in voting and shall be put to a single vote," unless the plenary decides to proceed with the vote on amendments.[28] There thus exists a "crucial link" between

[25] Ibid., para. 8.

[26] Council of the European Union, "Ordinary Legislative Procedure: Guide for the Presidency," 11 October 2016, at 6.

[27] Robert D. Putnam, "Diplomacy and Domestic Politics: The Logic of Two-Level Games" (1988) 42 *International Organization* 427–460 at 435 f., affirming that the two-level-game model may apply to a host of different contexts, such as "heads of government representing nations . . . or labor and management representatives, or party leaders in a multiparty coalition, or a finance minister negotiating with an IMP team, or leaders of a House-Senate conference committee, or ethnic-group leaders in a consociational democracy."

[28] Rule 59(3)(1) EP RoP.

negotiations in trilogues, on the one hand, and the discussions within each institution, on the other. What is more, the relation between the two levels is "iterative," meaning that negotiators test provisional agreements on their principals as negotiations progress. All these characteristics make the two levels so closely intertwined that they cannot be understood independently from one another.

The two-level-game model not only provides a descriptively accurate image of how trilogues work but also offers a theoretically convincing explanation as to why trilogues are so successful in bringing about legislative agreements. Due to what some authors have termed "double acts of delegation," the institutions empower their respective representatives to both facilitate intra-institutional policy-making and negotiate interinstitutional compromise.[29] In turn, this authorization puts pressure on the negotiators from the Parliament, the Council, and the Commission to work as hard as possible to fulfill the requests and expectations of both their principals and their negotiating counterparts. After all, it is their reputation as reliable negotiators that is at stake, and they are likely to do whatever it takes to reach satisfactory agreements and avoid involuntary defections, especially unplanned rejections of trilogue agreements by the principal(s).

Two further elements are likely to prompt negotiators to display generic goodwill to one another and to sustain mutual efforts to reach acceptable compromise. To begin with, trilogues belong to a dynamic that game theory experts call "infinitely repeated games," meaning that the institutions know they will meet again a potentially nonfinite number of times for negotiating other legislative files. In these circumstances, defections can have high political and reputational costs. Furthermore, despite being the prerogative of the Commission, most legislative initiatives follow "joint declarations on annual interinstitutional programming" signed by the Presidents of the three institutions. These declarations, expressly acknowledged by Article 17(1) TEU,[30] set out broad objectives and priorities for the following year and identify items of major political importance to be prioritized in the legislative process.[31]

[29] Tom Delreux and Thomas Laloux, "Concluding Early Agreements in the EU: A Double Principal–Agent Analysis of Trilogue Negotiations" (2018) 56 *Journal of Common Market Studies* 300–317.

[30] Art. 17(1) TEU stipulates that the Commission "shall initiate the Union's annual and multiannual programming with a view to achieving interinstitutional agreements."

[31] Interinstitutional Agreement between the European Parliament, the Council of the European Union and the European Commission on Better Law-Making, para. 7. See, however, Martínez Iglesias, "Better Law-Making and the Interinstitutional

So, when negotiators meet in trilogues, they operate in the knowledge that the successful completion of the negotiations corresponds to the common wishes of the three institutions' highest echelons. Arguably, this further motivates them to attain viable legislative compromises.

But there is more to it. Negotiators in trilogues can exploit the existence of two distinct yet interconnected negotiation levels and play them against each other. In other words, they use the political dynamics and policy preferences of one level to influence those of the other level and vice versa.[32] Negotiators may do that, in the first place, to improve their bargaining power. For instance, negotiators in trilogues may claim the following: "I could accept your proposal, but my colleagues won't ever go along with it."[33] Or they may exploit different policy preferences between the opposing negotiating team and its principal to establish cross-table alliances. Moreover, negotiators may exploit the two-level dynamics to broaden the so-called win-set, which is the range of possible trilogue agreements that "would 'win' . . . when simply voted up or down."[34]

The broadening of the win-set can result from package deals and logrolling, which exploit different preference intensities,[35] as well as from those tactics that negotiators employ to reinforce one another's standing in the eyes of their respective principals, especially the public praising of the counterparts for their good work.[36] When negotiator A publicly praises negotiator B, it is not only a gesture of institutional courtesy but is also seeking to increase the political capital of B. Perceived as an effective negotiator, B will gain a wider margin of maneuver and thereby a wider win-set. Owing to B's wider win-set, A's relative bargaining leverage will in turn be augmented, together with the chances of reaching an agreement that satisfies all the parties involved.

When trilogue agreements eventually come back to the responsible parliamentary committees and Coreper, before then moving on to the plenaries of the Parliament and the Council, they are rarely rejected or

(Dis)agreements," 112, pointing out that the current term "has disavowed the provisions on multiannual programming of the IIA."

32 Putnam, "Diplomacy and Domestic Politics," 433. On the different strategies that can be employed by trilogue negotiators to play both levels against each other while avoiding a situation of agency slack, Delreux and Laloux, "Concluding Early Agreements in the EU," 305.

33 Putnam, "Diplomacy and Domestic Politics," 440. 34 Ibid., 437.

35 On the importance of package deals in the European legislative process, Raya Kardasheva, "Package Deals in EU Legislative Politics" (2013) 57 *American Journal of Political Science* 858–874.

36 Putnam, "Diplomacy and Domestic Politics," 451.

amended. This happens for at least three reasons. First, because institutions fear the political costs of rejection – nobody wants to incur blame for failed negotiations. Secondly, because reopening potentially settled issues can bring about high transaction costs in terms of both time and resources, while being of limited benefit in terms of political achievements. Thirdly, because a set of failed negotiations risks returning the institutions to a worse situation than the one that existed at the time the negotiations began – the disagreement persists, but the institutions can no longer count on the previous reservoir of goodwill and trust. Last but not least, because trilogue agreements are the result of painstaking negotiations – negotiations which necessarily seek to accommodate the policy preferences of a wide majority of political actors.

The Confirmation Letter

What is the outcome of trilogues? How does this outcome acquire legal relevance for the European legislative procedures? As for the first question, the outcome of trilogues is an agreement. To be precise, it is an agreement over a set of amendments to the Commission's original proposal. As for the second question, an agreement attained through trilogues must be officially endorsed through a letter between the co-legislators, with a copy to the relevant Commissioner. The letter is a crucial element, as no other means can certify the existence of an agreement. In the case of first- and second-reading agreements, the sender is the chair of Coreper and the recipient is the chair of the relevant parliamentary committee; in the case of early-second-reading agreements, it is the other way around.[37] The letter may be sent only after the competent body, either Coreper or the relevant parliamentary committee, has agreed to send it and formalizes the sender's commitment to bringing the trilogue agreement to the attention of the institution for deliberation and vote.

Here is how the 2007 Joint Declaration on Codecision words this obligation regarding first-reading agreements:

> Where an agreement is reached through informal negotiations in trilogues, the chair of Coreper shall forward, in a letter to the chair of the relevant parliamentary committee, details of the substance of the agreement, in the form of amendments to the Commission proposal. That letter shall indicate the

[37] Joint Declaration on Practical Arrangements for the Codecision Procedure (Article 251 of the EC Treaty), paras. 14, 18, and 23.

Council's willingness to accept that outcome ... should it be confirmed by the vote in plenary.[38]

The wording of this provision is unfortunate. It seems to imply – and, in fact, it is believed to imply – that if the EP plenary adopts the agreement appended to the confirmation letter, the Council "commits itself to adopt [sic] the act."[39] From a legal perspective, however, this view must be rejected: no legislative agreement at Coreper level could ever bind the Council. The co-legislators enjoy unconstrained freedom when determining the content of European legislation. They remain free to disregard the outcome of trilogues if they so wish. Still, this provision clarifies how the agreements achieved in trilogues become relevant for the European legislative institutions. As coordinating mechanisms that partake in the structure of the European legislative process, trilogues produce agreements that, pursuant to the 2007 Joint Declaration, find their way into – and have an impact on – the internal procedures of the co-legislators.

3.2.3 *Administrative Circulars: Nature and Relevant Examples*

I have already mentioned that the 2007 Joint Declaration on Codecision requires "[e]ach institution, in accordance with its own rules of procedure, [to] designate its participants for each meeting, define its mandate for the negotiations and inform the other institutions of arrangements for the meetings in good time." I have also mentioned that whereas the Parliament has adopted a detailed set of provisions in its Rules of Procedure, the Council and Commission have complied with this requirement by adopting a set of administrative circulars. As for the legal status of the Rules of Procedure, there is no dispute: they are genuine legal provisions, which can be relied upon in judicial proceedings by the members of the institutions and, within certain limits, by affected third parties (for example, the infringement of Rules of Procedure can amount to a violation of essential procedural requirements under Article 263 TFEU).[40] Doubts may arise as to the legal status of administrative circulars. Space precludes an in-depth elaboration of this topic. Given

[38] Ibid., para. 14.

[39] European Parliament, "Thematic Sheet: Letter of the Chair of Coreper Confirming a 1st or 2nd Reading Agreement," April 2010.

[40] For the legal relevance of rules of procedure in proceedings before the CJEU, Koen Lenaerts, Ignace Maselis, and Kathleen Gutman, *EU Procedural Law* (Oxford University Press, 2014), p. 377 f.

the relevance of the matter, however, some flavor of it must nevertheless be conveyed.

Administrative circulars are a typology of instruments that administrations, at all government levels, adopt for the most diverse purposes. This typology is so wide-ranging that it can only be described, in very vague terms, as encompassing all those (usually written) formal and official instruments that are meant for circulation to a closed group of people or for general distribution. Administrative circulars do not have a typical content. They can be used to issue orders and to specify the behavior of public officials as well as to provide information and to perform acts of institutional courtesy. Also, administrative circulars can be issued by superior vis-à-vis equally ranking or subordinate personnel as well as by the latter vis-à-vis the former – in fact, the adoption of circulars does not postulate the existence of any specific organizational relationship between the author and the addressees.[41] Due to such diversity, one scholar has gone so far as to affirm that circulars are nothing but "container[s] suitable for all purposes."[42]

Administrative circulars are widely used in the EU, too. Their adoption rests not only on the administration's power of self-organization but also on Article 41 of the Charter of Fundamental Rights – insofar as they ensure the European citizens' right to good administration – and on Article 298(1) TFEU – insofar as they contribute to creating an "open, efficient and independent European administration." And circulars certainly are an effective instrument for the establishment, maintenance, and management of such an administration. Note, however, that the status of administrative circulars depends on their content. As a rule, it is possible to say that whereas those circulars that contain interpretative guides, instructions to officials, and codes of practice have normative effects, those that contain general policy guidelines, messages, or other statements are cognitive sources.[43] Reality can however be a little more

[41] On this topic, Robert Baldwin and John Houghton, "Circular Arguments: The Status and Legitimacy of Administrative Rules" (1986) *Public Law* 239–284; René David, "Sources of Law," in Konrad Zweigert and Ulrich Drobnig (eds.), *International Encyclopedia of Comparative Law* (J. C. B. Mohr (Paul Siebeck)-Martinus Nijhoff Publishers, 1984), vol. 2, p. 72 ff.; Massimo Severo Giannini, "Circolare," in *Enciclopedia del Diritto* (Giuffrè, 1960), vol. 7, p. 1 ff.

[42] Franco Bassi, "Circolari amministrative," in *Digesto delle Discipline Pubblicistiche* (Utet, 1989), p. 55.

[43] In a comparative perspective, Armin von Bogdandy, *Gubernative Rechtsetzung* (Mohr Siebeck, 2000), p. 449 ff.

complex. To begin with, circulars may comprise both legal and cognitive elements, giving rise to a *mélange* of indications and statements of different nature.[44] Secondly, interpretative guides, instructions to officials, and codes of practice are often couched in hortatory rather than deontic language, thereby making it more complicated to construe their effects. Finally, general policy guidelines "may have [normative] effects in certain circumstances or from some perspectives and they may lack them in a different context"; thus, "to adhere to rigid definitions or conceptual distinctions is ... to fall into a trap."[45]

Against this backdrop, one point is worth emphasizing. The choice of hortatory language in administrative circulars serves a precise purpose. By using recommendations, requests, and rules of thumb,[46] administrations seek to provide their civil servants with sufficiently clear behavioral indications, while allowing for a certain flexibility. This flexibility consists in the fact that the course of action encouraged by those indications may be ignored if the specific circumstances of the case so suggest. In so doing, administrations seek to avoid the "overinclusion" that characterizes norms of general and abstract nature – such norms are overinclusive because they become binding every time the conditions for their application are met, regardless of whether the consequences may be inappropriate, counterproductive, or even unjust.[47] But there is no doubt that they also intend to produce normative effects, with ramifications both inside and outside the circle of their addressees.[48] Two further observations support these considerations. First, the notion of normative effects is "clearly quite broad, accommodating all types of impact on/in the law, its interpretation and application."[49] Secondly, the indications set out in administrative circulars are often backed by other provisions

[44] For instance, to the extent that the Council's administrative circulars contain parts relating to how the European Parliament arranges its own participation in trilogues, those parts have cognitive rather than normative value.

[45] Baldwin and Houghton, "Circular Arguments," 245.

[46] Rules of thumb are rough but practical principles or guidelines based on experience, as different from hard-and-fast rules or precise measures. For this definition, James E. Clapp, Elizabeth G. Thornburg, Marc Galanter, and Fred R. Shapiro, *Lawtalk: The Unknown Stories behind Familiar Legal Expressions* (Yale University Press, 2011), p. 219.

[47] von Bogdandy, *Gubernative Rechtsetzung*, p. 467.

[48] Through circulars, administrations aim at striking a balance between equality and legal predictability, on the one hand, and attention to the single case with its specificities and needs, on the other.

[49] Opinion of Advocate General Bobek in Case C-16/16 P *Belgium* v. *Commission* EU:C:2017:959, para. 73.

(for example, Treaties, interinstitutional agreements, Rules of Procedure), of which they are a specification. I therefore submit that administrative circulars, in the form of interpretative guides, instructions to officials, and codes of practice, usually have normative effects.[50]

European case law does not stand in the way of my argument. On several occasions, the CJEU has acknowledged that administrative circulars have normative effects. However, it has also affirmed that in principle they "have effects only within the administration itself and give rise to no rights or obligations on the part of third parties."[51] On this understanding, the Court has often denied the admissibility of actions for annulment against administrative circulars.[52] In my opinion, this case law is problematic. It perpetuates the idea that the functions of the administration are closely linked to the notion of prerogative (*puissance publique*).[53] It validates an inside–outside dichotomy and thereby an outdated understanding of the role of public administrations in contemporary polities.[54] Why should the public be unable to control administrative practice? But answering this question, certainly not immaterial to the present analysis, might lead me a little out of the way.[55] For my purpose,

[50] von Bogdandy, *Gubernative Rechtsetzung*, p. 469 ff., who conceptualizes the legal status of administrative circulars in the following terms. First, unlike in the norms of general and abstract nature, the factual elements that are expressly set out in administrative circulars are meant to include further unwritten elements. Secondly, the factual elements expressly set out in those documents determine the behavior to be followed, until there exist "good reasons" to depart from it. Thirdly, it is only in the presence of good reasons that the addressees of administrative rules are allowed to deviate from the expected behavior. Good reasons exist when the single case presents specificities of such a kind and relevance as to make a different behavior seem appropriate. To this end, the relevant actors must assess the relationship between objectives, reasons, and effects, considering constitutional and legislative provisions. For instance, in Case C-171/00 P *Libéros* v. *Commission* EU:C:2002:17, para. 35, the ECJ held that even when "[internal] measures may not be regarded as rules of law which the administration is always bound to observe, they nevertheless form rules of practice from which the administration may not depart without giving the reasons which led it to do so."

[51] Case C-366/88 *France* v. *Commission* EU:C:1990:348, para. 9. See also Case C-443/97 *Spain* v. *Commission* EU:C:2000:190, para. 28.

[52] Lenaerts, Maselis, and Gutman, *EU Procedural Law*, p. 272 f.

[53] In the same vein, David, "Sources of Law," p. 74.

[54] For a fine-grained criticism of the inside–outside dichotomy, von Bogdandy, *Gubernative Rechtsetzung*, p. 453 ff.

[55] Administrative rules can be brought before the ECJ through a preliminary ruling request. According to settled case law, Art. 267 TFEU "confers on the Court jurisdiction to deliver a preliminary ruling on the validity and interpretation of all acts of the EU institutions without exception." See, among others, Case C-16/16 P *Belgium* v. *Commission* EU:C:2018:79, para. 44.

the relevant point is rather that the Court acknowledges the normative effects of circulars, albeit circumscribing them. Consequently, I have made broad use of administrative circulars to legally reconstruct the working of trilogues.

As reported above, these documents aim at informing political leaders and civil servants about how the Parliament,[56] the Council,[57] and the Commission[58] organize their internal workings under the Ordinary Legislative Procedure. They are issued by, or under the supervision of, specific administrative units inside the three institutions. They are available to the public, sometimes directly on the website of the institution concerned, sometimes through access-to-documents requests. To the extent that the issuing units enjoy a mandate to collect, process, and disseminate information about the organization and functioning of trilogues, it is reasonable to believe that they also vouch for the accuracy and relevance of that information.[59] And to attest that that information reflects how things in effect happen entails a normative – alongside a descriptive – dimension. By certifying that the information provided is accurate and relevant, the issuing units generate normative expectations about the behavior of their officials. So much so that the content of the administrative circulars at issue belongs to those "core standards expected of GSC [General Secretariat of the Council] officials";[60] and it also forms part of the institutional knowledge that civil servants are expected to be familiar with when applying for career advancements in internal competitions.[61] I would therefore say that administrative circulars are "formally descriptive statements with normative effects."[62]

One further specification is in order. The arrangements laid down in administrative circulars relate, almost exclusively, to how the

[56] European Parliament, "Handbook on the Ordinary Legislative Procedure: A Guide to How the European Parliament Co-legislates," PE 640.179, September 2020.

[57] Council of the European Union, "Ordinary Legislative Procedure: Guide for the Presidency"; Council of the European Union, "Ordinary Legislative Procedure: Guide for GSC Officials," 11 October 2016.

[58] European Commission, "Ordinary Legislative Procedure (Article 294 TFEU): Guide to Internal Procedures," SPI(2011)25.

[59] This notion is, e.g., made explicit in Council of the European Union, "Ordinary Legislative Procedure: Guide for GSC Officials," at 2, where it is stated that: "[t]his present version of the Guide is the outcome of the work of the Task Force on Codecision, whose mandate included reviewing the various existing GSC [General Secretariat of the Council] documents on the OLP and establishing a set of core standards which would provide the reference for the GSC's minimum service to the Presidency."

[60] Ibid., at 44. [61] Case T-371/03 *Le Voci* v. *Council* EU:T:2005:290, para. 9 f.

[62] Christoph Möllers, *Die Möglichkeit der Normen* (Suhrkamp, 2015), p. 139.

institutions organize themselves internally. They focus on those stages that lead to trilogues, including the definition of the negotiating mandates and the composition of the negotiating teams. However, they contain very few indications about trilogue negotiations as such – for instance, how the teams are expected to interact as they build agreement, who is responsible for chairing the meetings or setting the agenda. And there is no instrument with an interinstitutional character that covers those aspects systematically. For however strange it might appear – especially considering the level of detail that the 2007 Joint Declaration on Codecision shows when regulating the inner workings of the Conciliation Committee – this circumstance probably bespeaks the intention of the institutions to make trilogues a context for the spontaneous creation of structures such as practices and shared logics of action. In other words, it is a matter of creating "a powerful social framework – one that encapsulates and exhibits the celebrated strength and resilience of those structures."[63] I will return to this in the next chapter.

It is now possible to move on to a more fine-grained analysis of how the European legislative process functions. In doing so, I will not consider the conciliation stage. Two reasons stand behind this choice. First, the Conciliation Committee is essentially a dying breed. In the last parliamentary term, no conciliation took place, reflecting a well-evidenced trajectory of recent years towards adopting legislative acts at first and second reading.[64] Secondly, and relatedly, the focus of scholarly debates lies almost exclusively on the agreements reached at these two stages, as these are often said to be the main source of legitimacy problems that beset the European legislative process. In what follows, I will therefore deal with first- and early-second-reading agreements, including some observations about second-reading agreements. I will then sketch out the inner workings of trilogues, considering the (little) information I could find in the administrative circulars at my disposal. As compared to other accounts that mainly focus on the co-legislators, my reconstruction will also encompass the internal functioning and organization of the Commission, thereby

[63] Scott, *Institutions and Organizations*, p. 59.

[64] European Parliament, "Activity Report," at 3. These readings account for 99 percent of the overall number of adopted legislative files. Note, however, that 99 percent does not represent the overall percentage of first-reading and early-second-reading agreements. It is just the percentage of files that were adopted at those two stages. Among those files, some were not negotiated and some other were carried over from the previous parliamentary term.

acknowledging the independent contribution of this institution to the making of European legislation.

3.3 First-Reading Agreements

3.3.1 *The European Parliament*

After a legislative proposal reaches the Parliament, the EP's President refers it to the committee responsible.[65] This committee appoints a rapporteur, tasked with "preparing the committee's report and … presenting it to Parliament on behalf of that committee."[66] Each political group may appoint a "shadow rapporteur" to work alongside the rapporteur, tracking the relevant report and seeking compromise on behalf of the group.[67] By and large, a legislative file goes through three stages. First, the rapporteur tables the draft report. Secondly, MEPs – in principle, every MEP – may submit amendments to the draft report within a given deadline. Thirdly, the committee discusses and votes on the proposed amendments.[68] The entire text is eventually subject to a final vote by roll call to ensure greater accountability.[69] Both the votes on the amendments and the final vote on the entire text are taken by majority of the votes cast, meaning that only the votes for and against (without abstentions) count.[70]

Between the reception of the Commission's proposal and the end of the discussions in the committee responsible, the Council Presidency and the EP rapporteur contact each other to explore the possibility of launching trilogue negotiations. If both parties show interest in doing so, the EP can formalize its intention to begin negotiations through two different procedures. Prior to the general revision of the EP's Rules of Procedure of 2016, these procedures were called "standard procedure" and

[65] Rule 48(1) EP RoP. [66] Rule 55(1) EP RoP. [67] Rule 215 EP RoP.

[68] For an overview of the various stages a draft report is to go through before its enactment, European Parliament, "Handbook on the Ordinary Legislative Procedure," at 14 ff.

[69] Pursuant to Rule 190(3) and (4) EP RoP, a roll-call vote is taken using the electronic voting system and is recorded in the minutes of the sitting, with an indication of how each MEP voted. In general, however, the EP votes by show of hands, as provided for by Rule 187(1) EP RoP.

[70] Rule 187(3) EP RoP. On the meaning of "votes cast" as an autonomous concept of EU law, see Case C-650/18 *Hungary* v. *Parliament* EU:C:2021:426, para. 84: "the usual meaning of the concept of 'votes cast' covers only a positive or negative vote on a given proposal. Since abstention must be understood in its usual sense as a refusal to adopt a position on a given proposal, it cannot be treated in the same way as a 'vote cast.'"

"exceptional procedure," respectively.[71] The standard procedure stipulates that the committee responsible adopts a decision by majority of its component members. This decision must be publicly announced at the beginning of the following parliamentary session and put to the vote, if members or a political group or groups reaching at least one-tenth of the Parliament's component members so request.[72] The exceptional procedure stipulates that the decision to participate in trilogues is taken directly by the plenary, which then refers the matter back to the committee responsible. The decision to follow the exceptional procedure rests on a proposal by the chair or the rapporteur of the committee responsible or by a political group or members reaching at least one-twentieth of the Parliament's component members.[73]

Whereas in the first procedure the negotiating mandate consists of the draft report as adopted by the committee concerned, in the second procedure the negotiating mandate consists of the draft report as voted by the plenary. Of course, a plenary mandate carries more political weight than a committee mandate. However, it may also reduce the margin of maneuver that the EP's negotiating teams enjoy in trilogues. Therefore, about three-quarters of all negotiating mandates are committee mandates, with plenary mandates being reserved only to politically sensitive files.[74]

All the same, the main body entrusted with conducting trilogues is the responsible committee,[75] with its negotiating team composition varying in accordance with the nature of the trilogue negotiations to be attended. In the case of political trilogues, the Parliament's delegation is led by the rapporteur and presided over by the chair of the committee or by a vice-chair designated by the chair, and it includes at least the shadow

[71] The currently applicable EP RoP no longer call these procedures with those names, but they still provide for both. In what follows, I will therefore stick to the old terminology for facilitating the reading.

[72] Rule 71(2) EP RoP.

[73] Rule 59(4)(4) EP RoP. As regards the number of mandates adopted under the "standard procedure" and those adopted under the "exceptional procedure," available data show that between February 2017 and the end of the eighth parliamentary term in 2019, over three-quarters had been mandates adopted under the "standard procedure." For more detail, see European Parliament, "Activity Report," at 10.

[74] European Parliament, "Activity Report," at 10.

[75] European Parliament, "Code of Conduct for Negotiating in the Context of the Ordinary Legislative Procedure," 28 September 2017, para. 2. This Code is explicitly referred to in Rule 70 EP RoP, which states that trilogues "shall be conducted having regard to the Code of Conduct laid down by the Conference of Presidents."

rapporteurs from each political group.[76] In the case of technical trilogues, the Parliament's delegation consists of MEPs' assistants and advisors from the different political groups.[77] Besides the political actors, the EP's negotiating teams always comprise an "administrative project team," which is "coordinated by the secretariat of the committee responsible, and should include at least the conciliations and codecision unit, the legal service, the directorate for legislative acts, the Parliament's press service, as well as other relevant services to be decided on a case-by-case basis."[78]

Ahead of and between trilogues, the EP's negotiating teams hold internal preparatory meetings to find common ground on the issues to be discussed. It is indeed important for the Parliament to present itself as a cohesive whole, so that it can avoid internal differences weakening its bargaining position vis-à-vis the Council. After each trilogue, the chair of the negotiating team and the rapporteur are to inform the committee responsible of the results and overall state of the negotiations (report-back obligation) and seek updated negotiating mandates, as appropriate.[79] If trilogues result in a first-reading agreement, the EP's team then has to inform the committee responsible and provide it with the documents "reflecting the outcome of the concluding trilogue." This agreement is *ad referendum* because it requires the approval of the committee responsible "by way of a single vote by a majority of the votes cast."[80] If approved by the committee, the provisional agreement is tabled for consideration by the Parliament, "in a presentation which clearly indicates the modifications to

[76] Rule 74(1) EP RoP.

[77] For the distinction between "political trilogues" and "technical trilogues," see above Section 3.2.2.1.

[78] European Parliament, "Code of Conduct for Negotiating in the Context of the Ordinary Legislative Procedure," para. 4. As regards the consultation of the EP's Legal Service in connection with legislative procedures, the chairs of the parliamentary committees and the rapporteurs may submit a written request for a legal opinion. However, any advice that may come during the negotiations usually reflects the personal views of that specific member of the Legal Service and not the official views of the Legal Service, "save where those views are confirmed in writing." See European Parliament, "Decision on the Consultation of the Legal Service," PE 339.484/BUR, 28 January 2004.

[79] Rule 74(3) EP RoP. For an empirical study revealing the poor compliance with the report-back obligation, Gijs Jan Brandsma, "Transparency of EU Informal Trilogues through Public Feedback in the European Parliament: Promise Unfulfilled" (2019) 26 *Journal of European Public Policy* 1464–1483. See also Richard Corbett, Francis Jacobs, and Darren Neville, *The European Parliament*, 9th ed. (John Harper, 2016), p. 288.

[80] European Parliament, "Code of Conduct for Negotiating in the Context of the Ordinary Legislative Procedure," para. 2: "[a]ny agreement reached during negotiations shall be deemed to be provisional until it has been adopted by Parliament."

the draft legislative act."[81] In the voting procedure in plenary, the provisional agreement enjoys priority over other amendments and is put to a single vote, unless the Parliament decides – at the request of a political group or members reaching at least one-twentieth of its component members – to proceed with the vote on amendments. If the provisional agreement obtains the majority of the votes cast, the President declares the first reading of the Parliament concluded. Otherwise, the President sets a new deadline for amendments.[82]

3.3.2 *The Council*

When a legislative proposal reaches the Council, the policy Directorate-General responsible for the file at hand (also known as *Service traitant*) convenes, in agreement with the Presidency, the relevant working party to examine the proposal. The *Service traitant*, together with the Legal Service, assists the Presidency throughout the whole legislative cycle. In particular, it advises the Presidency on the legislative procedure; it supports it in the negotiation of legislative texts both in the Council and in trilogues; and it acts as "historical memory" for a dossier, guaranteeing continuity between the rotating Presidencies.[83] If the exploratory contacts between the Presidency and the EP's rapporteur reveal both co-legislators' interest in launching trilogue negotiations, the responsible working party starts preparing a negotiating mandate for the Presidency. To this end, the chair of the working party takes all necessary actions to tackle as many issues as possible, especially through bilateral and multilateral contacts with the Member States' delegations.[84] The negotiating mandate comes into being through rounds of markup sessions, in which the delegates sitting on the responsible working party concerned discuss, suggest changes, and rewrite the proposed piece of legislation.

When the working party has resolved all the issues it can resolve on its own, the dossier comes to the attention of Coreper, which intervenes to smooth out unsettled political differences and to endorse the negotiating mandate. However, when a dossier raises political issues that the (deputy) permanent representatives cannot settle among themselves, Coreper

[81] Rule 74(4) EP RoP. [82] Rule 59(3) EP RoP.

[83] Council of the European Union, "Ordinary Legislative Procedure: Guide for GSC Officials," at 2; Council of the European Union, "Ordinary Legislative Procedure: Guide for the Presidency," at 17 f.

[84] Gijs Jan Brandsma, Maja K. Dionigi, Justin Greenwood, and Christilla Roederer-Rynning, "Trilogues in Council: Disrupting the Diplomatic Culture?" (2021) 28 *Journal of European Public Policy* 10-31.

hands the dossier over to the Council, which may approve the negotiating mandate in the form of a "general approach."[85] Data from the 2014–2019 European legislature show that general approaches accounted for 36 percent of all the trilogue mandates adopted by the Council.[86] With an established mandate, trilogues can eventually begin. The incumbent Presidency is solely responsible for representing the Council throughout the negotiations. Its negotiating teams consist of its own officials as well as officials from the *Service traitant*, including officials from the Legal Service – usually two: one legal advisor and one lawyer-linguist – and the Press Office. Incoming presidencies are invited to send an observer, who does not, however, take an active role in the negotiations.

Although there are no hard-and-fast rules about the seniority of representation, the Presidency's teams are usually led by either the chair of Coreper or the chair of the responsible working party, depending on the subject matter. The former leads the Council's delegations in political trilogues, whereas the latter leads the Council's delegations in technical trilogues. Ministers usually do not participate in trilogues in those phases that precede the Conciliation Committee. At any rate, the Presidency remains free to determine the seniority of its representation on a case-by-case basis.[87]

During the negotiations, the Presidency "cannot commit the Council to anything beyond the negotiating mandate." This implies that whenever the Presidency puts forward a compromise proposal, it must specify that

[85] Council of the European Union, "Ordinary Legislative Procedure: Guide for GSC Officials," at 5; Council of the European Union, "Ordinary Legislative Procedure: Guide for the Presidency," at 3. As clarified by the Legal Service of the Council, "a formal vote may be taken only on a final text." Therefore, general approaches are usually adopted by consensus. See Council of the European Union, "Drawing up of Part 'B' of Council Provisional Agendas," 10575/1/01 REV 1, 1 March 2002, at 4. The use of general approaches was however criticized by the Commission for two reasons. First, their adoption by consensus impairs the Commission's ability to rely on the qualified majority within the Council to obtain an agreement as close as possible to its original proposal. Secondly, the fact that their adoption, unlike Coreper-level mandates, is accessible to public viewing – and the documents relating to general approaches are made publicly available – hardens the position of the Council and makes it significantly more difficult for the Presidency to consider the differing positions of the other institutions. In these terms, European Commission, "'Orientations générales' dans les travaux du Conseil," SI(2006) 1141/2, 24 November 2006, at 4 f. The adoption of general approaches is said to have been validated by the ECJ in Case C-417/93 *Parliament* v. *Council* EU:C:1995:127, para. 10.

[86] Brandsma et al., "Trilogues in Council," 21.

[87] Council of the European Union, "Ordinary Legislative Procedure: Guide for GSC Officials," at 9; Council of the European Union, "Ordinary Legislative Procedure: Guide for the Presidency," at 8 f.

it is acting on its own motion and that the proposal will require the endorsement of Coreper. The same applies to those proposals put forward by the Commission and the Parliament; the Presidency can certainly express a favorable opinion, but it always needs the approval of Coreper before undertaking any commitment. Likewise, any adjustment to the original negotiating mandate must be agreed upon by Coreper, even when the mandate was approved by the Council through a general approach.[88] By contrast, when "provid[ing] delegations with prompt updates ('feedback') on developments during trilogue negotiations," the Presidency enjoys significant latitude. Indeed, "each Presidency is entitled to determine for itself in what form and when to provide feedback on trilogue negotiations."[89]

Once the institutions reach an agreement, the *Service traitant* prepares a consolidated text, which clearly highlights the changes to the Commission's original proposal. This text is then put on the agenda of Coreper for discussion. If Coreper does not approve the agreement, the Presidency can continue negotiations with the Parliament, either in another trilogue or by direct contact with the rapporteur and shadow rapporteurs. If Coreper instead approves the agreement, the consolidated text is attached to a confirmation letter to be signed by its chair and sent to the responsible parliamentary committee. The Legislation Programming, Support and Coordination Team, together with the *Service traitant*, monitors the EP's plenary proceedings and, if the Parliament's first-reading position corresponds to the agreement approved by Coreper, they inform the delegations with a note and put the legislative file on the Council's agenda as an "A" item, which is an item that does not require further discussion.[90]

3.3.3 *The Commission*

After sending its legislative proposal to the Parliament and the Council,[91] the Commission does not simply stand by and watch. As acknowledged by

[88] Council of the European Union, "Ordinary Legislative Procedure: Guide for GSC Officials," at 6 and 10.

[89] Ibid., at 16; Council of the European Union, "Ordinary Legislative Procedure: Guide for the Presidency," at 16.

[90] Council of the European Union, "Ordinary Legislative Procedure: Guide for GSC Officials," at 24 f.

[91] The Commission's decision to submit a legislative proposal to the co-legislators is taken either by oral or by written procedure. The oral procedure is laid down in Art. 4(a) and Arts. 5 to 11 of the Commission's Rules of Procedure and usually applies to politically

the Court of Justice, "the Commission's power ... does not come down to submitting a proposal and, subsequently, promoting contact and seeking to reconcile the positions of the Parliament and the Council."[92] The Treaties entrust the Commission with important prerogatives and obligations throughout the whole legislative procedure. These prerogatives and obligations also account for the Commission's presence in trilogues, where, due to its in-depth technical knowledge, it not only provides the co-legislators with valuable assistance, but also greatly influences the progress of the negotiations. The goal is to make sure that the compromises between the Parliament and the Council are not such as to essentially alter the nature and objective of its original proposal, while allowing for the flexibility necessary to secure a successful outcome to the negotiations.[93]

The Commission's main actors in trilogues are the Directorates-General. They are responsible for representing the Commission vis-à-vis the other two institutions, and to that end enjoy a fair degree of autonomy.[94] However, they must always ensure that the principle of collegiality is respected.[95] They are therefore requested to "submit to the College – via the [*Groupe des relations interinstitutionnelles* (GRI)] – any important problem concerning the substance of the proposal or the operation and interpretation of the procedure and any decision on the position to be taken at the various stages of the procedure."[96] The composition of the Commission's negotiating teams varies in relation to the nature of the expected discussion. In the case of political trilogues, the lead DG usually sends a Director-General; in the case of technical

salient initiatives. It requires that decisions to submit legislative proposals be taken by majority during meetings of the College of Commissioners (in practice, however, the Commission decides by consensus). The written procedure is laid down in Art. 12 of the Commission's Rules of Procedure and provides that "if the Directorates-General directly involved are in agreement and the proposal has been endorsed by the Legal Service," the text of the proposal is circulated in writing to all members of the Commission, who can make reservations or amendments within an agreed time limit. If no reservations or amendments are made, the proposal is adopted. See Rules of Procedure of the Commission [C(2000) 3614], OJ 2000 No. L308/26.

92 Case C-409/13 *Council* v. *Commission*, para. 74. See also Case C-24/20 *Commission* v. *Council (Adhésion à l'acte de Genève)*, para. 87.

93 The conduct to be followed by the Commission's representatives is outlined in European Commission, "Ordinary Legislative Procedure (Article 294 TFEU): Guide to Internal Procedures," at 13.

94 Ibid., at 10 f.

95 On the meaning of this principle, Maria Patrin, *Collegiality in the European Commission: Legal Substance and Institutional Practice* (Oxford University Press, 2023).

96 European Commission, "Ordinary Legislative Procedure (Article 294 TFEU): Guide to Internal Procedures," at 7.

trilogues, it usually sends a director or a head of unit. As a rule, however, the level of the Commission's representation reflects the rank of the negotiators from the Parliament and the Council – in principle, commissioners go to trilogues only when the Council's Presidency sends ministers. In addition, the Commission's negotiating teams always include a representative of the Secretariat-General and, if necessary, of the Legal Service. At its discretion, the lead DG may also invite officials from other departments to participate.[97]

The participation of the Commission in trilogue negotiations must be authorized by the College. To this end, the lead DG must make a specific request, passing through the GRI.[98] Strictly speaking, the Commission does not have a negotiating mandate; it operates on the basis of its original legislative proposal. As negotiations advance, the lead DG may advise the College to adopt specific positions and lines of action (for example, declare its opposition to a set of compromise amendments or identify possible bargaining zones) and to modify the original proposal to facilitate the conclusion of the legislative procedure.[99] According to the principle of collegiality, however, the negotiating teams of the Commission cannot autonomously assent to major changes to the original proposal; they first need to obtain the approval of the College.[100]

In case of first-reading agreements, the Commission may amend the original proposal in accordance with the outcome of the negotiations, thereby enabling the Council to approve the legislative act by qualified majority – instead of unanimity, as requested by Article 293(1) TFEU. Save for exceptional cases, the Commission does not table a new formal proposal; it simply *empowers* the responsible Commissioner to amend the original one verbally, during the relevant plenary session.[101] To this end, the lead DG, in agreement with the cabinet of the responsible Commissioner, prepares a draft *fiche*, proposing the Commission's position to be brought before the Parliament. This *fiche* is given to the GRI,

[97] Ibid., at 11 (fn. 14).

[98] Ibid., at 14. In general terms, the task of the GRI "is to examine . . . the positions to be adopted by the Commission in interinstitutional discussions." See European Commission, "Annex to the Commission Decision Amending Its Rules of Procedure: Rules Giving Effect to the Rules of Procedure," C(2010) 1200, 24 February 2010, Rule 6-5.1.

[99] European Commission, "Ordinary Legislative Procedure (Article 294 TFEU)," at 14.

[100] European Parliament, "Handbook on the Ordinary Legislative Procedure," at 32.

[101] European Commission, "Ordinary Legislative Procedure (Article 294 TFEU): Guide to Internal Procedures," at 15 and 39. This practice has also been endorsed by the ECJ, notably in Case C-445/00 *Austria* v. *Council*, para. 37 ff. and in Case C-643/15 *Slovakia* v. *Council*, para. 184 ff.

which examines it and passes it on to the College for the final decision. After the plenary vote, and preferably within six weeks, the College ratifies the empowerment.[102] With an amended proposal, the ball is in the court of the Council, which can either approve the legislative proposal – thus successfully concluding the legislative procedure – or adopt its first-reading position – thus leading to the Parliament's second reading and the possible adoption of an early-second-reading agreement.

3.4 Early-Second-Reading Agreements

Before moving on, it must be said that the participation of the institutions in early-second- and second-reading agreements essentially follows the same arrangements as those outlined above, including the composition of the negotiating teams and the definition of the negotiating mandates. I will therefore refrain from repeating what has been already said, unless there are specific differences worth highlighting.

3.4.1 *The European Parliament*

When the European Parliament concludes its first reading without approving a trilogue agreement, the institutions still have the possibility to pursue a negotiated solution to their differences. After checking the availability of the Council, the responsible parliamentary committee may decide to (re)launch interinstitutional negotiations. Such a decision is taken by a majority of the committee's component members and is then announced in plenary. The EP's first-reading position constitutes the negotiating mandate, and this mandate cannot be challenged by the plenary – it is indeed the plenary itself that adopted it.[103] However, the EP's Rules of Procedure require that decisions to initiate trilogue negotiations be announced during the plenary following the vote in committee.[104] Negotiations can start immediately after the committee decision.

The specificities and intricacies of early-second-reading agreements arise mostly once negotiations have come to a successful end. In such a case, the provisional agreement goes back to the Parliament and the Council to obtain the endorsement of the responsible parliamentary committee and Coreper, respectively. In the parliamentary committee

[102] European Commission, "Ordinary Legislative Procedure (Article 294 TFEU)," at 15 f. and 30 ff.
[103] European Parliament, "Handbook on the Ordinary Legislative Procedure," at 32.
[104] Rule 72 EP RoP.

the vote takes place after the publication of the provisional agreement on the EP's website. The committee decides by a single vote, by majority of the votes cast.[105] This is the so-called confirmation vote, and it has the main purpose of authorizing the chair of the responsible parliamentary committee to send a confirmation letter to his or her counterpart in Coreper.[106] With this letter, the chair indicates "his recommendation to the plenary to accept the Council common position without amendment, subject to confirmation of the common position by the Council."[107] Before the confirmation vote, however, the parliamentary committee often seeks to obtain some informal confirmation (by email or telephone) that the Member States are in favor of the compromise text.[108] Needless to say, the confirmation vote is not binding on the Parliament, which remains free to reject or amend any final agreement in its second reading.

3.4.2 *The Council*

After the successful conclusion of the negotiations and the receipt of the confirmation letter from the Parliament, the Council initiates the internal procedures leading to the adoption of its first-reading position.[109] It is a two-step process: first, the Council adopts a "political agreement" on the outcome of trilogues – usually as an "A" item – and submits the draft act for legal-linguistic verification;[110] secondly, it proceeds with the formal adoption of its first-reading position. Coreper intervenes before both the adoption of the "political agreement" and the formal adoption of the Council's first-reading position.[111]

[105] Rule 74(4) EP RoP.

[106] European Parliament, "Early Second Readings – Step by Step," May 2016, at 2 f.

[107] Joint Declaration on Practical Arrangements for the Codecision Procedure (Article 251 of the EC Treaty), para. 18.

[108] Council of the European Union, "Ordinary Legislative Procedure: Guide for GSC Officials," at 27.

[109] It is worth highlighting that when the institutions negotiate ahead of the Council's first reading, the Presidency's negotiating teams are usually led by the chair of Coreper. See Council of the European Union, "Ordinary Legislative Procedure: Guide for GSC Officials," at 27.

[110] In the Council's lexicon, the term "political agreement" refers to "a decision adopting a definitive position on a text, subject to finalization of that text by the Legal/Linguistic Experts." Once the Council reaches a political agreement, substantive issues cannot be reopened without an explicit agreement. See Council of the European Union, "Drawing Up of Part 'B' of Council Provisional Agendas," at 6.

[111] In principle, any formation of the Council can adopt the Council's formal first-reading position as an "A" item. See Council of the European Union, "Ordinary Legislative Procedure: Guide for GSC Officials," at 28.

Depending on whether the Commission has consented to amend its proposal, the Council may adopt its first-reading position by qualified majority or by unanimity. After the vote, the position of the Council is transmitted to the Parliament, together with the accompanying statement of reasons and the Commission's opinion pursuant to Article 294(6) TFEU. This transmission usually takes place on the Monday of the plenary session following the Council's formal adoption of its position. It is only after the EP's President announces the receipt of both documents in plenary that the Parliament's second reading formally begins.[112]

3.4.3 *The European Parliament*

With its announcement in plenary, "the Council's position shall be deemed to have been referred automatically to the committee responsible at first reading."[113] As of this moment, the Parliament has three months (extendable to four) to complete its second reading. The committee discusses the dossier and draws up a draft recommendation for the plenary, proposing to approve the Council's position. Still, MEPs (at this stage only members or permanent substitutes of the lead committee) can propose the rejection of the whole legislative file or the adoption of amendments to the Council's position, provided that these amendments comply with a set of admissibility criteria set out in the EP's Rules of Procedure.[114] The committee adopts its draft recommendation by a majority of the votes cast and tables it for the plenary.[115] Here, only the committee responsible, a political group or at least one-twentieth of the

[112] Rule 63(1) EP RoP. See also European Parliament, "Early Second Readings – Step by Step," at 3 f. Some differences between Parliament and Council still exist as regards the day from which the European Parliament's second reading formally starts. For years, the EP has been arguing that its second reading starts from the day after the President acknowledges in plenary the receipt of the Council's position at first reading. On the other hand, the Council has been maintaining that the EP's second reading starts on the day the Parliament receives the Council's position at first reading. Be that as it may, these different interpretations of the Treaties amount in fact to a discrepancy of no more than three days. See European Commission, "Ordinary Legislative Procedure (Article 294 TFEU)," at 45 (fn. 1).

[113] Rule 63(2) EP RoP.

[114] According to Rule 68 EP RoP, amendments are admissible only if they seek (a) to restore wholly or partly the EP's first-reading position; or (b) to reach a compromise with the Council; or (c) to amend a part of the text of a Council's position which was not included in – or differs in content from – the proposal submitted at first reading; or (d) to take account of new facts or legal situations arisen after the adoption of Parliament's first-reading position.

[115] Rule 65(3) EP RoP.

Parliament's component members may put forward proposals for rejection and amendment (always subject to the same restrictive admissibility criteria).[116] For them to be adopted, they need to secure the votes of a majority of the component members of the Parliament.[117] If no proposal to reject and no amendments to the Council's position have been tabled, "it shall be deemed to have been approved," without formal vote.[118]

3.4.4 *The Commission*

Early-second-reading agreements are reached when the Council has not yet formally acted on the Commission's legislative text. Therefore, according to Article 293(2) TFEU, the Commission is still free to decide whether or not it wishes to amend its proposal, with all the consequences that this implies in terms of voting requirements in the Council. If the College supports the outcome of trilogues, it needs to give its assent to the provisional agreement and empower the responsible Commissioner to communicate its will to the Council.[119] This again occurs through a *fiche*, which is first drawn up by the departments responsible and then assessed by the GRI. Moreover, after the Council adopts its first-reading position, the Treaties oblige the Commission to inform the European Parliament of its view. This occurs through a communication where the Commission states the reasons that led it to accept, support, or oppose the Council's position at first reading. To that end, as soon as the Council reaches what we called above a "political agreement," the lead DG draws up a draft communication and submits it for adoption by the College. The adoption should be concluded in time for the Commission's communication to be transmitted to the EP together with the Council's first-reading position.

3.5 Second-Reading Agreements

3.5.1 *The European Parliament*

When no agreement is reached before the end of the first reading, the Parliament, Council, and Commission may pursue further negotiations

[116] Rule 68(1) EP RoP. [117] Art. 294(7)(c) TFEU.

[118] Rule 67(5)(3) and Rule 69 EP RoP. This rule might appear strange. However, it is worth noting that Art. 294(7)(a) TFEU provides that if the EP does not take a decision within three months of the communication of the Council's first-reading position, "the act concerned shall be deemed to have been adopted in the wording which corresponds to the position of the Council."

[119] European Commission, "Ordinary Legislative Procedure (Article 294 TFEU)," at 18.

"with a view to achieving a better understanding of the respective positions and thus to bringing the legislative procedure to a conclusion as quickly as possible."[120] The reason behind these negotiations is to avoid at all costs the conciliation procedure. To achieve that, the institutions need to proceed promptly. After the formal beginning of the second reading, the Parliament has only three months (extendable to four) to decide on the Council's first-reading position – this time constraint explains why second-reading agreements have increasingly fallen out of favor with the institutions.[121] On the upside, the co-legislators have by now become familiar with the margins of negotiations and can focus all their energy on a few key issues.

After the EP's President acknowledges receipt of the Council's first-reading position and the legislative file is referred to the responsible parliamentary committee, this committee votes to decide whether to enter negotiations. It usually does so at the first available meeting and decides by majority of the votes cast (and not by majority of its members, as in the case of first- and early-second-reading agreements).[122] The decision to start negotiations is not announced in plenary. The negotiating mandate consists of the EP's first-reading position, possibly supplemented by some guidelines, including in the form of amendments.[123] The EP's Rules of Procedure speak of "guidelines" because they are more flexible and can be adopted more quickly. Indeed, the adoption of amendments can be time-consuming and risks eroding a large segment of the three-month deadline set out in the Treaties.

If negotiations lead to a provisional agreement, and if Coreper endorses it, the chair of the responsible parliamentary committee is informed, with a confirmatory letter, that the Council is willing to approve the Parliament's second-reading amendments, on condition that these amendments reflect the outcome of trilogues.[124] The provisional agreement is published on the EP's website and put to a vote in the responsible committee, which approves a draft recommendation for the plenary by

[120] Joint Declaration on Practical Arrangements for the Codecision Procedure (Article 251 of the EC Treaty), para. 21.

[121] It must be noted, however, that nothing prevents the institutions from establishing initial contacts as soon as the Council has adopted its first-reading position, or even as soon as it has reached a political agreement. In this sense, see Council of the European Union, "Ordinary Legislative Procedure: Guide for GSC Officials," at 33.

[122] Rule 73(1) EP RoP. [123] Rule 73(2) EP RoP.

[124] Joint Declaration on Practical Arrangements for the Codecision Procedure (Article 251 of the EC Treaty), para. 23.

majority of the votes cast. As mentioned above, the parliamentary committee usually recommends the adoption of the second-reading agreement. However, MEPs – at this stage only members or permanent substitutes of the responsible committee – can propose the rejection of the whole legislative file or the approval of amendments that depart from the trilogue agreement, provided that those amendments comply with the admissibility criteria set out in the EP's Rules of Procedure.[125]

Once the second-reading agreement is tabled for plenary, only the committee responsible, a political group or at least one-twentieth of the Parliament's component members may put forward proposals for rejection and amendments – always subject to the same admissibility criteria. As a second-reading agreement is a modification of the Council's first-reading position, its adoption requires the majority of the component members of the Parliament. In the voting procedure, the second-reading agreement enjoys priority over other amendments and is put to a single vote, unless the plenary decides – at the request of a political group or members reaching at least one-twentieth of the Parliament's component members – to proceed immediately with the vote on amendments, including those in the provisional agreement.[126] If the provisional agreement secures the majority of the component members of the Parliament, the President declares the second reading of the Parliament concluded and forwards the text of the legislative resolution to the Council and the Commission.[127]

3.5.2 *The Council*

After receiving the EP's legislative resolution, the Council has three months (extendable to four) to conclude its second reading. If the co-legislators have reached a provisional agreement and Coreper has already sent a confirmatory letter, the Legislation Programming, Support and Coordination Team follows the plenary vote and checks with the *Service traitant* if the amendments adopted by the Parliament correspond to the text approved by Coreper. If that is the case, the Legislation Programming, Support and Coordination Team produces an information note and puts the legislative file on the Council's agenda as an "A" item. Otherwise, if the amendments adopted by the Parliament differ from those agreed upon in trilogues and the Council is not able to approve them all, the Council's President, in agreement with the President of the

[125] Rule 65(3) and (4) EP RoP. [126] Rule 67(2) EP RoP. [127] Rule 67(5)(1) and (2) EP RoP.

EP, convenes the Conciliation Committee. The date on which the Council decides not to approve the amendments marks the beginning of the six-week time limit (extendable to eight weeks) for convening the Conciliation Committee.[128]

3.5.3 *The Commission*

In the second reading, the Commission has to deliver an opinion on all the amendments adopted by the Parliament.[129] This opinion is important because it determines the type of vote required in the Council. Should the Commission express a positive opinion, the Council may act by qualified majority; if the Commission expresses a negative opinion, the Council must act by unanimity.[130] Generally, the Commission does not need more than three weeks from the vote in the Parliament to formulate and adopt a second-reading opinion. However, in most cases it adopts its opinion during the same plenary session in which the Parliament adopts its amendments to the Council's first-reading position. To this end, the responsible Commissioner needs to receive the empowerment from the College. This requires, as usual, the preparation of a *fiche*.[131] If all the initiatives undertaken by the legislative institutions do not lead to the adoption of the file at second reading, the Commission must gear up for conciliation.

3.6 A Look Inside Trilogues: Their Inner Workings

I have already mentioned that, except for very few provisions in the 2007 Joint Declaration, there exists no instrument common to the three institutions that regulates the inner workings of trilogues – how the teams are expected to interact as they build agreement, who is responsible for chairing the meetings and setting the agenda, and so on. Even administrative circulars, which are otherwise very detailed, hardly address those aspects. Arguably, this circumstance testifies to the institutions' wish to allow for practices and shared logics of action to emerge spontaneously as well as to entrust political actors with a greater level of flexibility, as compared to other institutional contexts. Nevertheless, by juxtaposing the different sources at my disposal, I was able to reconstruct

[128] Council of the European Union, "Ordinary Legislative Procedure: Guide for GSC Officials," at 34 ff.

[129] Art. 294(7)(c) TFEU. [130] Art. 294(9) TFEU.

[131] European Commission, "Ordinary Legislative Procedure (Article 294 TFEU)," at 22 f.

a few general principles and rules that undergird trilogues as autonomous joint bodies.

The inner workings of trilogues revolve around two basic, closely associated principles: the equality and joint responsibility of the Parliament and the Council. In fact, one principle is the flipside of the other, and they have several practical implications. To begin with, trilogues may take place in the premises of either co-legislator – although in practice the majority of trilogues are held in the premises of the Parliament, in Brussels or Strasbourg. Secondly, trilogues do not have a strong chair. Even though the host institution should in principle assume the chairmanship of the single trilogue, "it is often not explicitly stated that either institution is in the chair – so the co-legislators effectively co-chair the trilogue."[132] Also, the powers of the chair are not particularly strong, as any relevant initiatives concerning the advancement of the negotiations must be taken "in a consensual manner that respect the wishes of both co-legislators."[133] Thirdly, the equality of the co-legislators is also reflected in the nearly obsessive attention of the institutions to the seating arrangements. These arrangements must ensure that no negotiating team sits in a higher position than the others; that the co-legislators directly face each other, with the Commission sitting at one of the sides; and that the Council and the Parliament have an equal number of seats at the table.[134]

Moreover, there exist four rules relating to the conduct of the negotiations. The first rule is that as soon as a co-legislator modifies its negotiating mandate, it is expected to present and justify the changes to its counterparts at the earliest possible trilogue.[135] The second rule, also known as the rule of the "single undertaking," provides that trilogue negotiations proceed on a nothing-is-agreed-until-everything-is-agreed basis.[136] Accordingly, all sides accept that what is said or proposed during the negotiations can be withdrawn until an agreement on the whole file

[132] Council of the European Union, "Ordinary Legislative Procedure: Guide for the Presidency," at 12; Council of the European Union, "Ordinary Legislative Procedure: Guide for GSC Officials," at 10.

[133] Council of the European Union, "Ordinary Legislative Procedure: Guide for the Presidency," at 12.

[134] Ibid., at 13; Council of the European Union, "Ordinary Legislative Procedure: Guide for GSC Officials," at 12 f.

[135] Council of the European Union, "Ordinary Legislative Procedure: Guide for the Presidency," at 14 f.

[136] Case T-540/15 *De Capitani* v. *Parliament* EU:T:2018:167, paras. 7, 39, 45, 87, and 102.

is reached, and then all sides are bound by all parts of the agreement.[137] In turn, this creates an atmosphere where people enjoy "greater freedom to brainstorm different solutions and to experiment with being more conciliatory on parts of the deal, knowing that their right to retract any partial proposal or individual concession is protected by 'until everything is agreed.'"[138] Further, participants in trilogues may seek to establish more intimate social relations. For instance, they may choose to call each other by name and to celebrate the successful completion of the negotiations with a toast. To be sure, any changes to the negotiating mandates must be discussed and approved by the competent bodies, and the co-legislators cannot agree to amendments that, by their nature, might distort the Commission's proposal.[139] However, insofar as the delegations comply with those conditions, every route and solution can be explored, in line with the idea that the search for compromise inevitably implies some creativity.[140]

The third rule is that negotiations are based on so-called four-column tables. These are synoptic tables that include the negotiating positions of the three institutions (in the first three columns) and the draft compromises agreed upon throughout the negotiations (in the fourth column).[141] These documents are key to keeping track of what political actors discuss and decide during trilogues. The fourth rule requires that there be sufficient time between trilogue meetings, so that each team may have the chance to report back to its institution.[142] Therefore, the rationale of this rule is twofold. It not only aims at assuring the accountability of the

[137] The rule of the "single undertaking" derives its mandatory nature from the norm of reciprocity. This norm characterizes trilogue negotiations throughout their entire unfolding and is an essential element of any compromise-seeking process. On this issue, Elise Rouméas, "The Procedural Value of Compromise" (2021) 47 *Social Theory and Practice* 377–396.

[138] Deepak Malhotra, *Negotiating the Impossible* (Berrett-Koehler, 2016), p. 86.

[139] Case C-409/13 *Council* v. *Commission*, para. 80.

[140] On the creativity inherent in any compromise-seeking activity, Frank R. Ankersmit, "Representational Democracy: An Aesthetic Approach to Conflict and Compromise" (2002) 8 *Common Knowledge* 24–46 at 37 ff.

[141] Council of the European Union, "Ordinary Legislative Procedure: Guide for the Presidency," at 15 f.; Council of the European Union, "Ordinary Legislative Procedure: Guide for GSC Officials," at 6 f.; European Parliament, "Code of Conduct for Negotiating in the Context of the Ordinary Legislative Procedure," para. 3; European Commission, "Ordinary Legislative Procedure (Article 294 TFEU)," at 12.

[142] Council of the European Union, "Ordinary Legislative Procedure: Guide for the Presidency," at 10; Council of the European Union, "Ordinary Legislative Procedure: Guide for GSC Officials," at 11.

negotiating teams; it also seeks to protect the other institutions against unpleasant surprises that might come at the end of the negotiations, such as the complete rejection of the provisional agreement.

Two final points are worth making. First, the co-legislators are jointly responsible for the drafting and updating of a series of common negotiating documents, such as the negotiation timetables, the trilogue agendas, and the four-column tables. It is therefore considered "inappropriate for either Secretariat to place its institution's logo alone on the joint negotiating document."[143] Other, less sensitive documents, such as the invitations or the attendance lists, are prepared and sent by the host institution. Secondly, negotiations usually take place in English. This practice creates some disadvantages for the Parliament, as its negotiating teams often include members without full command of the language.[144] The host institution is therefore responsible for providing simultaneous interpretation, according to need.

The upshot of this reconstruction is that the above principles and rules have an essential function: they seek to ensure as fair and neutral a negotiation environment as possible, by reducing and keeping in check those power imbalances that characterize the relations among political actors. To use the blunt language of trade, the rationale of those principles and rules is to facilitate the emergence of a level playing field among negotiators as well as to support the development of interinstitutional relations based on trust. These considerations will provide the building block of the next chapter, which will investigate another essential feature of trilogues: their informality. But before moving on to that topic, some brief conclusions are in order.

3.7 Conclusions

The main objective of this chapter has been to reconstruct the European legislative process, with a special focus on trilogues. To this end, I have relied on different legal provisions, including the Treaties, the 2007 Joint Declaration on Codecision, the Rules of Procedure of the institutions

[143] Council of the European Union, "Ordinary Legislative Procedure: Guide for the Presidency," at 15; Council of the European Union, "Ordinary Legislative Procedure: Guide for GSC Officials," at 6.

[144] Anita Bultena, "Negotiations in the Ordinary Legislative Procedure: The Perspective of the European Parliament," in Flora A. N. Goudappel and Ernst M. H. Hirsch Ballin (eds.), *Democracy and Rule of Law in the European Union: Essays in Honour of Jaap W. de Zwaan* (Asser Press/Springer, 2016), p. 102.

(especially those of the EP), and other – often neglected – sources of law: the administrative circulars. This exercise has shown that European legislation is the result of an articulate and highly organized process, which sits between two apparently opposing principles, those of autonomy and cooperation. It has also shown that trilogues are a key device by which the European legislative institutions seek to operationalize this complex, sometimes messy normative environment.

The main takeaway of this chapter is that the success of trilogues, as means of legislative coordination, depends on them virtuously conflating two elements: the steering capacity of normative structures and the logic of two-level games. While the former element provides trilogues with a certain degree of stability, the latter creates conditions that – if properly exploited – can greatly increase the chances of reaching agreements. The efficacy of these two elements is further enhanced by the obligation, set out in the 2007 Joint Declaration, to bring any final trilogue agreement to the attention of the relevant internal bodies of the Parliament and the Council. The combination of these elements offers a convincing explanation of why trilogues are so successful in producing agreements that, in most cases, the co-legislators enact without amendments.[145]

[145] This does not mean that trilogue agreements always find unconditional support among the co-legislators. For instance, rejection of trilogue agreements by Coreper has occurred more frequently during the eighth parliamentary term. See European Parliament, "Activity Report," at 8.

4 Trilogues

Informality Meets Positive Law

4.1 Introduction

The 2007 Joint Declaration on Codecision states that "trilogues are usually conducted in an informal framework" and defines them as "informal negotiations." These statements raise the question as to what "informal" actually means or, better put, what characterizes trilogues *qua* informal frameworks and the negotiations that take place therein. This chapter is devoted to answering that question. I must immediately observe that although the term "informality" is liable to generate misunderstandings, "informality" is, as far as the EU is concerned, a genuine legal concept. It is used in the Treaties, in secondary law, and in a host of other official documents. Thus, instead of criticizing the use of the term, the task of legal doctrine should be to reconstruct its meaning and thereby to answer the following question: what does EU law really mean when it employs terms such as "informality," "informal," and "informally"?

When it comes to informality, legal scholarship often oscillates between two positions. On the one side, some contributions treat informality as a thoroughly and fully legally binding phenomenon. By so doing, however, they risk overlooking its distinguishing characteristics.[1] On the other side, some contributions sharply contrast informality and legally binding structures, thereby failing to notice the intensity and functionality of the relation between the two.[2] In fact, each of these

[1] These contributions usually espouse the approach that has been defined as "extended legal pluralism." See, in this respect, Denis J. Galligan, *Law in Modern Society* (Oxford University Press, 2007), p. 173 ff.

[2] For a critique of this approach, Jelena von Achenbach, "Verfassungswandel durch Selbstorganisation: Triloge im europäischen Gesetzgebungsverfahren" (2016) 55 *Der Staat* 1–39 at 10 ff. and 17.

positions tells half the truth. To bridge the gap between them, I have availed myself of the most basic notions of institutionalism. This approach offers a powerful explanatory framework for the study of political institutions in general and of informality in particular. Due to its broad theoretical compass, this analytical strand has typically proved sensitive to a great variety of structural elements that stand behind the creation and maintenance of institutions.

My analysis begins from two basic assumptions: first, institutions exist and persist thanks to norms that state what is acceptable and what is not; secondly, legally binding norms are just one – however decisive – normative element behind the creation and continuing existence of institutions. My constructivist argument is that informality is also one of those elements. It produces stability and provides social life with shared meaning, and this makes it a normative phenomenon in its own right.[3] Informality must therefore be included among those phenomena that public lawyers have to factor in when studying political institutions. In what follows, I will explore the informality of trilogues in the frame of the public law discourse (Sections 4.2 and 4.3) and point out its essential features (Section 4.4). By so doing, I desire to gain deeper insight into the essence of the European legislative process to propose a concept of democracy capable of making sense of and legitimizing it.

4.2 A Controversial Concept

Informality has drawn the interest of many scholars in different research fields, such as political science, sociology, economics, organization theory, and law. From a legal perspective, this concept is relevant for the European as well as for the national and international legal orders. Scholars have not only analyzed the role of informality in contemporary EU governance,[4] but have also analyzed its role and effects in the history

[3] W. Richard Scott, *Institutions and Organizations: Ideas, Interests, and Identities*, 4th ed. (Sage, 2014), p. 56.

[4] Matthias Ruffert, "The Many Faces of Rule-Making in the EU," in Elaine Fahey (ed.), *The Actors of Postnational Rule-Making: Contemporary Challenges of European and International Law* (Routledge, 2016), p. 47 ff.; Christoph Möllers, "European Governance: Meaning and Value of a Concept" (2006) 43 *Common Market Law Review* 313–336 at 333 ff.; Jan van Tatenhove, Jeannette Mak, and Duncan Liefferink, "The Inter-play between Formal and Informal Practices" (2006) 7 *Perspectives on European Politics and Society* 8–24.

of European integration.[5] Along similar lines, many studies have been dedicated to better understanding the effects of informality on constitutional structures.[6] Especially in Germany, the legal discourse has focused on the allegedly increasing informalization of state activities and its implications for the rule of law, the doctrine of sources, and the accountability of public institutions.[7] At the international level, informality has been the subject of an ambitious project called IN-LAW. This project has concluded that the future of the international legal discipline rests on its ability to take advantage of the "rich, effective and legitimate normative output stemming from informal international lawmaking."[8]

Yet, despite the general agreement on its importance, the meaning of informality is far from clear. An overview of the relevant literature leaves the impression that informality is treated as a residual category rather than a concept with epistemic validity. In legal studies, for instance, the notion is used in a rather indiscriminate manner. As one leading scholar in this field acknowledged not long ago, "'informality' is not a clearly defined legal concept."[9] Evidence of this is abundant. First, it is possible to

[5] On the importance of informality in the history of European integration, see the contributions in Lennaert van Heumen and Mechthild Roos (eds.), *The Informal Construction of Europe* (Routledge, 2019).

[6] Giorgio Berti, "Stato di diritto informale" (1992) 42 *Rivista trimestrale di diritto pubblico* 3–30.

[7] Friederich Schoch, "Entformalisierung staatlichen Handelns," in Josef Isensee and Paul Kirchhof (eds.), *Handbuch des Staatsrechts*, 3rd ed. (C. F. Müller, 2005), vol. 3, p. 131 ff.; Martin Morlok, "Informalisierung und Entparlamentarisierung politischer Entscheidungen als Gefährdungen der Verfassung?" (2003) 62 *Veröffentlichungen der Vereinigung der Deutschen Staatsrechtslehrer* 37–80; Matthias Ruffert, "Entformalisierung und Entparlamentarisierung politischer Entscheidungen als Gefährdungen der Verfassung?" (2002) 117 *Deutsches Verwaltungsblatt* 1145–1154; Helmut Schulze-Fielitz, "Das Verhältnis von formaler und informaler Verfassung," in Alex Görlitz and Hans-Peter Burth (eds.), *Informale Verfassung* (Nomos, 1998), p. 25 ff. In the field of administrative law, Michael Fehling, "Informelles Verwaltungshandeln," in Wolfgang Hoffmann-Riem, Eberhard Schmidt-Aßmann, and Andreas Voßkuhle (eds.), *Grundlagen des Verwaltungsrechts*, 2nd ed. (C. H. Beck, 2012), vol. 2, p. 1457 ff.

[8] Joost Pauwelyn, Ramses A. Wessel, and Jan Wouters (eds.), *Informal International Lawmaking* (Oxford University Press, 2012). As regards informality in international organization law, Jan Klabbers, "Institutional Ambivalence by Design: Soft Organizations in International Law" (2001) 70 *Nordic Journal of International Law* 403–421. See also Charles B. Roger, *The Origins of Informality: Why the Legal Foundations of Global Governance Are Shifting, and Why It Matters* (Oxford University Press, 2020).

[9] Helmut Schulze-Fielitz, "Konstitutionalisierung der Informalität? Nutzen und Grenzen einer Nachführung des Verfassungsrechts an informale Prozesse der Entscheidungsfindung," in Julian Krüper, Heike Merten, and Martin Morlok (eds.), *An den Grenzen der Rechtsdogmatik* (Mohr Siebeck, 2010), p. 95; Morlok, "Informalisierung und Entparlamentarisierung," 55.

consider the tautological definition employed in the IN-LAW project, according to which "IN-LAW is informal in the sense that it dispenses with certain formalities (related to the output, process, or the actors involved) traditionally linked to international law."[10] Secondly, there are those scholarly contributions that treat informality and soft law as overlapping, interchangeable concepts,[11] although informality – broadly speaking – concerns processes and organization (throughput), whereas soft law concerns legal instruments (output).[12] Thirdly, it is worth mentioning those studies, too, that employ informality to describe any everyday social practice not based on an exercise of public authority, such as the spontaneous forming of a line in front of a news stand.[13] This list could go on almost indefinitely.[14]

Against such a varied landscape, I will identify only those elements of informality that are relevant for European constitutional law, maintaining my focus on trilogues.[15] To this end, I have compared trilogues with two other European bodies that, according to standard readings, are also informal in nature. These bodies are the Euro Group and the so-called Informal Council meetings. The Euro Group, which provides the most influential forum to discuss questions relating to the single currency and the economy of the Eurozone, is under a EU primary law obligation to

[10] Joost Pauwelyn, Ramses A. Wessel, and Jan Wouters, "Informal International Lawmaking: An Assessment and Template to Keep It Both Effective and Accountable," in Joost Pauwelyn, Ramses A. Wessel, and Jan Wouters (eds.), *Informal International Lawmaking* (Oxford University Press, 2012), p. 499.

[11] See, e.g., Stephen J. Toope, "Formality and Informality," in Daniel Bodansky, Jutta Brunnée, and Ellen Hey (eds.), *The Oxford Handbook of International Environmental Law* (Oxford University Press, 2008), p. 107 ff.; Jan Klabbers, "Informal Instruments before the European Court of Justice" (1994) 31 *Common Market Law Review* 997–1023.

[12] As for the distinction between output and throughput, *locus classicus* is Vivien A. Schmidt, "Democracy and Legitimacy in the European Union Revisited: Input, Output and 'Throughput'" (2013) 61 *Political Studies* 2–22 at 7.

[13] See, e.g., Neil MacCormick, *Institutions of Law: An Essay in Legal Theory* (Oxford University Press, 2007), p. 21 ff.

[14] On the confusion surrounding the term "informality," Mechthild Roos and Lennaert van Heumen, "Introduction," in Lennaert van Heumen and Mechthild Roos (eds.), *The Informal Construction of Europe* (Routledge, 2019), p. 3 ff.

[15] Ibid., p. 9, where it is argued that informality is so multifarious that any research with a pretense of being scientifically sound "must clarify what kind of informality is studied and what actually makes a particular actor, procedure, network and so on informal." Similarly, Emmanuel Mourlon-Druol, "How Informality Can Play Out in European Integration," in Lennaert van Heumen and Mechthild Roos (eds.), *The Informal Construction of Europe* (Routledge, 2019), p. 219 ff.

meet informally[16] – not for nothing is it said to be "the most developed institutional infrastructure for informal policy dialogue so far."[17] Council presidencies can – and usually do – organize a certain number of informal ministerial meetings during their respective six-month mandates in order to ensure policy coordination in relation to specific matters, even outside the set of competences of the EU. The Informal Council meetings are organized in accordance with a set of basic "rules," whose objective is to preserve their informal nature.[18]

This comparative exercise has confirmed that trilogues, the Euro Group, and the Informal Council meetings share a set of common defining elements. In my take, these elements hypostatize – at least in part – the European concept of informality and can therefore be employed to clarify and deepen its understanding. True, these bodies operate in rather different areas of governance. Whereas trilogues are the center of political gravity in legislative matters, the Euro Group and the Informal Council meetings are relevant in the field of intergovernmental policy coordination. However, far from revealing a weakness of my reconstructive work, the fact that these bodies operate in different governance areas is apt to fortify my findings, as it shows that the European concept of informality enjoys consistency across different empirical contexts.[19] But

[16] Art. 1 Protocol (No. 14) on the Euro Group states: "The Ministers of the Member States whose currency is the euro shall meet informally." For an analysis of the Euro Group's "requirement of informality," Giacomo Rugge, "The Euro Group's Informality and *locus standi* before the European Court of Justice: *Council v. K. Chrysostomides & Co. and Others*" (2021) 81 *Heidelberg Journal of International Law* 917–936 at 927 ff.; Opinion of Advocate General Pitruzzella in Case C-597/18 P *Council v. K. Chrysostomides & Co. and Others* EU: C:2020:390, para. 84 ff. and fn. 60. Due to the express mentions of the Euro Group in EU primary law, such as in Art. 137 TFEU and the foregoing Protocol, it is quite surprising to read that the Euro Group has "a shadow existence . . ., which is not even mentioned in any legal document." In these terms, Hauke Brunkhorst, "Democracy under Siege: The Decay of Constitutionalization and the Crisis of Public Law and Public Opinion," in Poul F. Kjaer and Niklas Olsen (eds.), *Critical Theories of Crisis in Europe: From Weimar to the Euro* (Rowman & Littlefield International, 2016), p. 178.

[17] Uwe Puetter, *The European Council and the Council: New Intergovernmentalism and Institutional Change* (Oxford University Press, 2014), p. 156.

[18] Presidency Conclusions, "Helsinki European Council: 10 and 11 December 1999," Annex III.E; Council of the European Union, "Legal Service: Rules Governing the Holding of Informal Ministerial Meetings," 13818/03, 21 October 2003. Further information about the organization and workings of the Informal Council meetings can be found in Council of the European Union, "Internal Standing Instructions for GSC Staff," SN 1862/1/15 REV 1, May 2015, at 22.

[19] For consistency among different contexts as a key attribute of a "good concept," Tom Ginsburg and Nicholas Stephanopoulos, "The Concepts of Law" (2017) 84 *University of Chicago Law Review* 147–175 at 153 f.

before presenting and discussing my findings, namely the five common defining elements of European informal bodies, I will elaborate on a couple of more general observations. The aim of these observations is to provide a sharper theoretical and conceptual framework for the following analysis of European informality.

4.3 An Institutionalist Reading

From a terminological point of view, "informality" is the antonym of "formality." It would therefore be possible to believe that the former word is all that the latter is not, and vice versa. If formality means, for instance, regimentation, organization, and rigidity, informality might be associated with spontaneity, randomness, and flexibility. Yet in those scholarly works in which they assume relevance, the two concepts are not always conceived as being mutually exclusive. In fact, they are believed to relate to each other in interdependent and reciprocally reinforcing ways. First, formality (with its norms and structures) is the "bottom line" to fall back on if informality breaks down. For instance, if trilogues do not lead to an agreement, the institutions proceed to the next reading of the proposal with debate and vote, as provided for by EU primary law. Secondly, according to many institutional and governance theories,[20] informality gives rise to structures that "fashion, enable, and constrain political actors as they act within a logic of appropriate action."[21] Informality therefore amounts to a full-fledged institutional phenomenon, with its own characteristics. Among these characteristics, two are particularly worth specifying: its normative character and its functions and effects. I will consider them in turn.

[20] James G. March and Johan P. Olsen, "Elaborating the 'New Institutionalism,'" in Sarah A. Binder, R. A. W. Rhodes, and Bert A. Rockman (eds.), *The Oxford Handbook of Political Institutions* (Oxford University Press, 2008), p. 4, writing that institutionalism broadly denotes "a general approach to the study of political institutions, a set of theoretical ideas and hypotheses concerning the relations between institutional characteristics and political agency, performance, and change. Institutionalism emphasizes the endogenous nature and social construction of political institutions. Institutions are not simply equilibrium contracts among self-seeking, calculating individual actors or arenas for contending social forces. They are collections of structures, rules, and standard operating procedures that have a partly autonomous role in political life."

[21] Ibid., p. 4.

4.3.1 *A Normative Phenomenon in Its Own Right*

To better explain the normative character of informality, an anecdote is in order. In one of the most critical moments in recent EU history, the noncompliant behavior of Yanis Varoufakis – then Greek finance minister – with the Euro Group's informal norms was about to derail the successful completion of a key round of negotiations over a rescue package for Greece. This episode took place in April 2015 and resulted from the violation of one of the most essential norms of European informal bodies, according to which openly confrontational, rhetorical attitudes, as often observable in public arenas, are not acceptable. The episode was reported by Luuk van Middelaar in the following terms:

> The new Greek finance minister Yanis Varoufakis did not hold with the *informal club rules* of the Euro Group. He gave his colleagues lessons in Keynesian economic policy and refused any longer to be pushed into the position of a debtor confronting the bankers. The 18 other ministers expressed their impatience. After less than three months the newcomer was ejected from the circle at a quarrelsome meeting in Riga; he spoke of an ambush and of "character assassination" with the complicity of the press.[22]

The gist of this anecdote is that informality does not mean normative vacuum. As an institutional phenomenon, informality bespeaks the instinctive and irrepressible "efforts of individuals and subgroups to control the conditions of their existence."[23] As observed, "whenever people come together to carry out some activity, they form rules to govern and guide them. The tendency to do so appears deeply embedded in any context of shared activities."[24] The same applies to European informal bodies. As close-knit aggregates of individuals engaged in face-to-face interactions for a precise purpose,[25] they could not do without norms that guide the conduct of the actors involved, providing predictable and stable interactional dynamics. This also emerged at the end of the previous chapter,[26] as it was shown that the inner workings of trilogues rest on emerging practices and shared logics of action. In this

[22] Luuk van Middelaar, *Alarums & Excursions: Improvising Politics on the European Stage* (Agenda Publishing, 2019), p. 195 (emphasis added).

[23] Donald Chisholm, *Coordination without Hierarchy: Informal Structures in Multiorganizational Systems* (University of California Press, 1989), p. 16.

[24] Galligan, *Law in Modern Society*, p. 106

[25] "body, n., sense IV.13.a," in *Oxford English Dictionary* (Oxford University Press, July 2023): "a group of people with a common purpose or function acting as an organized unit, as for deliberation, government, or business."

[26] Chapter 3, Section 3.6.

sense, informality is a norms-based phenomenon.[27] The functioning of informal structures and bodies relies on expectations that political actors retain even in the face of disappointment – with Luhmann, one could say "contra-factually."[28]

That said, one aspect deserves closer scrutiny. The norms that govern informal structures and bodies, including European informal bodies, have their own characteristics, notably a certain degree of ambiguity and open-endedness.[29] The relevant actors enjoy a fair amount of discretion in adapting them to the circumstances; and this makes them "norms in self-administration."[30] From a practical viewpoint, this implies that the standards of behavior offered by these norms can be weighed against contingent factors and modulated accordingly; and this may lead to actors departing from the usually observed behaviors. In other words, the actual course of action results from empirical assessments that consider singularity and situatedness. The norms can be bent, within certain limits, to suit the needs and purposes of the specific case, provided that the actors concerned consent. In so doing, these norms allow political actors to cultivate a more balanced relationship between abstract and context-sensitive aspects,[31] between universal and particularistic considerations. An example might help to better explain how these norms operate.

[27] Roos and van Heumen, "Introduction," p. 8: "Particularly at the European level, informality is not without its rules, which are set by the participants of a particular sphere, forming an institution, body or network." See also Morlok, "Informalisierung und Entparlamentarisierung," 50; Christian Hanke, "Informale Regeln als Substrat des parlamentarischen Verhandlungssystems. Zur Begründung einer zentralen Kategorie der Parlamentarismusforschung" (1994) 25 *Zeitschrift für Parlamentsfragen* 410–440 at 420 f.

[28] Niklas Luhmann, *Soziale Systeme: Grundriß einer allgemeinen Theorie*, 16th ed. (Suhrkamp, 2015), p. 437.

[29] According to some of the first institutional theories, European informal bodies might seamlessly qualify as legal orders. Although those theories have the merit of placing these bodies close to the realm of the law – indeed locating them within such a realm – they also carry the risk of overlooking all their differentiating features. Among those theories, deserving of special mention is that of Santi Romano, as outlined in *L'ordinamento giuridico*, 2nd ed. (Sansoni, 1951), p. 29 ff. After about a century from its first Italian edition in 1918, the book was finally translated into English: Santi Romano, *The Legal Order* (Routledge, 2017), p. 17 ff. More recently, Galligan, *Law in Modern Society*, p. 173 ff.

[30] Morlok, "Informalisierung und Entparlamentarisierung," 53 f.; von Achenbach, "Verfassungswandel durch Selbstorganisation," 18. On the flexibility of those norms, Hanke, "Informale Regeln als Substrat des parlamentarischen Verhandlungssystems," 425.

[31] This feature of the norms of informal bodies is also highlighted by Morlok, "Informalisierung und Entparlamentarisierung," 50 ff.

Seating arrangements are of extreme importance. They give outward expression not only to specific political needs but also to particular political theories.[32] In the case of trilogues, for instance, "seating ... should always be arranged with a view to promoting a free and constructive exchange of views between the principal interlocutors." Seating arrangements are therefore meant to create an atmosphere conducive to genuine exchanges amongst the participants.[33] To operationalize this norm, the European Parliament drafted a "Manual on the Preparation of Meeting Rooms by Conference Ushers," which includes precise indications as to how to set up negotiation rooms. The manual is introduced by the following words: "These Rules are not written in stone and ushers are always willing to help to accommodate additional requests ...; however, it is important to understand that those changes should remain within a limited framework. This is a matter of image, coherence and efficiency."[34] This statement clearly lays bare the distinguishing nature of the norms at issue, the aspiration of which is to provide general standards of behavior while proving adjustable to the specific circumstances of the case.

Similar considerations apply to many other norms that govern informal structures and bodies. A case in point is the norm according to which negotiating teams in trilogues should have the same level of representation. To understand the rationale of this norm, let us assume that the team of the EP were headed by a parliamentary assistant, whereas the teams of the Council and the Commission were headed by a deputy permanent representative and a Director-General, respectively. In such a situation, the two latter teams, especially that of the Council, would have a bargaining disadvantage, as they would have to negotiate with someone who, owing to a lowly official position, is less capable of committing his or her home institution. Therefore, the norm has a twofold rationale, symbolic and practical, which ensures that the norm is obeyed. Still, after mutual consultations, the institutions may – and often do – agree to depart from the usual behavior, if they deem it expedient or appropriate.

[32] Philip Manow, *In the King's Shadow: The Political Anatomy of Democratic Representation* (Polity Press, 2010), p. 8 ff.

[33] Council of the European Union, "Ordinary Legislative Procedure: Guide for GSC Officials," 11 October 2016, at 12; Council of the European Union, "Ordinary Legislative Procedure: Guide for the Presidency," 11 October 2016, at 13.

[34] European Parliament, "Manual on the Preparation of Meeting Rooms by Conference Ushers," D(2015)14246, 16 June 2015.

In short, the expectations that these norms create and stabilize can be adapted to the circumstances, provided that the actors concerned consent to such adaptation. Their blunt violation may lead to political sanctions or high political costs, which can be rather effective in eliciting compliance, not unlike legal enforcement mechanisms.[35] Despite their flexibility, these norms have the obvious ambition of inducing obedience on the part of their addressees. Regardless of how these norms are treated in court, they certainly shape the range of conceivable (acceptable) normative solutions.[36] As for the anecdote of the Euro Group, the violation of what van Middelaar calls "informal club rules" was not – and could not have been – sanctioned by a European or domestic judge, but it was sanctioned politically. Varoufakis paid a high reputational price for his behavior, leaving his country hanging by a thread.

I would therefore argue that informality, at least in its European version, indicates institutional structures and bodies in which legal normativity is intentionally kept at bay.[37] This does not mean that type of normativity plays no role at all: ultimately, every institutional phenomenon must operate in the shadow of constitutional law. However, it is possible to have structures and bodies that are intentionally designed to be less susceptible to legal normativity – and therefore to be more informal – than others. In the European institutional system, the Euro Group is arguably less informal than trilogues; and trilogues are probably less informal than the Informal Council meetings. All these observations gain further traction after considering that, traditionally, the smooth functioning of political institutions has never counted so much on legally

[35] The risk of incurring sanctions does not per se account for norm-abiding behaviors. Such a risk might be a powerful tool for promoting compliance, but it is by no means a conclusive element for gauging the normativity of a given prescription. See Cristina Bicchieri, Ryan Muldoon, and Alessandro Sontuoso, "Social Norms," in Edward N. Zalta (ed.), *The Stanford Encyclopedia of Philosophy* (2018). See also Galligan, *Law in Modern Society*, p. 106 f.

[36] In these terms, see also von Achenbach, "Verfassungswandel durch Selbstorganisation," 14 ff. Unlike legally binding norms, many of those norms that govern informal structures and bodies are not – in and of themselves – enforceable in court. They can become relevant in judicial proceedings insofar as their content materializes that of a legal provision (e.g., the principle of loyal cooperation).

[37] Following some authors, informal structures and bodies may be said to display intermediate-to-low levels of "legalization." See Kenneth W. Abbott, Robert O. Keohane, Andrew Moravcsik, Anne-Marie Slaughter, and Duncan Snidal, "The Concept of Legalization" (2000) 54 *International Organization* 401–419 at 401, arguing that "legalization" refers to "a particular form of institutionalization characterized by three components: obligation, precision, and delegation." Accordingly, legalization ought to be understood as a multidimensional continuum, capable of accommodating the most diverse combinations.

binding norms.[38] Moreover, informal structures and bodies play an indispensable function: they contribute to the stability of the whole political system. Indeed, "[i]f this is rigidly determined in all its parts by legally binding norms . . . it is more exposed to the risk of falling underneath the impetus of the various and varying streams which always shake the political life."[39] These remarks form the basis for a second set of observations, which focuses on the functions and effects of informality.

4.3.2 *Its Multiple Functions and Effects*

The standard argument in favor of informality is that it provides "the nerves of governance";[40] it instantiates the connective tissues that make procedures work, becoming an ineliminable element of any working institutional system. However, informality should not simply be considered as a necessary evil or as the price to pay for the effectiveness of the European legal order or of any other legal order for that matter. In fact, informality can have legitimacy-enhancing effects.[41] In addition to signifying the existence of a consensus about how to implement constitutional procedures and prerogatives,[42] it can significantly improve the actual functioning of institutions.[43] For instance, it can clarify ambiguities, resolve apparent contradictions in legal provisions, adjust the institutions to changing societal conditions – absent a constitutional amendment[44] – and reduce transaction costs and uncertainty.[45] In short, informality can step up collective action capacity.[46]

[38] Legally binding norms are often regarded as "expensive." See Robert D. Putnam, *Making Democracy Work* (Princeton University Press, 1993), p. 165.

[39] Santi Romano, "Diritto e correttezza costituzionale," in *Scritti minori* (Giuffrè, 1950), vol. 1, p. 278.

[40] Klaus von Beyme, *Der Gesetzgeber: Der Bundestag als Entscheidungszentrum* (Westdeutscher Verlag, 1997), p. 44.

[41] Timo Grunden, "Informelle Machtarchitekturen im parlamentarischen Regierungssystem – Zur Analyse der Entstehung, Funktion und Veränderung informeller Institutionen," in Stephan Bröchler and Timo Grunden (eds.), *Informelle Politik: Konzepte, Akteure und Prozesse* (Springer, 2014), p. 23.

[42] Hanke, "Informale Regeln als Substrat des parlamentarischen Verhandlungssystems," 436.

[43] Grunden, "Informelle Machtarchitekturen," p. 27 f.

[44] Chisholm, *Coordination without Hierarchy*, p. 34 f., pointing out that "all formal designs have a built-in obsolescence that cannot be circumvented, thus virtually requiring that informal mechanisms be developed if the organization is to continue to prosper."

[45] The underlying idea is that, by putting the relevant institutional actors in direct contact, it is possible to reduce social complexity. See Morlok, "Informalisierung und Entparlamentarisierung," 49.

[46] Grunden, "Informelle Machtarchitekturen," p. 18.

As I will show in the next chapters, trilogues might be considered as the means by which the Parliament, the Council, and the Commission make up for the limitations of the European party system. In national parliamentary democracies, the legislative process is essentially based on negotiations among political parties and structured along party lines.[47] At EU level, the same negotiations occur through trilogues. In both cases, formal decisions are often the simple enactment of previously negotiated political compromise. In the absence of a strong European party system, capable of conveying a general policy direction, trilogues aim at bringing the Parliament, the Council, and the Commission together and arriving at a meeting point between otherwise strongly separated institutions. The Euro Group and the Informal Council meetings might be loosely compared to those informal institutions that underpin German "cooperative federalism," such as the ministerial conferences of the German *Länder* (*Fachministerkonferenzen*). Indeed, German "cooperative federalism" is not only intergovernmental in character,[48] but also largely informal.[49]

However, there is another aspect of informality which is particularly worth mentioning, especially in relation to the general argument of this book. Informality requires, and at the same time generates, trust among actors. Its development and maintenance feed off a mutually reinforcing logic: the stronger the disposition to cooperate, the likelier the emergence of informality, and vice versa. For if it is true that a certain amount of institutional trust is necessary to establish informal structures and bodies, once in place these structures and bodies consolidate and enhance that trust, "foster[ing] socialization into cooperative and constructive behavior"; and this is said to augment skills at political compromise.[50] In particular, informality is said to be a very effective way to create an atmosphere of reciprocity; an atmosphere that is extremely favorable for the elaboration of compromise. There is indeed both anecdotal and empirical evidence which confirms that the prevailing atmosphere in informal bodies,

47 In these terms, among others, Schoch, "Entformalisierung staatlichen Handelns," p. 180 ff.

48 Manfred G. Schmidt, *Political Institutions in the Federal Republic of Germany* (Oxford University Press, 2003), p. 62 f.

49 Morlok, "Informalisierung und Entparlamentarisierung," 41. See also Thomas O. Hueglin and Alan Fenna, *Comparative Federalism: A Systematic Inquiry*, 2nd ed. (University of Toronto Press, 2015), p. 238 ff.

50 Christine Reh, Adrienne Héritier, Edoardo Bressanelli, and Christel Koop, "The Informal Politics of Legislation: Explaining Secluded Decision Making in the European Union" (2011) 49 *Comparative Political Studies* 1112–1142 at 1126. On the relationship between informality and trust, Anna-Tina Pannes, *Informalität* (Springer, 2015), p. 209.

especially in trilogues, has the foregoing characteristics.[51] I will come back to this key point in the last section of this chapter.

To be sure, informality can also weaken the arrangements and safeguards that the Treaties provide in defense of basic democratic standards, such as transparency, accountability, and participation.[52] Two points therefore need emphasizing. First, legally binding decisions can emanate only from the procedures set out in the Treaties, and any agreement reached informally must be legitimized through those procedures.[53] Secondly, any normative assessment of informal structures and bodies should follow a *holistic* approach. Drawing on the German Federal Constitutional Court's doctrine about the "level of democratic legitimacy,"[54] informal phenomena should be analyzed in their broader context and within the framework of the Treaties generally, focusing on how they interplay and combine with other institutional components.[55]

To carry out a normative assessment, the yardsticks are not only the relevant procedural provisions but also the "founding principles."[56]

[51] As regards trilogues, María Gómez-Leal Pérez, "El procedimiento legislativo ordinario en la práctica: los acuerdos en primera lectura" (2015) *Cuadernos Europeos de Deusto* 101–118 at 115; Katrin Huber and Michael Shackleton, "Codecision: A Practitioner's View from inside the Parliament" (2013) 20 *Journal of European Public Policy* 1040–1055 at 1044; Olivier Costa, Renaud Dehousse, and Aneta Trakalová, "Codecision and 'Early Agreements': An Improvement or a Subversion of the Legislative Procedure?" (2011) *Notre Europe* 32; Reh et al., "The Informal Politics of Legislation," 1125 f. and 1133 f.; Jean-Paul Jacqué, "Une vision réaliste de la procédure de codécision," in Aline De Walsche and Laure Levi (eds.), *Mélanges en hommage à Georges Vandersanden: promenades au sein du droit européen* (Bruylant, 2008), p. 192 ff.; Michael Shackleton, "The Politics of Codecision" (2000) 38 *Journal of Common Market Studies* 325–342 at 333 ff.

[52] As to the challenges that informality poses to constitutional law, Möllers, *The Three Branches*, p. 227 ff. See also Mechthild Roos and Christine Neuhold, "Studying the Informal in European Integration: A Research Guide," in Lennaert van Heumen and Mechthild Roos (eds.), *The Informal Construction of Europe* (Routledge, 2019), p. 20, affirming that "[m]ost forms of informal action are seen to have a questionable level of legitimacy and accountability, given the lack of oversight, fair access, and often of visibility."

[53] This is what some authors call "asymmetrical dependence." See Reh et al., "The Informal Politics of Legislation," 1117

[54] See, e.g., German Federal Constitutional Court, Case No. 2 BvL 5/98, 5 December 2002 – *Lippeverband*, para. 159: "For the assessment of whether a sufficient level of democratic legitimacy is achieved, the forms of institutional, functional, substantive and personal legitimacy ... are not important for themselves, but only in their interaction" (my translation). In this respect, Paul Kirchhof, "Mittel staatlichen Handelns," in Josef Isensee and Paul Kirchhof (eds.), *Handbuch des Staatsrechts*, 3rd ed. (C. F. Müller, 2007), vol. 5, p. 75 ff.

[55] For a similar understanding, Morlok, "Informalisierung und Entparlamentarisierung," 65.

[56] On the meaning and relevance of the "founding principles," Armin von Bogdandy, "Founding Principles," in Armin von Bogdandy and Jürgen Bast (eds.), *Principles of European Constitutional Law*, 2nd ed. (Hart/C. H. Beck/Nomos, 2011), pp. 11 ff. and 21 ff.

As regards the legislative function of the EU, the procedural provisions are those set out in Article 293 TFEU and following; the founding principles are those set out in Article 9 TEU and following, including the principles of institutional balance and loyal cooperation. Whereas a normative assessment that analyzes a phenomenon in its "clinical isolation" may lead to an outright negative result, a normative assessment that studies the same phenomenon in a holistic perspective may lead to completely different conclusions. With this in mind, I can now turn to the five common defining elements of trilogues, the Euro Group, and the Informal Council meetings as informal bodies.

4.4 European Informal Bodies: Defining Elements

Despite being different from each other in numerous ways, the bodies under scrutiny show some common features that may be reasonably considered as defining elements of their informal nature. Indeed, trilogues, the Euro Group, and the Informal Council meetings all share the following characteristics: (a) limited number of participants; (b) confidentiality of the discussions, including – but not limited to – the nonpublic nature of the meetings; (c) importance of consensus, as distinguished from majority voting and unanimity; (d) absence of final decision-making powers; and (e) creation of genuine exchanges among the participants.

4.4.1 *Limited Number of Participants: Size Matters*

The debate about the size of representative institutions, especially legislative ones, is as old as the hills. On the one hand, large representative institutions are thought to provide a more faithful picture of societies: the higher the number of members, the broader the interests represented; the higher the number of representatives, the more mimetic the representation. On the other hand, small-sized representative institutions are thought to allow for a more active participation in deliberations while reducing transaction costs deriving from protracted, less focused discussions.[57] Whereas there are no theoretical reasons for excluding a positive-sum relationship between active participation and actual representativeness, institutional engineering in Western liberal democracies has largely proved unable to devise representative institutions that allow

[57] Giovanni Sartori, "Will Democracy Kill Democracy? Decision-Making by Majorities and by Committees" (1975) 10 *Government and Opposition* 131–158 at 153: "face-to-face small groups … allow for a 'reasoned', well-discussed elaboration of decisions."

for both needs to properly coexist. The pragmatic solution to this problem has been to have both large representative assemblies and cabinet-size bodies with varying degrees of institutionalization, with the latter working alongside and in cooperation with the former.[58]

The creation and burgeoning of small decision-making bodies are subject to widespread criticism. Some authors argue that their proliferation results from the deplorable tendency of politics to escape its natural place: the plenaries of parliamentary assemblies.[59] These criticisms are off-target though. Plenaries have never taken center stage in the legislative process,[60] despite authoritative voices to the contrary.[61] Their size makes them generally unsuitable for cooperation and deliberations in a thick sense,[62] pushing actors into other forums, especially parliamentary committees and political parties. This unsuitability of plenaries has been highlighted, with different nuances and purposes, by authors of different historical periods and intellectual sensibilities, such as John Stuart Mill, Niklas Luhmann, and Jeremy Waldron.[63] It would be wrong, though, to assume that plenaries are mere "outward countenance." They fulfill important democratic and legitimizing functions. They are the hinge between the legislative authority and the citizens. Debates and votes in plenaries force representatives and political parties to provide justifications and to take responsibility for legislative action, according to the idea of "bottom-line transparency."[64] They also urge them to inform the public at large on their objectives, intentions, and decisions; to clarify background information and consequences of specific policy choices; and to present interests and political forces involved, thereby allowing the

[58] Ibid., 149: "In democracies, committees remain and indeed augment."

[59] Eberhard Schuett-Wetschky, "Auswanderung der Politik aus den Institutionen: Schwächung der Demokratie? Zur Legitimation der Parteiendemokratie" (2001) 11 *Zeitschrift für Politikwissenschaft* 3–29.

[60] Armin von Bogdandy, "Parlamentarismus in Europa: eine Verfalls- oder Erfolgsgeschichte?" (2005) 130 *Archiv des öffentlichen Rechts* 445–464 at 456 ff.

[61] One of the staunchest supporters of the centrality of the plenary in legislative deliberations is the German Federal Constitutional Court. See, e.g., German Federal Constitutional Court, Case No. 2 BvR 301/98, 7 December 1999 – *Häusliches Arbeitszimmer*, para. 30.

[62] Putnam, *Making Democracy Work*, p. 166.

[63] Jeremy Waldron, *Law and Disagreement* (Oxford University Press, 1999), p. 51; Niklas Luhmann, *Legitimation durch Verfahren*, 9th ed. (Suhrkamp, 2013), p. 174; John Stuart Mill, "Considerations on Representative Government," in *On Liberty, Utilitarianism, and Other Essays* (first published 1861, Oxford University Press, 2015), p. 235 ff.

[64] For an account of what bottom-line transparency implies and how it works, "Mechanisms of Secrecy" (2008) 121 *Harvard Law Review* 1556–1577.

formation of political judgment.[65] Arguably, these were the functions that the ECJ had in mind when it held that debates and votes during the EP's plenary sittings must be carried out with "all the necessary attention, rigor and commitment."[66]

These considerations about the plenaries confirm that in politics size matters.[67] But how can the right size of an optimal decision-making unit be determined? Sartori claims that the maximal efficient size for small, interacting face-to-face bodies is some thirty members.[68] This figure is a rough approximation, but it may offer an authoritative point of reference to gauge how the EU handles size in informal bodies. Trilogues, for instance, comprise on average between thirty and fifty participants – and the Council looks unfavorably at the Parliament's ever-expanding trilogue delegations.[69] Similarly, the Euro Group and the Informal Council meetings keep the number of participants under a certain critical threshold to have more in-depth discussions. To this end, they follow the minister-plus approach, meaning that they usually include the responsible minister plus one or two senior advisors, impeding access not only to the public but also to other EU and national officials. As twenty ministers participate in the Euro Group and twenty-seven participate in the Informal Council meetings, the overall number of participants in each of those bodies usually ranges from fifty to eighty. The Euro Group, for instance, is attended by the President and two members from each Eurozone Member State, to which one has to add about a dozen further possible participants.[70] Similarly, the Informal Council meetings are attended by twenty-seven ministers with a maximum of two assistants each, plus the Council Presidency.[71] The Commission takes part in these

[65] Thomas Schürmann, "Plenardebatte," in Martin Morlok, Ute Schliesky, and Dieter Wiefelspütz (eds.), *Parlamentsrecht: Handbuch* (Nomos, 2016), p. 612 f.

[66] Case C-73/17 *France* v. *Parliament (Exercice du pouvoir budgétaire)* EU:C:2018:787, paras. 41, 50, 58, and 60.

[67] Hermann Heller, "The Nature and Structure of the State" (1996) 18 *Cardozo Law Review* 1139–1216 at 1182: "all exercise of power is subordinate to the law of the small number."

[68] Sartori, "Will Democracy Kill Democracy?," 143.

[69] Council of the European Union, "Ordinary Legislative Procedure: Guide for GSC Officials," at 12 and 14; Council of the European Union, "Ordinary Legislative Procedure: Guide for the Presidency," at 13.

[70] Euro Group, "Working Methods of the Eurogroup," ECFIN/CEFCPE(2008)REP/50842 rev 1, 3 October 2008, at 4 f. See also Roberto Baratta, "Diritto e prassi evolutiva dell'Eurogruppo" (2015) *Il Diritto dell'Unione Europea* 493–521.

[71] Presidency Conclusions, "Helsinki European Council," Annex III.E., para. 20(iii).

meetings as well and is usually represented by the portfolio commissioner (s).[72] Compared to the ordinary Council meetings, in which much more than 150 people might take part,[73] these numbers denote a significant downsizing in terms of attendance.

That said, there is no hard-and-fast rule as regards the size of bodies such as trilogues. Defining in general terms the point at which a quantitative change implies also a qualitative one is simply not realistic. As Sartori himself recognized, a small, interacting face-to-face group "may perform poorly with twenty members, and manage to perform nicely with forty."[74] He was aware that the maximum efficient size of a small decision-making body depends, to a large extent, on its operational code. Reducing the number of participants to a minimum is often not enough, on its own, to generate those feelings of reciprocity and sociability that characterize informal environments. For instance, it has been reported that even after reducing the size of the national delegations participating in the ECOFIN meetings, ministers still avoided engaging in forthright exchanges when they were in public session.[75] The creation of an atmosphere of open dialogue calls for other elements. And indeed, the success of European informal bodies is intrinsically linked to their taking place far from the public eye or, to be more precise, to their being largely confidential.

4.4.2 *The Confidentiality of the Discussions*

To begin with, the meaning of "confidential" needs qualification. As regards European informal bodies, confidentiality not only implies that the public, video cameras, and audio recording devices do not have access to meeting rooms, but also that no minutes are available, making

72 European Commission, "The Commission's Presence in Meetings of the European Parliament, the Council, the Conciliation Committee and Trilogues, the European Economic and Social Committee, the Committee of the Regions and of National Parliaments," SEC(2010)102, 25 March 2010, para. 3.2, stating that "in order to preserve the informal nature of [the Informal Council meetings], the presence of officials is normally kept to a strict minimum."

73 Puetter, *The European Council and the Council*, p. 153, where the author affirms that "when the EU comprised only 15 members, over 100 people could be found in the meeting room. Enlargement exacerbated this problem dramatically." It is therefore safe to assume that, at present, at least 150 people participate in ordinary Council meetings. See also Opinion of Advocate General Pitruzzella in Case C-597/18 P *Council* v. *K. Chrysostomides & Co. and Others*, fn. 53.

74 Sartori, "Will Democracy Kill Democracy?," 143.

75 Puetter, *The European Council and the Council*, p. 161 f.

it difficult to know who said what and when. Until recently, agendas, negotiating documents, and results of the proceedings also used to be completely confidential. However, things have been slowly changing, due in part to the CJEU leaning towards transparency and to the work of the European Ombudsman.[76] In a 2018 judgment, for instance, the General Court expressly acknowledged that, in principle, EU citizens must be granted access to the main trilogue negotiating documents: the four-column tables.[77] The Euro Group has started to publish, on a more regular basis, draft annotated agendas, summing-up letters, and relevant meeting documents, including the press conferences that follow Euro Group meetings. Further measures are said to be in the pipeline.[78] The Informal Council meetings are also becoming less confidential. Presidencies are developing the practice of publishing on their websites the agendas and final statements of all the informal meetings that take place during their incumbency.

Despite recent moves towards increasing transparency, the working of these bodies still occurs in a regime of ("weak") confidentiality.[79] In the absence of video, audio, or written proceedings, it is hard to get an idea of which policy preferences and contributions animated the negotiations, and how they were integrated into a common position. What is more, many of the negotiating documents are not easily accessible, either because the institutions deny access or because citizens are not aware of their existence and cannot file appropriate and successful access requests. Even the publication of the foregoing documents, due to their extreme brevity, does not offer a full account of the relevant discussions.

[76] With a focus on trilogues, Maarten Hillebrandt and Päivi Leino-Sandberg, "Administrative and Judicial Oversight of Trilogues" (2021) 28 *Journal of European Public Policy* 53–71. See also European Ombudsman, "Decision of the European Ombudsman Setting Out Proposals following Her Strategic Inquiry OI/8/2015/JAS Concerning the Transparency of Trilogues," OI/8/2015/JAS, 12 July 2016.

[77] As regards the four-column tables, see Chapter 3, Section 3.6. The General Court based its reasoning on the assumption that only by having full access to those documents can EU citizens keep abreast of political actors' (changing) positions and exercise their democratic rights. See Case T-540/15 *De Capitani* v. *Parliament* EU:T:2018:167. For a comment of this judgment, Giacomo Rugge, "Trilogues and Access to Documents: *De Capitani* v. *Parliament*" (2019) 56 *Common Market Law Review* 237–258.

[78] Euro Group, "Press Release: Remarks by Mário Centeno following the Eurogroup Meeting of 13 September 2019," 13 September 2019.

[79] As different from secrecy, a regime of weak confidentiality implies that people are aware that proceedings are taking place, but they are not aware of their content. See Adrian Vermeule, *Mechanisms of Democracy: Institutional Design Writ Small* (Oxford University Press, 2007), p. 188.

But here is the predicament: the moment these bodies become (too) public, candor risks vanishing, and participants might be less open to listen to each other's concerns and interests. Although some recent studies begin to question the theoretical and empirical validity of such a predicament,[80] common opinion still has it that confidentiality facilitates negotiations in different ways, including by fostering openness and trust in discussions.[81] Hence, Simone Chambers states: "we will always need to have closed door sessions."[82]

So, the crux of the matter is how to prevent excessive confidentiality from transforming European informal bodies into "smoke-filled rooms," while preserving some moments for truly candid deliberations. To be clear, I do not claim that the EU institutions should not improve their transparency.[83] I argue, however, that unfettered transparency is not the solution. Scholarly literature is replete with contributions that highlight not only the "bright" but also the "dark" side of transparency, especially in the context of legislative deliberations and accountability.[84] Unfettered transparency can lead, for instance, to actors engaging in

[80] Sandrine Baume and Stéphanie Novak, "Compromise and Publicity in Democracy: An Ambiguous Relationship," in Sandrine Baume and Stéphanie Novak (eds.), *Compromises in Democracy* (Palgrave Macmillan, 2020), p. 78 ff.; Gijs Jan Brandsma and Albert Meijer, "Transparency and Efficiency of Multi-actor Decision-Making Processes: An Empirical Analysis of 244 Decisions in the European Union" (2022) 88 *International Review of Administrative Sciences* 626–643.

[81] Carrie Menkel-Meadow, *Negotiation: A Very Short Introduction* (Oxford University Press, 2022), p. 40; Mark E. Warren and Jane Mansbridge, "Deliberative Negotiation," in Jane Mansbridge and Cathie Jo Martin (eds.), *Negotiating Agreement in Politics: Report of the Task Force on Negotiating Agreement in Politics* (American Political Science Association, 2013), p. 108, who maintain that: "By now, the empirical evidence on the deliberative benefits of closed-door interactions seems incontrovertible"; David Stasavage, "Open-Door or Closed-Door? Transparency in Domestic and International Bargaining" (2004) 58 *International Organization* 667–703. See also Puetter, *The European Council and the Council*, p. 109 f., who, as regards the European Council's proceedings, observes that "the preoccupation with the question of what is communicated to the press after a meeting is an obstacle to more substantial policy debate . . . Informal meetings are considered to reduce such pressure."

[82] Simone Chambers, "Behind Closed Doors: Publicity, Secrecy and the Quality of Deliberation" (2004) 12 *Journal of Political Philosophy* 389–410 at 398.

[83] European Ombudsman, "Special Report of the European Ombudsman in Strategic Inquiry OI/2/2017/TE on the Transparency of the Council Legislative Process," OI/2/2017/TE, 16 May 2018.

[84] The literature is rich. Here is a partial sample of some very helpful works: Martin Hartmann, *Vertrauen: Die unsichtbare Macht* (S. Fischer, 2020), p. 200 ff.; David E. Pozen, "Transparency's Ideological Drift" (2018) 128 *Yale Law Journal* 100–165; Byung-Chul Han, *The Transparency Society* (Stanford University Press, 2015); Vermeule, *Mechanisms of Democracy*, ch. 6; John R. Hibbing and Elizabeth Theiss-Morse, *Congress as Public Enemy* (Cambridge University Press, 1995).

pandering and posturing, providing the public with poorly reasoned and generally appealing justifications, and pushing deliberations further to more opaque forums. As transparency cuts both ways, the objective should be to advance what good transparency can do, while suppressing its negative effects to the extent possible and desirable. As it is, it all boils down to a problem of optimization;[85] and the solution of this problem can lead – so I argue – to the recognition of stages in the European decision-making processes where confidentiality is legitimately envisaged, without thereby violating the democratic principles set out in the Treaties.

Such an exercise comports with EU primary law. Taking as a starting point the recent statement of the General Court, according to which "the principle of openness … is not absolute,"[86] I submit that when Article 1(2) TEU stipulates that in the Union "decisions are taken as openly as possible … to the citizen," it does not demand the maximization of transparency but rather its optimization. This reading finds confirmation in the fact that, in the very same clause, the Treaties also refer to the principle of subsidiarity ("decisions are taken … as closely as possible to the citizen"). As known, the subsidiarity principle requests the optimal allocation of authority in relation to the issue at stake and the resources available to address it. Hence the question: why should the Treaties put transparency and subsidiarity together in the same provision – in fact, in the same grammatical relationship ("as … as possible") – and then demand the optimization of the one and the maximization of the other? In addition, and with specific regard to the legislative process, the recognition of some confidential stages would not violate the requirement of Article 15(2) TFEU, according to which the Parliament and the Council shall deliberate and vote on draft legislation in public. In its current wording, such requirement does not extend to the activities carried out by internal preparatory bodies.[87] In fact, in making its committee meetings "normally" public,[88] the EP has ensured a level of transparency

[85] On the optimization problem, Vermeule, *Mechanisms of Democracy*, ch. 6.

[86] Case T-163/21 *De Capitani* v. *Council* EU:T:2023:15, para. 56.

[87] This is the widespread interpretation in legal scholarship. See, among others, Markus Krajewski and Ulrich Rösslein, "Art. 15 AEUV [Grundsatz der Offenheit]," in Eberhard Grabitz, Meinhard Hilf, and Martin Nettesheim (eds.), *Das Recht der Europäischen Union* (C. H. Beck, 2013), vol. 1, paras. 15 and 21; Johann Schoo and Niklas Görlitz, "Artikel 15 AEUV [Grundsatz der Offenheit]," in Jürgen Schwarze (ed.), *EU-Kommentar*, 3rd ed. (Nomos, 2012), paras. 12 and 15.

[88] Rule 121(3) EP RoP.

higher than that prescribed by EU primary law and ensured by many national parliaments (for instance, in Austria, Denmark, Finland, Germany, Italy, and Sweden).[89]

Without prolonging the debate excessively, I would like to add that the optimization of transparency may be achieved through the adoption or improvement of small-scale design mechanisms, following three guiding ideas: first, representing within European informal bodies all possible points of view, thus impeding a particularistic view from dominating the debate (reproducing the critical function of pluralism); secondly, ensuring "a back and forth between closed bargaining and open public debate"[90] – the report-back obligation after each trilogue is an example of this;[91] thirdly, promoting better insight into the working of informal bodies through more proactive publication of relevant documents. These ideas articulate the analogy that any "decisional system resembles a traffic system," for both systems can be controlled at a few strategic crossing points, through appropriate mechanisms placed at the appropriate junctures.[92]

European informal bodies, especially trilogues, are not that far from realizing those guiding ideas.[93] The EP takes part in trilogues with a delegation that comprises one MEP from each political group (creating a situation of overrepresentation of the smaller groups). The Commission is also present and fully involved in the negotiations, although its

[89] In all those countries, committee meetings usually take place *in camera*. See the data available on the website of the Inter-Parliamentary Union at: https://data.ipu.org/content/parline-global-data-national-parliaments (accessed on 8 August 2023).

[90] Chambers, "Behind Closed Doors," 408 f.

[91] The actual functioning of this obligation should be certainly improved. See Gijs Jan Brandsma, "Transparency of EU Informal Trilogues through Public Feedback in the European Parliament: Promise Unfulfilled" (2019) 26 *Journal of European Public Policy* 1464–1483, providing evidence that the EP's negotiating teams fail to satisfactorily comply with the report-back obligation set out in the Rules of Procedure. See also Christine Reh, "Is Informal Politics Undemocratic? Trilogues, Early Agreements and the Selection Model of Representation" (2014) 21 *Journal of European Public Policy* 822–841.

[92] The analogy is taken from Sartori, "Will Democracy Kill Democracy?," 149.

[93] On a more general note, it is worth highlighting that, according to many authors, the EU's political system is more transparent than those of its Member States. See, e.g., María José Martínez Iglesias, "The Accidental Democracy: A European Model," in Sacha Garben, Inge Govaere, and Paul Nemitz (eds.), *Critical Reflections on Constitutional Democracy in the European Union* (Hart, 2019), p. 209; van Middelaar, *Alarums & Excursions*, p. 226 f.; PK, "On Transparency – But Do Not Mention Brexit!" (2019) 44 *European Law Review* 587–588; Daniel Innerarity, *Democracy in Europe: A Political Philosophy of the EU* (Palgrave Macmillan, 2018), p. 57.

participation is – strictly speaking – not necessary.[94] Furthermore, the Presidency, in its capacity as the Council's unitary representative in trilogue negotiations, ensures that all Member States are aware of, and updated on, what happens in those negotiations, with its mandate and any subsequent changes thereto being agreed by the Member States in Coreper or in the Council. As a keen expert of European affairs recognized, information circulates fast between the Parliament and the Council, and any breach of trust on the part of the Presidency certainly becomes known and is punished accordingly (for example, through disavowal and the ensuing damage to credibility).[95] This form of indirect control is also fostered by the presence of civil servants in all three negotiating teams.

What might be defined as the uneasy alliance between trilogues and national parliaments deserves special mention. In particular, scholars consistently highlight that, due to the poor availability of information about legislative negotiations, trilogues turn out to have a negative impact on the capacity of national parliaments to hold their governments to account.[96] And even though, as Protocol (No. 1) notes, "the way in which national Parliaments scrutinize their governments … is a matter for the particular constitutional organization and practice of each Member State," I believe that the EU institutions cannot turn a blind eye to such a crucial question. That said, I also believe it is important to understand where to intervene in order to enable national parliaments to carry out their scrutiny function while preserving a margin of confidentiality for the European institutions. To this end, it is perhaps not necessary to publish all trilogue documents in a proactive manner – the lists of participants and the draft agendas might be enough. It is crucial, instead, to document and disseminate the results of the discussions within the Council and its preparatory bodies, especially the different lines of conflict. Such an idea would be in sync with a recommendation that the European Ombudsman advanced a few years ago and reiterated

[94] Una O'Dwyer, "La dynamique historique des relations interinstitutionnelles. Le point de vue d'un praticien sur l'évolution de la procédure de codécision" (2010) *Revue du droit de l'Union européenne* 487–526 at 505.

[95] Jacqué, "Une vision réaliste," p. 199.

[96] Rik de Ruiter and Christine Neuhold, "Subsidiarity Watchdogs and the Kennel of Trilogues: When Do They Bark? The Role of National Parliaments in Trilogue Negotiations" (2021) 28 *Journal of European Public Policy* 93–111; Diane Fromage, "How to Ensure That National Parliaments (Truly) 'Contribute Actively to the Good Functioning of (Tomorrow's) EU'?" (2020) 26 *European Law Journal* 472–483.

in the wake of a 2020 initiative called "Strengthening Legislative Transparency," through which the Council extended the list of legislative documents to be issued publicly.[97] While welcoming the new steps to transparency, the Ombudsman also encouraged the Council "to continue its efforts to improve legislative transparency, particularly by recording Member State positions on draft laws."[98] In the end, what matters for the purposes of ensuring appropriate democratic control are the positions national governments take in the Council. The comparison between those positions and the outcome of trilogues should be adequate to allow the national parliaments and public opinions to assess their government's actions.

The upshot of all the foregoing considerations is that, in principle, the closer one gets to establishing optimal transparency in the sense described above, the less relevant other spaces, such as hideaways, cloakrooms, choirs,[99] football teams,[100] become.[101] These spaces are facts of politics and no institutional arrangement will ever eliminate them completely. In fact, they not only represent important contexts for preparing political decisions, for socializing, and for providing institutional stability;[102] they also bear witness to the existence of nonhierarchical power structures.[103] These spaces should, however, be kept in check to impede them from becoming like the secret dinner table meeting where Hamilton, Jefferson, and Madison reached the momentous Compromise of 1790, as dramatized in the musical "Hamilton." To that end, European informal bodies are an effective tool, on the condition that some of their

97 Council of the European Union, "Presidency/General Secretariat of the Council: Strengthening Legislative Transparency," 9493/20, 9 July 2020, at 2 f.

98 European Ombudsman, "Ombudsman Welcomes Steps to Make EU Law Making more Accessible to the Public," Press Release No. 2/2020, 16 July 2020.

99 Rebecca Mead, "In Brexit Britain, the Parliament Choir Is in Purgatory: In a Thirteenth-Century Chapel Deep inside Westminster, a Choral Society Crosses Party Lines," *The New Yorker*, 4 November 2019.

100 Roger Willemsen, *Das Hohe Haus: Ein Jahr im Parlament*, 6th ed. (S. Fischer, 2014), p. 19.

101 Another example are those meetings that went by the name of "G5" and used to take place at the dining room of the Stanhope Hotel in Brussels between Jean-Claude Juncker (then President of the Commission), Manfred Weber (then Chair of the EPP Group), Frans Timmermans (then Vice-President of the Commission), Martin Schulz (then President of the European Parliament), and Gianni Pittella (then Chair of the S&D Group). See Tara Palmeri, "The Most Exclusive Dining Club in Brussels: Inside the G5 Where 'the Best Jokes Are Told' and Major EU Policies Are Pre-cooked," *Politico*, 18 June 2015.

102 Philip Norton, "Power behind the Scenes: The Importance of Informal Space in Legislatures" (2019) 72 *Parliamentary Affairs* 245–266 at 247 f. See also Reh et al., "The Informal Politics of Legislation," 1115.

103 Schulze-Fielitz, "Konstitutionalisierung der Informalität?," p. 100.

confidentiality is preserved and cherished. If properly organized, they can channel, tame, and frame the inclination of officials to escape from structured arenas and to yield to self-indulgent bargaining, with a lower degree of responsiveness.

4.4.3 *The Importance of Consensus*

Someone entering a trilogue room and observing how the negotiations play out would probably be surprised to see that votes (almost) never take place. People are so accustomed to the idea that legislative decision-making implies voting that its absence might appear an anomaly. Instead, this aspect is a crucial feature of trilogues as well as the Euro Group and the Informal Council meetings. All these bodies reach agreements by *consensus*.[104] It is important to point out that, in the EU institutional system, a decision is taken by consensus "when there is no obvious act of disapproval that repeals the final 'confirmation act.'"[105] What does this entail, practically? When it appears that those who participate in the deliberations have reached an understanding, the chair recapitulates the discussion; if no one objects to what the chair has said, it is presumed that everyone agrees with it; consensus is thereby reached. This decision-making method has a long tradition. In its contemporary form, consensus has three core characteristics worth highlighting.[106]

First, consensus does not always feature a clear demarcation between deliberation and aggregation of preferences. Decisions may seem to emerge directly from the discussion. Secondly, consensus does not demand the express approval of each participant, but it does require the less demanding assent of those who agree, alongside the acquiescence of those who hesitate. Thirdly, consensus guarantees the participation of everyone in the discussion, but it cannot – and does not mean to – ensure equal weight for everyone in the decision. In fact, it is employed with the precise aim of legitimizing and implicitly valorizing the different influence of the participants;[107] that different influence may derive from a

[104] For the "ongoing search for consensus" as a defining feature of the decision-making processes that play out in the Euro Group and the Informal Council meetings, see Puetter, *The European Council and the Council*, p. 59.

[105] Eva Krick, "The Myth of Effective Veto Power under the Rule of Consensus. Dynamics and Democratic Legitimacy of Collective Decision-Making by 'Tacit Consent'" (2017) *Négociations* 109–128 at 113.

[106] Philippe Urfalino, "La décision par consensus apparent. Nature et propriétés" (2007) 45 *Revue européenne des sciences sociales* 47–70 at 60.

[107] Ibid., 66.

variety of factors, both institutional and personal, such as voting weight, technical knowledge, reasoning power, gravitas. Consensus therefore rests on a very delicate balance. On the one hand, it preserves the existing political differences among the actors, recognizing greater sway for majorities and skilled negotiators. On the other hand, it prompts everyone to work for the attainment of compromises that are acceptable to all, including the minorities. It engenders an atmosphere in which minorities have their say and actively participate in the decision-making process, while taking account of the existing power relations among the participants.

But why do European informal bodies reach agreements by consensus? The answer to this question has an intimate connection with the essential purpose of those bodies, which is to negotiate compromise. The success of this activity also relies on the possibility for political actors to exploit individuals' different intensities of preference. In fact, the existence of uneven preference intensities is a valuable prerequisite for compromise; and those negotiation techniques that help political actors take advantage of them, such as logrolling and vote trading, belong to the notion of "gains from trade."[108] Let us clarify this with an example.

Negotiators meet in a trilogue to find agreement on a legislative proposal which aims at curbing pollution through a new tax on vehicles. Whereas the European Parliament's negotiating team is in favor of both the objective (curbing pollution) and the means (the new tax), the Council's negotiating team is in favor of the objective but opposes the means. If each party equally held on to its policy preferences and were never open to any – even minor – concessions, reaching an agreement would be difficult or impossible. Fortunately, the most common scenario in politics looks different. In our example, the Council's negotiating team will express its support for the legislative proposal if the tax is kept below a certain amount; or if it gets the promise that, in another legislative proposal under negotiation, the European Parliament will abstain from opposing its amendments, and so on. The EP's negotiating team will show its willingness to change the tax to a different type of deterrent, or it will give its assent to less demanding pollution levels to keep down the tax on vehicles, for example. All these dealings are possible because political actors usually defend their positions with different intensity, depending

[108] Raya Kardasheva, "Package Deals in EU Legislative Politics" (2013) 57 *American Journal of Political Science* 858–874.

on the interests of their constituencies, the party lines, or their personal career prospects.

As distinguished from other rules of aggregation, consensus considerably facilitates the attainment of compromise in the sense described above; and it is more consonant, both logically and practically, with the adoption of comprehensive package deals, many of the components of which would be rejected if taken in isolation.[109] The main problem with majority voting is that it "equalizes unequal intensities"; it "rests on a *fictio*, indeed on a very thin and unrealistic stipulation: let us pretend that preferences are equal in their intensity."[110] In addition, majority voting pits winners against losers, thereby introducing the prospect of a final "moment of truth," a showdown in a context where political actors seek the exact opposite. Figuratively, it would be possible to say that majority voting "uses the psychological structure of opposing armies."[111] On the other hand, unanimity requires everyone's full endorsement of a proposal and therefore entails the power of each member to veto a decision, causing high transaction costs or the costs of failure. This is not the case with consensus, as its logics and application render veto options far more restricted, if not moot.[112]

All this leads us to a short consideration. Consensus, especially in the context of trilogues, is often referred to as the epitome of a more general tendency of European institutions to marginalize conflicts and opposition from decision-making. Insofar as this viewpoint derives from a majoritarian understanding of democracy, it is worth remembering that "[t]he EU ... is not an imperfectly majoritarian institution but deliberately keeps the application of majoritarian procedures under close limitations."[113] In the same spirit, the most common fruits of decisions by consensus (political compromises) do not per se imply the relinquishment of contentious politics.[114] In fact, contentious politics is an

[109] Sartori, "Will Democracy Kill Democracy?," 140 ff.

[110] The analogy is taken from ibid., 141. For a critique of this "founding fiction" of modern democracy, Pierre Rosanvallon, *Democratic Legitimacy: Impartiality, Reflexivity, Proximity* (Princeton University Press, 2011), p. 1 ff.

[111] This thought belongs to Elias Canetti, *Crowds and Power* (Continuum, 1981), p. 188, who employed it to describe the nature of the two-party system of modern parliaments.

[112] Krick, "The Myth of Effective Veto Power," 120 f.

[113] Jürgen Neyer, *The Justification of Europe: A Political Theory of Supranational Integration* (Oxford University Press, 2012), p. 161. See also Armin von Bogdandy, "The European Lesson for International Democracy: The Significance of Articles 9–12 EU Treaty for International Organizations" (2012) 23 *European Journal of International Law* 315–334 at 322 f.

[114] Jacqué, "Une vision réaliste," p. 198, who argues that sharing the sense of a joint undertaking does not make political differences disappear; rather, it helps to frame

"inevitable context" in the search for compromise. As agreements "in which all sides sacrifice something in order to improve on the status quo ... and in which the sacrifices are at least partly determined by the other sides' will," compromises always "express an underlying and continuing conflict of values." Actually, "the disagreements among the parties are embodied in the compromise itself," which encapsulates a suboptimal settlement open to additional discussions and criticisms, especially in the light of its subsequent implementation.[115] Compromises do not imply the absence of partisanship; they rather imply openness of partisanship. Therefore, as observed by a keen expert of EU politics, trilogues and the compromises reached therein do not seem to forestall an increased politicization of the interactions of European actors.[116]

Compromises are not only the outcome of successful negotiation activities, but also the occasion for further social and political debate. Whereas I believe that the EU stands to gain from "the goods that conflicts can bring to social life,"[117] I also believe that this could be done without jettisoning those institutional structures, such as trilogues or other informal European bodies, that allow for the effective and legitimate composition of political differences. What is more, decision-making processes are multistage processes. They can – and should – reconcile moments of compromise and consensus with moments of antagonism and voting. Indeed, both consensus and voting perform strong legitimizing functions, despite their conspicuous differences.[118] Whereas consensus operationalizes the notion of intensity of preference, voting ensures the equality of individual preferences.[119] I thus do not see the reason to abandon one for the other, when both can coexist and contribute in

those differences in the light of a common objective, namely the adoption of the best possible legislation, applicable in all Member States.

115 Amy Gutmann and Dennis Thompson, *The Spirit of Compromise: Why Governing Demands It and Campaigning Undermines It* (Princeton University Press, 2012), p. 10 ff. Similarly, Christine Reh, "European Integration as Compromise: Recognition, Concessions and the Limits of Cooperation" (2012) 47 *Government and Opposition* 414–440 at 422.

116 Vivien A. Schmidt, "Politicization in the EU: Between National Politics and EU Political Dynamics" (2019) 26 *Journal of European Public Policy* 1018–1036 at 1026.

117 Marco Dani, "Rehabilitating Social Conflicts in European Public Law" (2012) 18 *European Law Journal* 621–643 at 623.

118 Krick, "The Myth of Effective Veto Power," 121 ff.; Manfred G. Schmidt, *Demokratietheorien: Eine Einführung*, 6th ed. (Springer, 2019), p. 270 ff.

119 For a similar argument, Wojciech Sadurski, "Legitimacy, Political Equality, and Majority Rule" (2008) 21 *Ratio Juris* 39–65 at 41 f., who also points out that majority voting is "not totally blind to unequal intensities of preferences."

different ways to the legitimacy of supranational decision-making processes.[120] And this leads me to another defining feature of European informal bodies: their being devoid of *final* decision-making power.

4.4.4 *The Absence of Final Decision-Making Power*

This feature refers to the fact that, from a *formal* viewpoint, political agreements reached in informal bodies are not meant to wield public authority. More precisely, they are not meant to generate legal effects vis-à-vis third parties. Indeed, in the European legal order, decisions are final only when enacted by bodies with autonomous decision-making powers.[121] Official documents thus indicate that any agreement reached in trilogues "has to be approved by the formal procedures applicable within each institution";[122] that the Informal Council meetings "cannot arrive at formal conclusions or decisions";[123] and that "[t]he Eurogroup is an informal body and therefore it does not adopt any formal conclusions."[124] In spite of this, European informal bodies often constitute genuine loci of decision-making and exert a significant influence on the actual outcome of formal procedures, framing the final instruments in a decisive way.[125] In a recent judgment, the General Court even seems to maintain that since the co-legislators usually adopt trilogue agreements without the addition of substantial amendments, the decision-making process should be deemed closed – at least for the purposes of the rules on access to documents – at the moment when the (Presidency of the) Council reaches a provisional agreement with the EP.[126]

[120] For a similar argument, Michael Zürn, "Democratic Governance beyond the Nation-State: The EU and Other International Institutions" (2000) 6 *European Journal of International Relations* 183–221.

[121] In line with this reading, Case C-25/94 *Commission* v. *Council* EU:C:1996:114, para. 26, where the Court of Justice affirmed that Coreper cannot take final decisions, arguing that it "is not an institution of the Communities upon which the Treaty confers powers of its own but an auxiliary body of the Council, for which it carries out preparation and implementation work."

[122] European Parliament, "Handbook on the Ordinary Legislative Procedure: A Guide to How the European Parliament Co-legislates," PE 640.179, September 2020, at 29.

[123] Presidency Conclusions, "Helsinki European Council," Annex III.E., para. 20(v).

[124] Euro Group, "Working Methods of the Eurogroup," at 6.

[125] This certainly is true for trilogues, but it also applies to the Euro Group and – though less frequently – to the Informal Council meetings. See, in this respect, Puetter, *The European Council and the Council*, pp. 152 and 156 ff.

[126] Case T-682/21 *ClientEarth* v. *Council* EU:T:2024:165, para. 99. Although the General Court made the above statement in a specific context (the assessment of a refusal of access to

However, the fact that European informal bodies do not have final decision-making powers has some legal implications, especially as regards the judicial control of the political agreements reached in those bodies. To be precise, it implies that those agreements are usually excluded from the scrutiny of the Court, at least directly. As regards the action for annulment, for instance, the Court has repeatedly affirmed that judicial proceedings can be initiated only against acts that embody the final position of institutions, bodies, offices, or agencies.[127] Indeed, an action against intermediate measures whose purpose is to prepare the final act would oblige European courts to "arrive at a decision on questions on which the [institution] has not yet had an opportunity to state its position and would as a result anticipate the arguments on the substance of the case, confusing different procedural stages."[128] Moreover, the Court seems to deny that European informal bodies qualify as "bodies, offices or agencies of the Union" within the meaning of Article 263 TFEU. In *Mallis*, for instance, the ECJ held that the Euro Group is not a decision-making body but a forum for discussion without legal personality, and it

legislative documents based on the exception relating to the protection of the decision-making process), that statement is problematic both in relation to the specific court case and in general. It fails to acknowledge that, as far as the Council is concerned, provisional agreements reached in trilogues are agreements reached by the Presidency. The General Court is therefore disregarding the crucial democratic power of the Council to vote down those agreements of its Presidency that do not align with its political interests and, thereby, to keep the legislative process open. Acknowledging the existence of that power is even more important whenever the negotiating mandates for trilogues are preliminarily approved only by Coreper. In such instances, the decision-making process would be over, according to this judgment of the General Court, even before the Council has had a single opportunity to consider the legislative proposal under discussion.

127 Koen Lenaerts, Ignace Maselis, and Kathleen Gutman, *EU Procedural Law* (Oxford University Press, 2014), p. 260 f. Recently, the General Court has declared the inadmissibility of an action for annulment against a legislative resolution containing the first-reading position of the Parliament in the course of an Ordinary Legislative Procedure. The General Court has justified its order in the following terms: "the contested act, which is part of a legislative process that takes place in several phases, constitutes … only an intermediate act whose objective is just to prepare the adoption of a final act, namely a regulation of the Parliament and the Council, without definitively fixing the position that the co-legislators will jointly adopt at the end of the procedure." See Case T-360/19 *Jalkh* v. *Parliament* EU:T:2019:899, para. 23. Following the same logic, the General Court had already excluded the judicial reviewability of the legislative proposals of the Commission. See Case T-175/96 *Berthu* v. *Commission* EU:T:1997:72, para. 21.

128 Case C-463/10 P *Deutsche Post and Germany* v. *Commission* EU:C:2011:656, para. 49 ff.

ruled out the reviewability of its statements.[129] Considering that the Euro Group perhaps is the most institutionalized informal body among those thus far considered, the political agreements reached in trilogues and Informal Council meetings are even less likely to fall within the scope of Article 263 TFEU.

Somewhat different is the situation in the case of preliminary ruling requests. To begin with, the formula "bodies, offices or agencies of the Union" as employed by Article 267 TFEU has traditionally been subject to a more flexible interpretation.[130] According to settled case law, "the Court of Justice has jurisdiction to give a preliminary ruling on the validity and interpretation of all acts of the institutions of the European Union *without exception*,"[131] meaning that the Court may intervene irrespective of the form of those acts (for example, statements, press releases, draft minutes) and regardless of the nature of the issuing body. However, this route, too, could prove ineffective in practice. For starters, it seems unlikely that political agreements reached in informal bodies may be relevant to the determination of main proceedings before a national judge. In addition, despite its flexible approach about preliminary ruling requests, the Court still demands that all those preparatory measures brought to its attention under Article 267 TFEU enjoy an independent existence vis-à-vis the process in which they come into existence.[132] As things stand, preliminary ruling requests do not appear to be an effective judicial means to scrutinize the political agreements reached in informal bodies. A further obstacle is that the submission of a preliminary ruling request falls within the discretionary power of

[129] In *Mallis*, the ECJ was asked to decide about the annulment of some orders of the General Court. Through those orders, the GC had dismissed a set of legal actions seeking, among others, the annulment of a Euro Group statement concerning the restructuring of the banking sector in Cyprus. In its judgment, the Court upheld many of the findings of the General Court, affirming that "as the Eurogroup is not a decision-making body, a statement by it cannot be regarded as a measure intended to produce legal effects with respect to third parties." Also, it held that, due to its informal nature and its lack of legal personality, the Euro Group does not qualify as "a body, office or agency of the European Union within the meaning of Article 263 TFEU." In these terms, Joined Cases C-105/15 P to C-109/15 P *Mallis and Malli* v. *Commission and ECB* EU:C:2016:702, paras. 49 and 61, respectively. For a negative appraisal of this judgment, especially with regard to its consequences in terms of effective judicial protection, Paul Craig, "The Eurogroup, Power and Accountability" (2017) 23 *European Law Journal* 234–249 at 241 ff.

[130] Lenaerts, Maselis, and Gutman, *EU Procedural Law*, pp. 220 ff. and 460 f.

[131] Case C-137/08 *VB Pénzügyi Lízing* EU:C:2010:659, para. 38.

[132] Lenaerts, Maselis, and Gutman, *EU Procedural Law*, p. 224 f.

national judges and cannot be prompted at the behest of one of the parties to the main proceedings.

That said, the situation is less dramatic than it may seem. As for those political agreements reached in trilogues, they are always absorbed into legislative procedures and, in most cases, transformed into legal acts, in the sense of final, judicially reviewable acts.[133] The same generally applies to those political agreements reached in the Euro Group and Informal Council meetings. When challenging the final act, applicants – privileged and nonprivileged alike – will be able to invoke all those irregularities that were supposedly committed in the stages leading up to the adoption of that act.[134] For instance, they will be able to submit the violation of specific principles of EU law or the rules of procedure of an institution. They will even be able to claim that, by adopting a legislative act through trilogue negotiations, the institutions violated the principle of democracy as set out in the Treaties.

True, it cannot be ruled out that some political agreements reached in the Euro Group and Informal Council meetings do not flow into formal decision-making procedures and nonetheless be capable of affecting the legal position of third parties. Under the current European case law, those political agreements risk remaining stuck in a no man's land,[135] though this has so far been an exceptional occurrence. Should this unusual constellation present itself more frequently, the CJEU would have reason to reconsider its case law, perhaps arguing in terms of the right to an effective judicial protection as guaranteed by Article 47 of the Charter of Fundamental Rights. It is conceivable that, in the case of an action for annulment, the Court might allow the review of those political agreements reached in informal bodies, although such bodies do not have legal personality. As Advocate General Jääskinen put it, "even in the absence of an express provision endowing the entity in question with legal personality, I consider that ... if the institutions create an entity which is capable of taking decisions affecting individuals, a remedy must none

[133] As pointed out by Möllers, *The Three Branches*, p. 81: "informality becomes more questionable when it is no longer directed towards and does not result in a legally formalized decision, for in this case the state [read: the EU] exercises a form of power which is opaque, difficult to oppose, and for which there is no form of procedural accountability."

[134] Lenaerts, Maselis, and Gutman, *EU Procedural Law*, p. 274.

[135] Opinion of Advocate General Wathelet in Joined Cases C-105/15 P to C-109/15 P *Mallis and Malli v. Commission and ECB* EU:C:2016:294, para. 66.

the less exist."[136] And, in the most recent case law, there indeed seem to be encouraging signs that the Court might be willing to follow this conception.[137] As regards preliminary ruling requests, if political agreements reached in informal bodies do not flow into formal decision-making procedures while exerting legal effects vis-à-vis third parties, the Court should consider them to enjoy an independent existence and therefore express itself on their interpretation or validity under Article 267 TFEU. In sum, informal bodies' lack of final decision-making powers does not give rise to major concerns in terms of rights protection. Or to be more precise, it does not imply more issues than those that are already inherent in the judicial system set out in the Treaties, as interpreted by the CJEU.

4.4.5 *The Creation of Genuine Exchanges among the Participants*

Trilogues, the Euro Group, and the Informal Council meetings are all devised for generating genuine exchanges among the participants. This can be inferred from many different sources. As for trilogues, this feature is acknowledged both in numerous official documents and in the case law of the CJEU.[138] For instance, in its most recent activity report, which included an evaluation of the impact of the Covid-19 pandemic on legislative activities, the European Parliament affirmed that the "presence of the main negotiators from Parliament, the Council and the Commission in one room . . . appeared to be essential to establishing trust between the actors in the procedure, as well as contributing to successful negotiations."[139] As for the Euro Group, its Working Methods specify that "the informal character of the Eurogroup provides for . . . in-depth political discussions."[140] Finally, the "rules" concerning the organization of the Informal Council meetings are introduced by the following statement:

[136] Opinion of Advocate General Jääskinen in Case C-439/13 P *Elitaliana* v. *Eulex Kosovo* EU:C:2014:2416, para. 51.

[137] In a recent judgment, the ECJ affirmed that "an intermediate measure which has independent legal effects may form the subject matter of an action for annulment in so far as the illegality attaching to that measure cannot be remedied in an action brought against the final decision for which it represents a preparatory step." See Case C-650/18 *Hungary* v. *Parliament* EU:C:2021:426, para. 46.

[138] Case T-540/15 *De Capitani* v. *Parliament*, para. 106.

[139] European Parliament, "Mid-Term Activity Report: Developments and Trends of the Ordinary Legislative Procedure: 1 July 2019–31 December 2021 (9th Parliamentary Term)," PE 703.724, at 4 f.

[140] Euro Group, "Working Methods of the Eurogroup," at 1. See also Opinion of Advocate General Pitruzzella in Case C-597/18 P *Council* v. *K. Chrysostomides & Co. and Others*, para. 85.

"Informal meetings of Ministers are designed to permit as free as possible an exchange of views."[141] It is of course possible to object that the creation of genuine exchanges among the participants is just a consequence of the four common features identified above. Still, this aspect is so crucial for the understanding of informality in the European institutional system that it deserves separate, autonomous treatment.

Here the term "exchange" should be stripped of its trivial meaning, for it signals a specific type of interaction. Barbara Misztal defines it as follows:

> Exchange ... is about transactions among people who occupy certain social positions. Their conduct is not merely a function of their individual character and personality, it also reflects the social roles that they are enacting ... Others, that is, people in their roles, are seen here as important to achieving various goals, therefore mutual relations can be both instrumental and non-instrumental.[142]

These features distinguish "exchange" from other informal types of interactions, such as casual encounters or friendly relations. In "exchanges" actors remain aware of their roles and reciprocal standing, but they seek to strike a balance between self-revelation and self-restraint to create an atmosphere of reciprocity. They are expected to adopt an open attitude towards each other, without completely abandoning the detachment and objectivity inherent in their social roles. In an institutional environment, reciprocity usually implies a realm where actors may engage in positive-sum games. In such games everyone stands to gain something, sometimes in immediate and sometimes in deferred forms – these are the so-called specific and diffuse reciprocity, respectively. In this sense, reciprocity is not only descriptive, but also prescriptive.[143] In fact, it is one of the most basic norms to be followed when it comes to exchanges in informal bodies. This explains why actors usually call each other by their first names; or why pompous or self-assertive attitudes may lead to disaffection or to an abrupt termination of the exchanges.

The "genuine exchanges" must be distinguished from other types of social exchanges, such as "bureaucratic exchange" or "clientelism."

[141] Presidency Conclusions, "Helsinki European Council," Annex III.E., para. 20.

[142] Barbara A. Misztal, *Informality: Social Theory and Contemporary Practice* (Routledge, 2000), p. 70.

[143] See also Putnam, *Making Democracy Work*, p. 172, arguing that the norm of diffuse reciprocity is a "highly productive component of social capital," and that its coherent application "can more efficiently restrain opportunism and resolve problems of collective action."

Bureaucratic exchange refers to a purely "role-based and instrumental exchange, which is rooted in abstract, universal rules of the rational culture of modern organization"; clientelism involves "asymmetrical personal relations and obligations."[144] The former may not provide the flexibility necessary to reach compromise; the latter is inappropriate for public institutions. More important, neither characterizes genuinely cooperative relations. "Genuine exchanges" and reciprocity, instead, are characterized by "sociability." The main characteristic of sociability is that it postulates, and is furthered by, an adjustment between instrumental and noninstrumental types of motivation.[145] And this perspective activates, sustains, and reinforces a process characterized by discussion, compromise, and a positive mutual disposition among actors. It allows these actors to tune into each other's needs and to reconcile self-interest with solidarity.[146] Needless to say, reciprocity and sociability do not rule out strategic and tactical behaviors but ensure that these are embedded in contexts dominated by a generalized willingness to cooperate.

Moreover, cooperation brings about trust, and vice versa. Cooperation is hard to achieve without trust; and trust is hard to produce without cooperation. They stand in a self-reinforcing and cumulative relationship: the greater the likelihood of cooperation, the greater the level of trust.[147] This relationship might also explain the success of informal bodies, especially trilogues. Indeed, cooperation and trust tend to expand rather than shrink through use.[148] Once set on a path of cooperation and trust, a group of people or institutions is likely to rely on those resources to an increasing degree. This may be a positive development, in terms of both institutional performance and institutional forbearance – forbearance which is an increasingly scarce good in today's politics.[149]

[144] Misztal, *Informality*, p. 80. [145] Ibid., p. 80.

[146] Chambers, "Behind Closed Doors," 400. With regard to face-to-face, confidential meetings, Chambers writes: they "are meant to promote dialogue, not monologue; they are places to exchange ideas not deliver speeches; communication is unmediated and symmetrical. The result is that opinions are better informed and more reasonable in the sense that participants are more likely to take other people's concerns and interests into account."

[147] Putnam, *Making Democracy Work*, p. 171 and 177; Gutmann and Thompson, *The Spirit of Compromise*, p. 120.

[148] Putnam, *Making Democracy Work*, p. 169.

[149] For an account arguing that the lack of forbearance in contemporary US institutions was a decisive factor in Trump's accession to power, Steven Levitsky and Daniel Ziblatt, *How Democracies Die* (Viking, 2018).

To be sure, I am not oblivious of the possible negative impact of excessive cooperation and trust, especially in complex and detached contexts like institutions. Even assuming that some level of autonomy is a key element of democratic representation, such autonomy cannot lead to legislative institutions falling prey to particular interests (regulatory capture) or becoming socially disconnected. Hence, I fully acknowledge the importance of accountability channels, especially transparency. Still, holding political actors to account postulates the ability of those actors to decide; and doing so in an environment where reciprocity, cooperation, and trust dominate is likely to produce greater benefits for as diverse and plural a society as the one envisaged in Article 2 TEU.

All these observations allow me to stress again one vital point. The limited number of participants, confidentiality, consensus, and the absence of final decision-making powers serve the purpose of creating realms where actors can find reciprocity and sociability.[150] This objective also requires a specific type of norms. They must be flexible enough to adjust to the needs of the situation and constraining enough to provide a predictable frame of reference for fair institutional interactions. And that brings me to the following argument: the benefits of informality, such as "genuine exchanges" and the ensuing cooperation and trust, build up a compelling normative case for the existence of informal structures and bodies. As far as trilogues are concerned, they have proved rather successful in generating reciprocity among actors. They have not only established themselves as effective means to manage institutional interdependence in the legislative domain, thereby fulfilling an important practical need of the European system of government.[151] They have also institutionalized a mechanism for reaching collective decisions at the heart of which stands an essentially democratic quest of European politics: the quest for compromise. I will come back to this point in Chapter 6. For now, some concluding remarks are in order.

4.5 Conclusions

This chapter started from the assumption that informality is a concept of EU law, and it set about deepening its understanding with a special focus

[150] Putnam, *Making Democracy Work*, p. 166.

[151] See, e.g., Florian Meinel, *Selbstorganisation des parlamentarischen Regierungssystems* (Mohr Siebeck, 2019), p. 303, arguing that trilogue negotiations represent an institutional necessity of the European legislative process, in that they counterbalance the Commission's near monopoly over the legislative initiative.

on trilogues. The exercise was conducted, and the task accomplished, by employing a (new) institutionalist approach. This approach appeared particularly suited to getting to grips with a phenomenon that, despite its widely acknowledged relevance, often eludes the analytical capacity of legal doctrine.[152] In fact, legal doctrine becomes even more profound and powerful in its analysis when it addresses institutions in their concrete existence. In this case, it would be a mistake not to take note that informality *is* a concept of EU law, and it therefore gives rise to a paradox: "the hyper-rationality trap of formally demanding informality."[153]

To analyze informality at EU level, I juxtaposed trilogues with two other European bodies that, according to standard readings, are also informal in nature, namely the Euro Group and the Informal Council meetings. As a result of that juxtaposition, I could discover that the former share with the latter a set of elements: (a) limited number of participants; (b) confidentiality of the discussions, including – but not limited to – the nonpublic nature of the meetings; (c) importance of consensus, as distinguished from majority voting and unanimity; (d) absence of final decision-making powers; and (e) creation of genuine exchanges among the participants. The combination of these elements is part of what makes those bodies informal. I therefore analyzed those elements conflating descriptive and critical observations. The intent of those observations was not to provide a full-blown normative justification of informal bodies in general, and trilogues in particular. Rather, they meant to prove that informality is not conspicuously inconsistent with the democratic tenets that mold the constitution of the EU.

The fact is that constitutional orders are not only fixed systems of competences, but also open institutional arrangements among political actors. This is the basic assumption that leads, for instance, Christoph Möllers to maintain that "one key function of a working system of separated powers is to protect areas of political informality from juridification."[154] By using the legal concept of "informality" and its variants ("informally," "informal," and so on), the supranational legal order seeks to do precisely that, namely to create structures and bodies where the penetration of legal normativity is not totally excluded but significantly limited. In so doing, the European legal order mobilizes the law against the law. A paradox indeed. Openness to paradoxes and dilemmas,

[152] Florian Meinel, *Vertrauensfrage. Zur Krise des heutigen Parlamentarismus* (C. H. Beck, 2019), p. 156 ff.

[153] Misztal, *Informality*, p. 44.

[154] Möllers, *The Three Branches*, p. 81.

however, is a vital feature of both legal doctrines and legal orders – as Böckenförde teaches us. What counts are the solutions given by institutions to the different and sometimes opposing demands produced by, and surfacing in, the living constitution.

This mobilization of the law against the law is the expression of a very specific need of the European Union, which is often said to suffer from an endemic juridification (*Verrechtlichung*) of its decision-making processes.[155] Still, demarcating informal spaces implies also that power is concentrated within specific, tangible boundaries. European informality can therefore contribute to making power channels less dispersed, easier to locate, and, ultimately, more accountable. Furthermore, informal spaces are not black holes, and the accountability of those who act within their perimeters could always be improved through small-scale design mechanisms. In sum, the existence and relevance of European informal bodies rest on a balance between juridification and political power. Too much of the former leads to decision-makers finding other (probably more secluded) loci,[156] while too much of the latter leads to public authority being nontransparent, opaque, and possibly illegitimate. I believe that European informal bodies, especially trilogues, are the product of an elegant equilibrium. To find the most suitable concept of democracy for legitimizing them will be the core task of the next two chapters.

155 The law has always played a very prominent role in the European integration process. See the ground-breaking project *Integration through Law*, started in 1978 at the European University Institute in Florence and directed by M. Cappelletti, M. Seccombe, and J. H. H. Weiler. The project led to the publication of a series of volumes in the second half of the 1980s. More recently, and from different perspectives, Aldo Sandulli, *Il ruolo del diritto in Europa: L'integrazione europea dalla prospettiva del diritto amministrativo* (FrancoAngeli, 2018); Antoine Vauchez, *Brokering Europe: Euro-Lawyers and the Making of a Transnational Polity* (Cambridge University Press, 2015).

156 Extensively on the reasons that militate against the juridification of informality, Schulze-Fielitz, "Konstitutionalisierung der Informalität?," p. 112 ff. See also Pauwelyn, Wessel, and Wouters, "Informal International Lawmaking," p. 518; Josef Isensee, "Verfassungsrecht als 'politisches Recht,'" in Josef Isensee and Paul Kirchhof (eds.), *Handbuch des Staatsrechts*, 3rd ed. (C. F. Müller, 2014), vol. 12, p. 534.

5 Interchamber Coordination in a Comparative Perspective

5.1 Introduction

A fruitful discussion of those issues that affect the legitimacy of the European legislative process requires a clear appreciation of what it is realistic to expect from a set of institutions that operates beyond the state. By saying this, I am not suggesting an apologetic understanding of that process.[1] Such an understanding would run counter to the letter and spirit of the Treaties, which posit an ambitious conception of supranational legislation, especially through their "Provisions on Democratic Principles" (Articles 9 to 12 TEU). The scope of those provisions makes the Treaties an exacting foundational text in terms of democratic standards. Rather, I am suggesting a contextualist comparative account.[2] Grounded in the current practice of other legislative institutions, such an account aims at avoiding the creation of unreasonable expectations about the European legislative process, while allowing for a better understanding of the importance of trilogues for that process.

To this end, I will consider two countries that, although different from the EU, still present several similarities, especially as regards the design and arrangement of their legislative institutions. Those countries are the

[1] In a similar vein, Daniel Innerarity, *Democracy in Europe: A Political Philosophy of the EU* (Palgrave Macmillan, 2018), p. 15, arguing that "we must understand the nature of the EU in order to be able to answer the question of its democraticness. This does not only mean that we should understand the real institutional modus operandi and surrender to what is, so often, a mediocre game, but that we should understand the logic and the objectives for which that institutional level is meant to exist, as well as the global context in which it has to act."

[2] The premises, methods, and objectives of this approach have been articulated by Günter Frankenberg, "Critical Comparisons: Re-thinking Comparative Law" (1985) 26 *Harvard International Law Journal* 411–455.

United States and Germany. Despite nonnegligible differences (for instance, the United States has a two-party system, whereas Germany has a multiparty one; the United States has a competitive system, whereas Germany has a noncompetitive one), both countries are predicated on a compound mode of government, with two chambers participating in the adoption of legislation; both, moreover, provide for a multiplicity of veto points.[3] But, first and foremost, both countries are federal states, meaning that their legislation must amalgamate diverse interests as well as diverse legitimization and functional principles.[4] These circumstances, and the corresponding need for enhanced interchamber coordination, make the United States and Germany natural fits for a comparison with the EU, as many authoritative works have already posited.[5]

In what follows, I will focus on those interchamber coordination mechanisms that are provided for by constitutional law and parliamentary practice. In particular, I will examine the US conference committees and "ping-pong" procedure as well as the German Mediation Committee, and then explain their current relationship with party politics. Let me anticipate that this relation is of paramount importance. Referring to available data, I will show that these mechanisms have experienced a remarkable decline in both countries, and that this decline has run parallel to a growing role of party systems in ensuring effective coordination between legislative bodies. In other words, there seems to be a strong correlation – if not a causal relationship – between the relevance and success of interchamber coordination mechanisms, on the one hand, and how much conflict is preempted by and resolved within political parties, on the other.

The purpose of my analysis is threefold. First, and more generally, I would like to contribute to closing a research gap. Indeed, research on trilogues has proved reluctant to employ the rich analytical toolkit that

[3] Christoph Möllers, *The Three Branches: A Comparative Model of Separation of Powers* (Oxford University Press, 2015), p. 113 f., arguing that, from a separation-of-powers standpoint, the difference between a parliamentary and a presidential system is in fact "overestimated." In both systems "informal structures of cooperation dominate in parties and in programs and are ultimately expressed in the form of legislation."

[4] Daniel J. Elazar, *Exploring Federalism* (University of Alabama Press, 1987).

[5] Sir Francis Jacobs, "Comparative Law and European Union Law," in Mathias Reimann and Reinhard Zimmermann (eds.), *The Oxford Handbook of Comparative Law*, 2nd ed. (Oxford University Press, 2019), p. 551 ff. (and the literature cited therein).

comparative law offers, save for few exceptions.[6] The existence of such a gap appears even more striking considering that all complex legislative processes based on significantly heterogeneous institutions employ coordination devices. Secondly, I would like to highlight that, in contexts where political parties are weak (as is the case in the EU), the creation of different interchamber coordination mechanisms, such as trilogues, is essential. Thirdly, I would like to suggest that the institutionalization of trilogues has its own democratic advantages, as compared to those coordination mechanisms that hinge on party structures.

The following is organized into three sections. The first is dedicated to the United States (Section 5.2) and the second to Germany (Section 5.3). These sections will include a brief presentation of the basic constitutional principles regulating the legislative function in that country; an analysis of the formal conflict resolution mechanism(s) that that legal order provides; and an explanation of how polarization and grand coalition governments, respectively, have led to political parties acquiring further dominance over the legislative process. Then I will summarize the main findings of this chapter; show the specific democratic advantage of trilogues; and draw some general conclusions (Section 5.4).

5.2 The United States

5.2.1 The Constitutional Framework

The United States has a presidential system of government, based on the well-known principle of checks and balances. It features a bicameral legislature in which power is divided equally between two differently constituted chambers, the House of Representatives and the Senate. According to the Great Compromise as originally enshrined in the US Constitution, the House was to be composed of "Members chosen every second Year by the People of the several States," while the Senate was to be composed of "two Senators from each State, chosen by the Legislature thereof, for six Years."[7] As a result, the House was viewed as representing the people, while the Senate was viewed as representing the states. All this changed with the ratification and entry into force of the Seventeenth

6 Justin Greenwood and Christilla Roederer-Rynning, "Taming Trilogues: The EU's Law-Making Process in a Comparative Perspective," in Olivier Costa (ed.), *The European Parliament in Times of EU Crisis: Dynamics and Transformations* (Palgrave Macmillan, 2019), p. 121 ff.

7 Art. I, s. 2, Cl. 1 and Art. I, s. 3, Cl. 1.

Amendment in 1913, according to which the Senate "shall be composed of two Senators from each State, elected by the people thereof, for six years." Since then, US citizens have cast their votes not only for their representatives but also for their senators; and this has certainly contributed to making the Senate "more of a national policymaking institution than a federal chamber or a states' house."[8]

In the United States, the exercise of the legislative function requires, in the words of the Supreme Court, "bicameral passage followed by presentment to the President."[9] "Bicameral passage" implies that all legislation must be adopted by both chambers in the same legislative text and bill number. Neither chamber can act alone, save for those few "exceptional and unambiguous" cases set out in the Constitution.[10] As for the "presentment," it entails that all legislation must, before becoming law, be presented to the President, who enjoys "a limited and qualified power to nullify proposed legislation by veto."[11] Therefore, lawmaking is a function "to be shared by both Houses and the President,"[12] with bicameralism and presentment as interdependent concepts. The rationale behind this construction has been explained by the US Justices in *INS* v. *Chadha*:

> The Framers were acutely conscious that the bicameral requirement and the Presentment Clauses would serve essential constitutional functions. The President's participation in the legislative process was to protect the Executive Branch from Congress and to protect the whole people from improvident laws. The division of the Congress into two distinctive bodies assures that the legislative power would be exercised only after opportunity for full study and debate in separate settings. The President's unilateral veto power, in turn, was limited by the power of two-thirds of both Houses of Congress to overrule a veto thereby precluding final arbitrary action of one person.[13]

However, despite the President's important role in legislative matters, the "introduction" of a bill is an exclusive prerogative of the members of Congress. To implement a legislative program, the President may "propose" a draft bill (urging, for instance, a member of Congress to present it, or sending a presidential message), but the President cannot formally "introduce" it. Of course, bills passed by one chamber frequently differ from those passed by the other, especially when the two chambers are

[8] Frances E. Lee, "Bicameral Representation," in George C. Edwards III, Frances E. Lee, and Eric Schickler (eds.), *The Oxford Handbook of the American Congress* (Oxford University Press, 2011), p. 274.

[9] *INS* v. *Chadha*, 462 US 919, 954 f. (1983). [10] Ibid., 955. [11] Ibid., 947. [12] Ibid., 947.

[13] Ibid., 951.

dominated by different parties. The House and the Senate must therefore seek to resolve their differences, and they must do so expeditiously. Each congressional term lasts slightly less than two years, and all those measures that have not become law by the end of the term "automatically die and must be reintroduced in a new Congress to start the legislative process anew."[14] Given this stringent time limit, the House and Senate have developed two formal methods of legislative reconciliation, namely conference committees and "ping-pong" procedure (officially known as interchamber amendment exchange). Let us analyze them in turn.

5.2.2 *The Formal Interchamber Coordination Mechanisms: Conference Committees and "Ping-Pong" Procedure*

Conference committees are "ad hoc joint committee[s] composed of members selected from each chamber to resolve differences on a particular bill in disagreement."[15] Conference committees are not provided for by the Constitution. They were created by a House–Senate committee at the beginning of the first Congress in 1789, through the adoption of a joint rule.[16] Nowadays, the power of conference committees rests on a body of rules and precedents that, taken as a whole, give rise to what is often referred to as the "conference committee system." This system works by and large as follows. Conference committees are convened upon request of one chamber, with the agreement of the other. For instance, if the House passes a Senate bill with amendments, it may request a conference; once the bill returns to the Senate, this may decide to declare its disagreement with the amendments put forward by the House and agree

[14] Walter J. Oleszek, Mark J. Oleszek, Elizabeth Rybicki, and Bill Heniff Jr., *Congressional Procedures and the Policy Process*, 11th ed. (Sage/CQ Press, 2019), p. 26. This depends on the fact that the House of Representatives, unlike the Senate, is reelected completely every two years. In this regard, see also *McGrain* v. *Daugherty*, 273 US 135, 181 f. (1927), where the US Supreme Court defined the Senate a "continuing body," with the consequence that "its rules remain in force from Congress to Congress except as they are changed from time to time, whereas those of the House are readopted at the outset of each new Congress."

[15] Oleszek et al., *Congressional Procedures*, p. 327.

[16] For an account of how conference committees came into existence, Ada C. McCown, *The Congressional Conference Committee* (Columbia University Press, 1927), p. 38 ff. It should be noted, however, that conference committees "may be asked in all cases of difference of opinion between the two Houses on matters depending between them" (e.g., the respective prerogatives of the Houses, matters of procedure, impeachment proceedings, etc.). See section XLLVI of the Jefferson's Manual of Parliamentary Practice available at: www.govinfo.gov/content/pkg/HMAN-116/pdf/HMAN-116.pdf (accessed on 8 August 2023).

to go to conference.[17] In this case, each chamber separately elects a few representatives and senators responsible for carrying out conference negotiations, also known as conferees. Depending on the political salience and complexity of a legislative file, the number of conferees may vary significantly, from 6 to over 250.[18] Politicians and experts of congressional procedures have observed that large conferences present an impediment to successful negotiations. It is therefore not uncommon for the final stages of large conference committees, when many of the House–Senate differences have already been dealt with, to be conducted only by a handful of senior conferees.[19]

According to rules and precedents, the selection of conferees is a matter for the Speaker and the presiding officer of the Senate, respectively. However, the two chambers usually ask the chairman and the ranking minority member of the committee that originally considered and reported the bill to present them with a list of possible conferees. The Speaker and the presiding officer of the Senate will usually choose from that list.[20] This implies that House and Senate party leaders exert significant influence over the appointment of conferees, often naming members who – they believe – will favor their positions on the legislation at hand. As a rule of thumb, party ratios in conference committees should always mirror party membership in the two chambers. However, due to the lack of stricter rules about conferee selection, cross-party controversies, especially in relation to the number of conferees and the ratio between majority and minority members, are commonplace.

The objective of the negotiations is to draft a report to be presented to the chambers for a final vote. In doing so, conferees face some limits. For instance, they cannot "add new matter, reopen provisions that both chambers agreed to, or exceed the range of the matters in disagreement committed to them."[21] They must remain within the so-called scope of

[17] In such a case, instead of declaring its disagreement with the bill as amended by the House and agreeing to go to conference, the Senate could deal with the House amendment(s): "(1) by adopting a motion to refer the amendment(s) to the competent standing committee; (2) by further amending the House amendments; (3) by agreeing to the House amendments (thus clearing the bill); (4) by tabling the House amendments, in which case they are returned to the House with a message that the Senate has disagreed to them." See Oleszek et al., *Congressional Procedures*, p. 339.

[18] To be sure, with over 250 Senators and Representatives the conference was exceptional. It concerned the 1981 omnibus budget reconciliation bill, and it has been said to be "[t]he largest conference in congressional history." Ibid., p. 343.

[19] Ibid., p. 343. [20] Ibid., p. 340. [21] Ibid., p. 349.

the differences. Conferees can receive instructions from their respective chambers, but these are not binding and can be totally disregarded, especially when seeking to reach compromise.[22] To establish if there is an agreement, the two delegations vote as separate units. After that, reports must be signed by a majority of conferees from each delegation. The chambers cannot amend them; they can only vote them up or down.[23]

Both House and Senate rules prescribe that conference committee meetings be open to the public (occasionally, they can also be televised), unless a majority of conferees from either delegation votes in public to hold secret sessions (for example, when discussing issues relating to national security). That said, the publicity of conference committees is, in practice, very limited. As some experts point out, "[c]ompliance with the rules requiring open meetings is usually achieved by holding a single, public session, either at the start of the process where conferees make opening statements or at the end of the process to sign off on the compromise already reached."[24] Either way, the public is left essentially unaware of how interchamber negotiations play out.

As an alternative to conference committees, Congress may resort to amendments between the houses, also known as "ping-pong procedure." The functioning of this method is easily explained. If one chamber amends a bill from the other chamber, House and Senate may decide to shuttle the bill back and forth between themselves a few times, until all differences are cleared. To avoid endless discussions, a parliamentary principle prescribes that the amending process in each chamber be limited to two degrees (that is, an amendment and an amendment to it).[25] However, each chamber, in accordance with its internal rules, can exceptionally lift this limitation, thereby extending the number of rounds of amendment exchange. Compared to conference committees, this method provides political actors with greater flexibility. For instance,

[22] Ibid., p. 343 ff.

[23] The first chamber to act on a conference report has three options. It can adopt, reject, or recommit (send the report back to conference for further discussion). Once the first chamber has adopted the report, the conference committee is automatically dissolved, and the other chamber can only cast a "yes" or "no" vote on the report. Ibid., p. 355.

[24] Ibid., p. 346. As regards the publicity of conference committees in the practice, Elizabeth Rybicki, "Amendments between the Houses: Procedural Options and Effects," CRS Report R41003, 14 March 2022, at 13 f. and 21 ff.

[25] Oleszek et al., *Congressional Procedures*, p. 223 f.; Rybicki, "Amendments between the Houses," at 7.

amendments between the houses can be initiated without any formal decision being necessary; they are not subject to the same content restrictions as conference reports; and they do not require joint explanatory statements.[26]

Until the beginning of the 1990s, about 15 to 25 percent of all bills went to conference. These may seem minor figures, but among those bills were the most controversial and important measures. This made conference committees "central arenas of legislative power" or, as someone used to call them, the "third house" of Congress.[27] However, since the mid-1990s, the US legislative process has undergone a transformation.[28] A different political culture has taken root on Capitol Hill. Data show that, during the 103rd Congress (1993/1994), 62 bills reached the conference stage (about 13 percent of 465 enacted public laws). During the 116th Congress (2019/2020), however, only 3 bills were negotiated in conference (about 1 percent of 344 enacted public laws). A decline, although less marked, can also be observed as regards the other method of legislative reconciliation. During the 103rd Congress (1993/1994), 112 bills were subject to amendment exchange (about 24 percent of 465 enacted public laws). During the 116th Congress (2019/2020), however, no more than 50 bills were subject to this method (about 15 percent of 344 enacted public laws).[29] How could this transformation happen?

5.2.3 *Interchamber Coordination in Times of Strong Partisanship*

It is the generally accepted view that, until the beginning of the 1990s, political parties in Congress were rather weak relative to their counterparts in other democratic legislatures.[30] US political culture has

[26] For a comparison between the two procedures, Rybicki, "Amendments between the Houses," at 13 and 23.

[27] Lawrence D. Longley and Walter J. Oleszek, *Bicameral Politics: Conference Committees in Congress* (Yale University Press, 1989), p. 4 ff.

[28] The forerunners of this transformation had been long in the making. Many authors agree that the turning point coincided with the tenure of Newt Gingrich (R-GA) as Speaker of the House (1995–1999). See, e.g., Robert G. Kaiser, *Act of Congress: How America's Essential Institution Works, and How It Doesn't* (Vintage, 2014), p. 330; Thomas E. Mann and Norman J. Ornstein, *The Broken Branch: How Congress Is Failing America and How to Get It Back on Track* (Oxford University Press, 2006), p. 97 ff.

[29] The data concerning the 103rd Congress (1993/1994) can be found in Oleszek et al., *Congressional Procedures*, p. 329. The data concerning the 116th Congress (2019/2020) can be found in Rybicki, "Amendments between the Houses," at 30.

[30] Randall W. Strahan, "Party Leadership," in George C. Edwards III, Frances E. Lee, and Eric Schickler (eds.), *The Oxford Handbook of the American Congress* (Oxford University Press, 2011), p. 378 ff.

traditionally shown ambivalent feelings about the proper role of parties in the political system. Immediately after the Second World War, a report issued by the American Political Science Association (APSA) affirmed that US politics was not partisan enough. It therefore recommended establishing an effective party system with an effective opposition in order to improve the democratic accountability of the political institutions.[31] In a recent report on legislative negotiations, however, the self-same APSA advanced the following, opposite claim: "Washington's ailments center on the emergence of excessive partisanship and deep ideological divisions among political elites and officeholders."[32] The Association is simply voicing a widely shared diagnosis among congressional experts. Even accounts that seek to present a less dire picture must eventually concede that "[t]he current level of congressional polarization is the highest since the Civil War."[33] The rising partisanship has gone hand in hand with the spread of an uncompromising mindset and tightened party discipline, a reality that some authors have not hesitated to liken to tribalism.[34] And no agreement exists about the causes of, and the solutions to, this situation. Paradoxically, some suggested battling partisanship with stronger parties.[35]

In these circumstances, it is no wonder that those methods that were expressly devised to help political actors reconcile their differences have been experiencing a persistent decline. The conference committee system is a case in point. This institutional arrangement calls for a political culture that puts a premium on compromise, institutional comity, and basic fairness. However, the uncompromising mindset that prevails in today's US politics is rendering that system largely unworkable.

[31] American Political Science Association, "Toward a More Responsible Two-Party System: A Report of the Committee on Political Parties" (1950) 44 *American Political Science Review* 1–96.

[32] Michael Barber and Nolan McCarty, "Causes and Consequences of Polarization," in Jane Mansbridge and Cathie Jo Martin (eds.), *Negotiating Agreement in Politics: Report of the Task Force on Negotiating Agreement in Politics* (American Political Science Association, 2013), p. 37. For an introduction to this topic, Brian F. Schaffner, "Party Polarization," in George C. Edwards III, Frances E. Lee, and Eric Schickler (eds.), *The Oxford Handbook of the American Congress* (Oxford University Press, 2011), p. 527 ff.

[33] Cynthia R. Farina, "Congressional Polarization: Terminal Constitutional Dysfunction?" (2015) 115 *Columbia Law Review* 1689–1738 at 1705. For a recent empirical confirmation of the increased polarization in US politics, Drew Desilver, "The Polarization in Today's Congress Has Roots That Go Back Decades," Pew Research Center, 10 March 2022.

[34] Mann and Ornstein, *The Broken Branch*, p. 212.

[35] Nathaniel Persily, "Stronger Parties as a Solution to Polarization," in Nathaniel Persily (ed.), *Solutions to Political Polarization in America* (Cambridge University Press, 2015).

Conference committees are of little or no avail if parties are not interested in negotiating with one another. Similar considerations apply to the other method of legislative reconciliation, the "ping-pong" procedure. Indeed, amendment exchanges start only after the second-acting chamber had the chance to debate and amend the original bill. This requires a political process characterized by a certain degree of openness and decentralized power structures, which the inflexibility of today's US politics has largely undermined.

A pragmatic example of this situation is the so-called Hastert rule. The rule takes its name from former Republican politician Dennis Hastert, who served as Speaker of the House from 1999 to 2007. According to this rule, announced in 2004, a bill can reach the floor for a vote only if a "majority of the majority" (that is, a majority of representatives of the ruling party) supports it. Applied at the Speaker's discretion, the rule seeks to limit the power of the minority party to bring bills to the floor, "in order to reduce the danger of bipartisan passage."[36] On several occasions, its application has impeded significant pieces of legislation from reaching the floor of the House (for example, an important immigration law passed by the Senate in 2013).

Hence, it is reasonable to ask: how does contemporary Congress get legislation done? It has been said that "in contemporary Congress the Chambers generally arrive at a resolution of the substantive differences between House and Senate versions of a measure through informal, bicameral discussions that might resemble conference committee meetings even though neither house has officially appointed conferees to consult over a bill."[37] More precisely, a "leadership-influenced bicameral bargaining process" has taken over,[38] to the detriment of rank-and-file members and the minority party.[39] Nowadays, a good chunk of US legislation results from negotiations in party caucuses, among few majority leaders.[40] The outcome of these negotiations is then presented to representatives and senators on a take-it-or-leave-it basis and, in most cases, forced on them through party discipline. This provides evidence of the

[36] Sam Tanenhaus, "The Power of Congress: Before L.B.J., Progressives Saw Bipartisanship as a Blight. What Happened?," *The New Yorker*, 12 January 2015.

[37] Rybicki, "Amendments between the Houses," at 1.

[38] Oleszek et al., *Congressional Procedures*, p. 332.

[39] Lee, "Bicameral Representation," p. 278.

[40] Steven S. Smith, Jason M. Roberts, and Ryan J. Vander Wielen, *The American Congress*, 9th ed. (Cambridge University Press, 2015), p. 196 f.; Adrian Vermeule, *Mechanisms of Democracy: Institutional Design Writ Small* (Oxford University Press, 2007), p. 189.

weakening of Congress' autonomy vis-à-vis executive power and party politics. These meetings among majority leaders are often prepared by staff aides, who enjoy significant latitude throughout the whole legislative cycle. As Senator Ted Kennedy once put it: "[n]inety-five percent of the nitty-gritty work of drafting and negotiating is now done by staff."[41]

Data corroborate these findings. They show that the overall number of *simple adoptions* by one chamber of the bill version sent to it by the other chamber has increased by about 22 percentage points between the 103rd and the 116th Congress (1993/1994–2019/2020), passing from 63 to 85 percent.[42] However, this way of doing legislative business has been subject to sharp criticism. The more frequent use of conference committees in the past – so the standard account goes – testified to a more democratic legislative process.[43] Indeed, conference committees and amendments between the houses belong to what in Congress jargon is called "regular order," namely those procedural expectations and norms that emerged during the 1950s, 1960s, and 1970s and promoted consensus-based forms of decision-making, giving a role also to minority members, in a political system that Maurice Duverger could define as "*pseudo-bipartisme*."[44] The erosion of that order has led many scholars and political commentators to complain about the declining openness and civility of the US legislative system.[45]

As a result, debates about Congress focus on how to restore a stronger sense of comity. Indeed, the inability of US politicians to "cross the aisle" appears to be damaging not only for Congress' ability to deliver, but also for its social legitimacy. Even the informal device known as "budget summit," which has been increasingly used to facilitate interchamber negotiations in the budgetary procedure, could not help avoiding the

[41] As cited in Kaiser, *Act of Congress*, p. 28.

[42] The data concerning the 103rd Congress (1993/1994) can be found in Oleszek et al., *Congressional Procedures*, p. 329. The data concerning the 116th Congress (2019/2020) can be found in Rybicki, "Amendments between the Houses," at 30.

[43] Kaiser, *Act of Congress*, p. 331.

[44] Maurice Duverger, *Introduction à la politique* (Gallimard, 1964), p. 166. As regards the main features of the Congress' "regular order," Winfried Steffani,"Grundzüge des amerikanischen Regierungssystems," in Parlamentarische und präsidentielle Demokratie: Strukturelle Aspekte westlicher Demokratien (Springer, 1979), p. 307 ff.

[45] According to a 2019 inquiry, an overwhelming 85 percent of the general US population believes that "the tone and nature of political debate in the United States has become more negative in recent years – as well as less respectful, less fact-based and less substantive." See "Public Highly Critical of State of Political Discourse in the U.S.," Pew Research Center, 19 June 2019.

2018/2019 US federal government shutdown – the longest in US history.[46] According to data collected in July 2023, Gallup found that an overwhelming majority of those interviewed (77 percent) disapproved of the way Congress was doing its job. And the main reasons for this lack of approval were, in order of relevance: party gridlock, bickering, not compromising (28 percent); not getting anything done, not making decisions (21 percent); caring too much about politics and not enough about the country (11 percent).[47] Against this backdrop, a group of political scientists (again from the American Political Science Association) have argued that the existence of a political culture that favors bipartisan negotiations and compromise may help improve the situation.[48]

Be that as it may, my intention was to highlight an evolution in the US political system and its consequences for congressional politics. Today's public debates about Congress and legislation are dominated by the polarization/partisanship issue. Scholars and pundits observe, mostly with regret, that contemporary congressional politics has become hierarchical and polarized, and that the culture of compromise has been lost. Decisions are taken by senior figures, and then passed to – and in some cases, foisted on – lower-ranking colleagues for enactment. And such a situation cannot only be attributed to the specific characteristics of the US political system (for example, two main parties, first-past-the-post voting rules, and a spoils system). As the next section will show, this evolution finds some striking similarities in the German political system, despite all the differences.

5.3 Germany

5.3.1 The Constitutional Framework

Germany has a parliamentary system of government. Due to its federal structure, the Basic Law provides for the direct participation of the state

[46] On the budget summit, Vermeule, *Mechanisms of Democracy*, p. 191.

[47] Gallup, "Congress and the Public," available at https://news.gallup.com/poll/1600/congress-public.aspx (accessed 8 August 2023). The public support enjoyed by the practice of compromise among US citizens was the subject of a recent study by Jennifer Wolak, *Compromise in an Age of Party Polarization* (Oxford University Press, 2020), p. 31 f. By using surveys, the author showed that US citizens think about political compromise in principled ways and that public support for compromise resists also in the face of competing values.

[48] Cathie Jo Martin, "Negotiating Political Agreements," in Jane Mansbridge and Cathie Jo Martin (eds.), *Negotiating Agreement in Politics: Report of the Task Force on Negotiating Agreement in Politics* (American Political Science Association, 2013), p. 1 ff.

governments' representatives in the adoption of federal legislation. The Bundestag (BT), which is the directly elected representation of the German people, is the main federal legislative body. The Bundesrat (BR), which comprises members of the state governments, participates in the legislative process through its decisions on consent bills (*Zustimmungsgesetze*) or its involvement in objection bills (*Einspruchsgesetze*). Usually, consent bills concern specific matters that have a relevant impact on state governments' interests, notably amendments to the Basic Law, bills affecting the state budgetary revenue, and bills affecting the administrative jurisdiction of the states. In these cases, legislation can be enacted only insofar as the Bundesrat gives its consent. All other bills – the majority – are objection bills. In these cases, the BR can express its disagreement by entering an objection, but it cannot prevent the BT from enacting the legislation at hand. To that effect, the BT must overturn the objection by either absolute majority or qualified majority, depending on the majority in the BR that supported the objection.[49]

Although legislation may be initiated by the federal government, the Bundestag, or the Bundesrat, data indicate that from 1949 to 2021 by far the largest share of legislative initiatives originated from the federal government (74 percent), followed by the BT (15 percent), and the BR (11 percent).[50] It must also be said that the first figure is probably higher, as the federal government not infrequently makes use of its parliamentary majority to bring legislation directly to the floor of the Bundestag. This workaround allows it to fast-track the procedure, avoiding the opinion that the BR would otherwise be entitled to give before the BT may formally start considering the draft bill.[51] In official statistics, these cases count as initiatives of the Bundestag, but they are de facto initiatives of the federal government. All the same, these figures reflect a broad trend of contemporary democracies whereby governmental bureaucracies own the lion's share of legislative initiatives. This situation stems from the fact that, within the state, the administration is the almost exclusive

[49] Art. 77(4) Basic Law provides as follows: "If the objection is adopted by the majority of the votes of the Bundesrat, it may be rejected by a decision of the majority of the Members of the Bundestag. If the Bundesrat adopted the objection by a majority of at least two thirds of its votes, its rejection by the Bundestag shall require a two-thirds majority, including at least a majority of the Members of the Bundestag."

[50] These data are available at: www.bundesrat.de/DE/dokumente/statistik/statistik-node.html (accessed on 8 August 2023).

[51] Art. 76(2) Basic Law.

repository of the technical and scientific knowledge necessary to draft increasingly complex legislation.

One further observation is in order. The Bundesrat does not amount to a genuine "second chamber," but to what legal scholarship and the German Federal Constitutional Court call a "*mitwirkendes Organ*" (cooperating institution).[52] This reading is based on Article 77(1) Basic Law, which stipulates that "[f]ederal laws shall be adopted by the Bundestag." Here is one of the most significant differences between the United States and Germany. Whereas the United States is a genuinely bicameral system, Germany is not – the Bundesrat is not considered, from a strictly legal viewpoint, as a parliamentary chamber.[53] That said, it would be a mistake to conclude that the BR is simply ornamental. Since its inception in 1949, the Bundesrat has become "one of the most powerful institutions in the Federal Republic."[54] Its consolidation at the heart of the German political system is the effect not only of the BR's political ingenuity but also of the case law of the Federal Constitutional Court, which showed a certain generosity when interpreting the prerogatives of the Bundesrat.[55] As a result, *Zustimmungsgesetze* have been rather frequent, probably a lot more frequent than anticipated by the framers of the Basic Law.[56] In the nineteenth parliamentary term (2017–2021), for instance, those laws accounted for about 38 percent of all enacted legislation.[57]

The strong influence of the Bundesrat, however, has also increased the chance of legislative frictions. Moreover, since the Bundestag election in 1969, the political majorities in the BT and the BR have often differed,

52 Ralf Müller-Terpitz, "Art. 50 GG," in Theodor Maunz and Günter Dürig (eds.), *Grundgesetz: Kommentar* (C. H. Beck, 2017), vol. 4, para. 59. See also German Federal Constitutional Court, Cases No. 2 BvF 2/73 and 2 BvF 3/73, 25 June 1974 – *Zustimmungsgesetz (Bundesrat)*, para. 78 ff.

53 Donald P. Kommers and Russell A. Miller, *The Constitutional Jurisprudence of the Federal Republic of Germany*, 3rd ed. (Duke University Press, 2012), p. 114.

54 Ibid., p. 119.

55 Probably, this was a reaction to partially counter the phenomenon that Konrad Hesse defined as *unitarischer Bundesstaat* (unitary federal state). On this topic, Ernst-Wolfgang Böckenförde, "Sozialer Bundesstaat und parlamentarische Demokratie: Zum Verhältnis von Parlamentarismus und Föderalismus unter den Bedingungen des Sozialstaats," in *Staat, Nation, Europa* (Suhrkamp, 1999), p. 189 f. This debate is far from outdated, as continuing media attention testifies. See Wolfgang Renzsch, "Deutschland, einig Bundesstaat?," *Frankfurter Allgemeine Zeitung*, 9 March 2020.

56 Christoph Möllers, "Vermittlungsausschuss und Vermittlungsverfahren" (2010) 32 *JURA – Juristische Ausbildung* 401–407 at 402.

57 Bundesrat, "Statistik der parlamentarischen Arbeit des Bundesrates (Sitzungen im Zeitraum der 19. Wahlperiode des Bundestages)," 8 October 2021.

further adding to the risk of gridlock.[58] It is precisely to cope with such a risk that the Basic Law provides for a mediation procedure through a committee (*Vermittlungsausschuss*). In the words of the Federal Constitutional Court, the aim of this committee is "to bring a specific legislative procedure to a positive conclusion either by avoiding the objection of the Bundesrat or by obtaining its consent, initially withheld, to a Bundestag enactment."[59] Note that this procedure is also applicable to the adoption of constitutional amendments. The outcome of the mediation is a compromise proposal that the BT may adopt on a take-it-or-leave-it basis. The Basic Law requires that the composition and proceedings of the Mediation Committee be regulated by rules of procedure adopted by the Bundestag upon consent of the Bundesrat. The currently applicable "Joint Rules of Procedure," however, are far from comprehensive, as they encompass thirteen succinct provisions. This concision is the result of a precise choice: leaving to parliamentary practice the regulation of as many operational aspects as possible.[60] With this in mind, I can now provide a brief explanation of how the Mediation Committee works.

5.3.2 *The Formal Interchamber Coordination Mechanism: The Mediation Committee (*Vermittlungsausschuss*)*

According to the Joint Rules, the BT and BR each send sixteen of their members to the permanent Mediation Committee. From among its members, the Committee elects one member from the BT's delegation and one from the BR's delegation to alternate in the chair every three months – these features make the German Mediation Committee a permanent body, unlike the US conference committees. The chair carries out a set of important tasks: besides presiding over the meetings of the Committee, it draws the main lines of the discussions; it makes suggestions, both procedural and substantive; and it declares a compromise proposal reached. In fulfilling these tasks, the chair is not – and is not expected to be – neutral or impartial: it has its own interests in the

[58] Möllers, "Vermittlungsausschuss und Vermittlungsverfahren," 402, arguing that such a constellation "was previously considered unlikely."

[59] German Federal Constitutional Court, Case No. 2 BvE 3/02, 8 December 2004 – *Sitzverteilung im Vermittlungsausschuss*, para. 58. The English translation of this excerpt is taken from Kommers and Miller, *The Constitutional Jurisprudence*, p. 230.

[60] Jens Kersten, "Art. 77 GG," in Theodor Maunz and Günter Dürig (eds.), *Grundgesetz: Kommentar* (C. H. Beck, 2012), vol. 5, para. 70. See also German Federal Constitutional Court, *Sitzverteilung im Vermittlungsausschuss*, para. 71.

success of the procedure.[61] Neither the Basic Law nor the Joint Rules say anything about how the BT and the BR are to appoint their members to the Mediation Committee. The matter is therefore regulated by the internal rules of procedure of the two institutions, which have opted for different criteria. Whereas the delegation of the Bundestag shall reflect the composition of the plenary session (*Grundsatz der Spiegelbildlichkeit*), the delegation of the Bundesrat shall include one representative from the government of each *Land*. These distinctions lay bare the tensions between the various legitimizing principles that surround the Mediation Committee (for example, the majority principle, the principle of proportional representation, effectiveness, democracy), tensions that also characterize the case law of the Federal Constitutional Court in this field.

According to the Basic Law, neither the members of the BT's delegation nor those of the BR's delegation are bound by instructions. This is an important element, especially as far as the members of the Bundesrat are concerned. While the Basic Law already provides that the members of the Bundestag are "responsible only to their conscience,"[62] the same does not apply to the members of the Bundesrat, who are generally subject to the orders and instructions of their governments. In this sense, Article 77(2) Basic Law enshrines an exception, which was originally meant to facilitate the attainment of compromise proposals.

However, deviations from majority–opposition logics are quite rare in the working of the committee,[63] which may adopt compromise proposals by "majority of the votes of the member present." To that end, at least seven members from each delegation must take part in the vote. Although the Joint Rules provide that usually the mediation procedure shall end with the adoption of a compromise proposal, they also allow for its earlier conclusion whenever, after the first two meetings, the committee is still unable to reach a compromise proposal and a member expressly requests its termination. In such a case, the committee meets one last time, in the hope of building a majority around a compromise proposal. If this last attempt fails as well, the draft legislative act goes

[61] Jasmin Merati-Kashani, "Vermitteln im Vermittlungsausschuss – Mediation in der Bundesgesetzgebung?" (2011) 30 *Neue Zeitschrift für Verwaltungsrecht – Extra* 1–7 at 3 f.

[62] Art. 38(1) Basic Law.

[63] As empirically demonstrated by Matthias Lehnert, "Der Einfluss der Parteipolitik auf das Vermittlungsverfahren: Eine Analyse der Einigungsvorschläge (1949–2005)," in Helmar Schöne and Julia von Blumenthal (eds.), *Parlamentarismusforschung in Deutschland* (Nomos, 2009), p. 279 ff.

back to the Bundesrat, which may adopt it or reject it (in case of consent bills) or express its agreement or its objection (in case of objection bills). To counter a possible failure of the mediation procedure, it is the committee's standard practice to prepare its official meetings in informal working groups, from which minority parties are often excluded.[64] This practice, which the Federal Constitutional Court recently upheld,[65] is further facilitated by the fact that neither the Basic Law nor the Joint Rules set a maximum time limit for the conclusion of the procedure.[66]

The Mediation Committee follows the principle of confidentiality. This means that its meetings are not open to the public, and the minutes of its deliberations are not publicly available until at least the beginning of the second parliamentary term after the meeting in question (that is, between four and eight years, depending on when the relevant Mediation Committee meeting took place).[67] However, the principle of confidentiality is sometimes infringed. It is indeed not uncommon that the press and the public get wind of what is being discussed in a meeting of the Mediation Committee – information leakage may be a very useful means to force the hand of the opponents or the undecided.[68]

This raises another important question: to what extent can the Mediation Committee propose changes to a draft legislative act? The Federal Constitutional Court has ruled on the issue several times over the years.[69] However, it was in its 1999 *Häusliches Arbeitszimmer* judgment that the court laid down the tenets of what has been its case law ever since. According to that judgment, the Mediation Committee may

[64] Winfried Kluth, "Der Vermittlungsausschuß," in Josef Isensee and Paul Kirchhof (eds.), *Handbuch des Staatsrechts*, 3rd ed. (C. F. Müller, 2005), vol. 3, p. 1019 f.

[65] German Federal Constitutional Court, Case No. 2 BvE 1/11, 22 September 2015 – *Spiegelbildlichkeit von Ausschüssen*.

[66] As for consent bills, should a first mediation procedure end unsuccessfully a new procedure may be initiated. In such a case, the new procedure must be initiated by an organ other than the one that initiated the first (unsuccessful) procedure. In practice, this possibility does not occur frequently. The initiation of a third mediation procedure is very rare. As for objection bills, this possibility does not exist, as the only organ entitled to initiate a mediation procedure is the Bundesrat. See Thomas Mann, "Art. 77 [Verfahren bei Gesetzesbeschlüssen]," in Michael Sachs (ed.), *Grundgesetz: Kommentar*, 8th ed. (C. H. Beck, 2018), para. 13.

[67] Kersten, "Art. 77 GG," para. 74.

[68] Merati-Kashani, "Vermitteln im Vermittlungsausschuss," 3.

[69] On the two main phases that characterize the case law of the German Federal Constitutional Court in this specific field, Kersten, "Art. 77 GG," para. 83 ff. For a convincing negative appraisal of this case law, Möllers, "Vermittlungsausschuss und Vermittlungsverfahren," 405 ff.

"propose amendments, additions or deletions to provisions adopted by the Bundestag only if and insofar as this compromise proposal remains within the scope of the request for a mediation procedure [*Anrufungsbegehren*] and of the legislative procedure on which that request is based." Furthermore, the committee's objective should be to "bridge the gap between alternatives already discussed in the legislative organs without introducing a legislative initiative."[70] This judgment, with its vague maxims, has brought about further judicial proceedings, with the court showing a rather restrictive approach, further limiting the scope of action of the Mediation Committee.[71]

An in-depth normative assessment of the role and function of the mediation procedure falls outside the scope of this comparative law exercise. What I mean to highlight here is that, in the last fifteen years or so, the importance of this "institutional core of Germany's grand coalition state" has been shaky.[72] From 1949 to 2017, a total of 897 draft legislative acts was sent to the Mediation Committee, with a remarkable success rate – only 109 (that is, a little more than 12 percent) of all those acts did not hit the statute book.[73] However, after enjoying significant popularity during the twelfth, thirteenth, fourteenth, and fifteenth parliamentary terms (the last two chancellorships of Helmut Kohl and the following two of Gerhard Schröder), the number of draft bills sent to mediation experienced a staggering drop. From the fifteenth to the sixteenth parliamentary term, that number fell from 100 to 18, going down to 3 in the eighteenth term.[74] This trend is characterizing the

70 German Federal Constitutional Court, Case No. 2 BvR 301/98, 7 December 1999 – *Häusliches Arbeitszimmer*, para. 31 f.

71 German Federal Constitutional Court, Case No. 2 BvL 1/09, 15 January 2019 – *Vermittlungsausschuss (Kompetenzgrenzen)*, para. 62. In this judgment, the Federal Constitutional Court declared a provision of the 1999 German corporation tax legislation (*KStG*) unconstitutional on the ground that, in introducing that provision in the compromise proposal (*Einigungsvorschlag*), the Mediation Committee had in effect acted *ultra vires*. Since the request for a mediation procedure (*Anrufungsbegehren*) referred to specific provisions of the legislative decision (*Gesetzesbeschluss*), among which was not the one at stake in the judicial proceedings, the Mediation Committee was not allowed to extend its reach into those parts of the legislative decision that were not expressly covered by the request.

72 Manfred G. Schmidt, *Political Institutions in the Federal Republic of Germany* (Oxford University Press, 2003), p. 84 f.

73 Silke Podschull-Wellmann, "Die Tätigkeit des Vermittlungsausschusses in der achtzehnten Wahlperiode des Deutschen Bundestages: Neunzehnte zeitliche Übersicht mit Fundstellen" (2018) *Schriftenreihe der Geschäftsstelle des Vermittlungsausschusses des Deutschen Bundestages und des Bundesrates* 1–62 at 30.

74 Ibid., 30.

current legislature as well, with only two draft legislative acts sent to mediation so far.[75]

The reasons behind the declining importance of the Mediation Committee are manifold. The case law of the Federal Constitutional Court, for instance, certainly does not contribute to making the procedure attractive to German politicians. While it is too early to proclaim the obsolescence of this important institution of German constitutional law (the Mediation Committee has indeed experienced other periods of prolonged near latency, especially during the 1980s), it is fair to say that it has lost some ground. Hence, the question: where are differences in contemporary German politics solved? To answer this question, it is important to look once more at the role and function of political parties. As I will show in the next section, the chief reason for the declining importance of the Mediation Committee lies in the fact that Germany has had grand coalition governments for the better part of the last two decades.

5.3.3 *Interchamber Coordination in Times of Grand Coalitions*

Political parties have traditionally occupied a prominent position in the democratic life of the Federal Republic. So much so that an expert of German political institutions could affirm that legislation in Germany "takes place within the shadow of the party state."[76] Due to several structural elements, such as the multiparty system and the structure of executive federalism, the German legislative process has traditionally required a great deal of political coordination. Since ruling parties at federal level can be – and often are – in the opposition at state level, this coordination may not only concern the partners of a coalition government, but may also extend to one or more opposition parties. This is especially the case when the opposition commands a blocking majority in the Bundesrat. As a result, legislative action in Germany almost invariably prompts "the prior formation of a formal or tacit grand coalition of the major established parties and a coalition between the federal government and state governments." Ernst-Wolfgang Böckenförde called it

[75] Bundesrat, "Statistik der parlamentarischen Arbeit des Bundesrates (Sitzungen im Zeitraum der laufenden Wahlperiode des Bundestages)," 10 July 2023.

[76] Schmidt, *Political Institutions*, p. 91. See also Eberhard Schuett-Wetschky, "Regierung, Parlament oder Parteien: Wer entscheidet, wer beschließt?" (2005) 36 *Zeitschrift für Parlamentsfragen* 489–507 at 497, arguing that MPs do not decide on legislation in the Parliament, but in the context of their respective parties. Schuett-Wetschky also adds that the Parliament does not make legislation, it only sanctions it.

"all-party government";[77] Manfred G. Schmidt defines it as "a grand coalition State";[78] Florian Meinel speaks of a continuous participation of the opposition in a "cooperative parliamentary co-government."[79] Regardless of its formulation, the message is clear: the close coordination between parties is an entrenched feature of the German political system. As widely acknowledged, this coordination has essentially occurred outside the main legislative organs (for example, the cabinet and the Bundestag) and has mainly relied on party politics.[80]

This feature of the German political system underwent a notable intensification in the four consecutive governments of Angela Merkel. Three interconnected factors can explain that intensification. First, the German political system has developed into a multiparty system, with a less clear predominance of some parties over others.[81] This development, including the proliferation of veto positions that has come with it, has significantly boosted the need for interparty coordination.[82] Secondly, during her sixteen years at the helm of the Federal Republic, Merkel was the chancellor of three grand coalition governments, also known as *GroKo*, which is the acronym of the German term *Große Koalition*.[83] Although the first grand coalition of postwar Germany dates back to Kurt Georg Kiesinger's chancellorship (1966–1969), this oft-criticized type of government became "conventional" only after Merkel's accession to power in 2005.[84] Thirdly, Merkel embraced a style of politics that put a

[77] Böckenförde, "Sozialer Bundesstaat und parlamentarische Demokratie," p. 201 ff., arguing that an all-party government (*Allparteienregierung*) is not a parliamentary government, but not necessarily undemocratic.

[78] Schmidt, *Political Institutions*, p. 22 f.

[79] Florian Meinel, *Vertrauensfrage. Zur Krise des heutigen Parlamentarismus* (C. H. Beck, 2019), p. 137.

[80] Thomas Saalfeld, "Germany: Stable Parties, Chancellor Democracy, and the Art of Informal Settlement," in Wolfgang C. Müller and Kaare Strøm (eds.), *Coalition Governments in Western Europe* (Oxford University Press, 2000), p. 32.

[81] So much so that someone has been pleading in favor of minority governments. See Werner J. Patzelt, "Minderheitsregierung? Warum eigentlich nicht!," *Frankfurter Allgemeine Zeitung*, 9 December 2019. Skeptical, and with convincing arguments, Meinel, *Vertrauensfrage*, p. 197 ff.

[82] Meinel, *Vertrauensfrage*, p. 137.

[83] Strictly speaking, the term "grand coalition" indicates the political alliance of those two parties that, following an election, obtained the largest number of political mandates. In German federal politics, grand coalition governments have so far always resulted from an alliance between CDU/CSU and SPD.

[84] Meinel, *Vertrauensfrage*, p. 35 f., arguing that even during Merkel's second mandate (2009–2013), which resulted from an alliance with the FDP, the SPD operated more like a "reserve majority" than a genuine opposition party. As regards the criticisms of grand

premium on resolving differences through negotiations within and among political parties rather than through majoritarian procedures in the Parliament. As evidence of the intensification of interparty cooperation, it is possible to consider how the grand coalition partners organized and managed their alliances in recent years, with a special focus on two instruments, namely the coalition bodies (*Koalitionsgremien*) and the coalition agreements (*Koalitionsverträge*).

Among the coalition bodies, scholars usually assign a prominent role to coalition committees (*Koalitionsausschüsse*).[85] Their composition is not fixed, but it usually comprises the Chancellor, the Vice-Chancellor, the party chairpersons, the group leaders, and other possible key politicians, including *Länder* politicians.[86] Decisions in coalition committees are usually taken by consensus in order to recognize the interests of all partners. Coalition committees have two functions: a decision-making function – to adopt strategic, key coalition-relevant decisions – and a conflict-resolution function – to settle conflicts that cannot be solved otherwise. For this reason, they can (and often do) weaken legal bodies, such as the Mediation Committee, parliamentary committees, or the cabinet, that are entrusted with similar tasks.[87] Arguably, the more prominent coalition committees are, the less relevant other fora become. In this respect, Angela Merkel's governments not only made extensive use of coalition

coalitions, they usually revolve around the weakening of the opposition's role. For an analysis of this issue in the light of the 2016 judgment of the Federal Constitutional Court in *Oppositionsfraktionsrecht*, Paulina Starski, "Die 'Große Koalition' als Problem des Verfassungsrechts: Recht auf effektive Opposition vs. Gleichheit der Abgeordneten" (2016) 69 *Die Öffentliche Verwaltung* 750–761.

[85] The creation of coalition committees dates to the famous "circle of Kreßbronn" ("Kreßbronner Kreis"), from the location where the main figures in Kiesinger's grand coalition government used to meet to discuss important matters informally.

[86] Bernhard Miller, *Der Koalitionsausschuss: Existenz, Einsatz und Effekte einer informellen Arena des Koalitionsmanagements* (Nomos, 2011), p. 254 f., who could assign up to 153 different official roles to those who participated in *Koalitionsausschüsse* during the chancellorship of Helmut Schmidt, between 1974 and 1982. Participants also included state politicians (*Ministerpräsidenten* and *Landesministern*). See also Klaus Stüwe, "Der Bundesrat in Zeiten Großer Koalitionen" (2008) *Aus Politik und Zeitgeschichte* 24–31 at 29 ff., arguing that, in the second grand coalition, the Mediation Committee played a significantly less prominent role because the Merkel government had in place well-functioning informal negotiation bodies, especially in the area of federal–state relations.

[87] Coalition committees are often said to run counter to some provisions of the Basic Law, especially its Art. 65, which attributes the power to determine policy guidelines and to resolve differences of opinion between federal ministers to the Chancellor and the government. See Wolfgang Rudzio, *Das politische System der Bundesrepublik Deutschland*, 9th ed. (Springer, 2015), p. 266 ff.

committees – grand coalitions are significantly more reliant on coalition committees than traditional coalitions. They also placed a lot of important decisions directly in the hands of *Spitzenpolitiker*. During the 2013–2017 coalition government, for instance, committees were considered to be too "populous." Angela Merkel, Horst Seehofer, and Sigmar Gabriel thus preferred to meet separately, among themselves. They enjoyed relatively undisputed control over their party members and could do without regular coalition committee meetings.[88]

The coalition agreements, furthermore, are political pacts between those parties that intend to form a government. They are by no means a novelty of recent years – the first, official coalition agreement at federal level dates to 1961 and was concluded between the CDU/CSU and FDP. However, their scope and level of detail, including the time needed to negotiate them, have grown visibly over the years, especially after the 2005 federal elections. The coalition agreement signed in 2002 between the SPD and Bündnis 90/Grüne consisted of 71 pages; the grand coalition agreement signed in 2005 between the CDU/CSU and SPD consisted of 143 pages; and the last grand coalition agreement signed in 2018 between the CDU/CSU and SPD had 175 pages, the longest among all its predecessors.[89] The latter was even surpassed, albeit slightly, by the coalition agreement currently in place between the SPD, Bündnis 90/Grüne, and FDP, which consists of 177 pages. Such growth in scope and detail reflects not only the increased number of people involved in the negotiations of the agreements – which nowadays includes several representatives from the *Länder*.[90] It also reflects the need, felt particularly by the parties to a grand coalition, to prevent changing preferences and opportunism from threatening the smooth continuation of the alliance. Above all, however, it reflects the desire of the parties to exert a tighter control over the government's work program: the more detailed the coalition agreements, the more constraints on governmental discretion.[91]

88 Patrick Horst, "Das Management der dritten Großen Koalition in Deutschland 2013 bis 2015: unangefochtene Dominanz der drei Parteivorsitzenden" (2015) 46 *Zeitschrift für Parlamentsfragen* 852–873 at 854 ff.

89 Meinel, *Vertrauensfrage*, p. 138 f.; Ingo von Münch, "Anmerkungen zur Koalitionsdemokratie und ein Plädoyer für die Beendigung des Lagerdenkens" (2015) 46 *Zeitschrift für Parlamentsfragen* 874–886 at 880 f.

90 For a table that summarizes the structures and the main protagonists of the coalition negotiations after the 2017 federal elections, Sven T. Siefken, "Regierungsbildung 'wider Willen' – der mühsame Weg zur Koalition nach der Bundestagswahl 2017" (2018) 49 *Zeitschrift für Parlamentsfragen* 407–436 at 422.

91 Meinel, *Vertrauensfrage*, p. 140.

How is all this relevant to the issue of interchamber coordination? The political system of the Federal Republic has always featured a domination of political parties (*Parteiendemokratie*) and a prominent role of coalition governments. The normalization of grand coalition governments, however, has led to an even greater need for coordination and conflict prevention. Indeed, the survival of those governments relies heavily on the ability of political actors to identify and manage conflict in advance – the opposition is always ready to capitalize on internal differences and uncertainties. These functions have increasingly been taken over by party structures. It is certainly no coincidence that, after the beginning of the second grand coalition government in 2005, the Mediation Committee has met a lot more sporadically than in previous legislatures and that, despite a recovery during the 2009–2013 legislature, its current activity is at a record low.

It would be a mistake to dismiss this situation as temporary, as something that will slowly but surely return to "normal" now that Merkel has handed over the reins of power to her successor. It seems that the trends are the result of more structural changes, including the deepening of European integration.[92] Be that as it may, the upshot of this account is that although interchamber coordination has always benefitted from the contribution of party structures, the rise of grand coalition governments have led to those structures acquiring even more importance, at the expense of the constitutionally mandated Mediation Committee. In fact, today's interchamber coordination appears firmly in the hands of the parties, and this makes the traditional instruments provided for by constitutional law significantly less warranted.

5.4 Conclusions

The analysis of interchamber coordination mechanisms in the United States and Germany has brought to light an important development: the interchamber mechanisms provided for by constitutional law and parliamentary practice are receding into the background, almost to the point of becoming obsolete. In the United States, the role of conference committees has been taken over by a "leadership-influenced bicameral bargaining process."[93] In Germany, the Mediation Committee has been significantly weakened through a more precise and systematic use of

[92] Ibid., pp. 35 f. and 209. [93] Oleszek et al., *Congressional Procedures*, p. 334.

those instruments that go under the name of "coalition management instruments." In this development, it is possible to see a parallel with the European political system. This system, too, is experiencing the complete disappearance of the Conciliation Committee, the formal interchamber coordination mechanism set out in the Treaties. The 2014–2019 European legislature was the first parliamentary term since the entry into force of the Treaty of Maastricht in which no legislative file reached conciliation. Arguably, this development is evidence of a challenge that is common to several legislative systems. An analysis of this topic, however, falls outside the scope of the present work.

I believe the above account hints at a convincing explanation for why trilogues are so prevalent at European level. They embody the need of political actors for interchamber coordination in an institutional context characterized by weak political parties. Of course, it could be argued that the Treaties already provide for an interchamber coordination mechanism: the Conciliation Committee. However, this mechanism has a major shortcoming, as it intervenes after two full readings by both co-legislators. This is too advanced a stage in the procedure; positions are often too entrenched – US conference committees and the German Mediation Committee, for instance, can be convened immediately after the first reading. What is more, formal interchamber coordination mechanisms do not exclude – in fact, they have always existed alongside – other structures with a similar function, as the role of parties in the United States and Germany testifies.

In a highly divided governmental setup with weak political parties and complex procedures, interchamber coordination cannot only rest on the Conciliation Committee. The role the Treaties assign to conciliation makes it more of a last resort than an everyday solution to coordination issues. In these circumstances, trilogues alleviate institutional fragmentation and the status quo bias that comes with it. From a functional standpoint, trilogues partly fulfill the mediating function that, in national contexts, is played by political parties. That said, considering the contribution of trilogues only in functional terms would be a mistake. I believe that since interchamber coordination is needed, leaving it to party structures does not provide more (and possibly less) democratic accountability than entrusting it to trilogues. If the "iron law of oligarchy" formulated by Robert Michels has some explanatory power,[94]

[94] Robert Michels, *Zur Soziologie des Parteiwesens in der modernen Demokratie*, 2nd ed. (Alfred Kröner Verlag, 1925), p. 479 ff.

party structures are less likely to ensure more equality and inclusiveness than the structures created by legislative institutions under the constraints of constitutional law.

As observed in the previous chapter, trilogues are institutionalized joint bodies, based on a developed set of rules. They are part of the legislative process and subject to those principles that regulate it. Although much remains to be done, trilogues already present tangible advantages, as compared to decision-making in parties. They ensure a higher level of transparency, accountability, and protection of minorities. All actors in the Parliament and the Council must be given access to the documents used in trilogues; they are entitled to exhaustive information about the unfolding of the negotiations, for the EP's Rules of Procedure demand that this information be given publicly in committee meetings. Smaller parties in the EP, moreover, have not only access to the negotiations but also the possibility to voice their interests through their "shadow rapporteurs." A poor implementation of the rules that regulate trilogues is certainly a problem worth addressing, but it is not a sufficient reason for throwing trilogues overboard altogether.

A recent article argues that the European Union and the United States epitomize opposite trends. On the one hand, the European Union is working for the institutionalization of "informal politics," especially through trilogues. On the other hand, the United States is working for the deinstitutionalization of Congress' "regular order," especially through a "'gangmen style' of legislative politics." Against this backdrop, that article provides a compelling conclusion: the institutionalization of trilogues reveals a positive – although "unfinished" – development.[95] These findings show an interesting consistency with the conclusions set out by the American Political Science Association in its report on legislative negotiations. Worried about the disrupting consequences of strong partisanship in US politics, that report recently suggested looking at the "compelling example" of Europe.[96] Of course, trilogues are by no means perfect. Their workings must be significantly improved; their rules can be better implemented. The aim of the foregoing analysis, however, was to

[95] Greenwood and Roederer-Rynning, "Taming Trilogues," p. 134 f.

[96] Cathie Jo Martin, "Conditions for Successful Negotiation: Lessons from Europe," in Jane Mansbridge and Cathie Jo Martin (eds.), *Negotiating Agreement in Politics: Report of the Task Force on Negotiating Agreement in Politics* (American Political Science Association, 2013), p. 125.

provide an account that allowed me to place trilogues in a more appropriate perspective and to possibly mitigate the negative judgment that usually surrounds them.

On this basis, I will now turn to the final part of this book, which investigates the relationship between trilogues and European democracy, with a special focus on Articles 9–12 TEU.

6 Trilogues and European Democracy

6.1 Introduction

The previous chapters traced the historical origins of trilogues; outlined the institutional setup within which trilogues operate; described and analyzed their workings, also in a comparative perspective; and explained their informal nature. Against this backdrop, I am now concluding with a chapter that observes trilogues from a normative angle. Given their incidence in the EU legislative process, trilogues raise the issue of democracy as a core value of the EU, as expressly embraced in the Preamble, Article 2, and Articles 9–12 of the Treaty on European Union. Hence, there are two research questions behind this chapter. First, are trilogues truly democratic and, if so, what makes them so? Secondly, and adopting a reverse logic, what type of democracy is compatible with – and makes sense of – the existence and prevalence of trilogues in the EU legislative process? In what follows I will answer the first question by arguing that trilogues offer an important democratic contribution because they put compromise at the very heart of the EU legislative authority.[1] I will answer the second question by claiming that the existence and prevalence of trilogues reveal a structural closeness of the EU to those polities that go under the name of "negotiation democracies."

These two arguments must be developed in the light of an important stipulation. Since democracy is an "essentially contested concept" and none of its conceptions can claim conclusive cognitive prevalence over

[1] In doing so, the EU shows a typical feature of a genuine federal polity. In this respect, Thomas O. Hueglin and Alan Fenna, *Comparative Federalism: A Systematic Inquiry*, 2nd ed. (University of Toronto Press, 2015), p. 34 ff.; Daniel J. Elazar, *Exploring Federalism* (University of Alabama Press, 1987), p. 67.

the others,[2] I specify that democracy is a regime in which the exercise of power is based on the political freedom and equality of the citizens as well as on extensive political participation rights.[3] It is the citizen that stands at the heart of the democratic order. In this order, political decisions are to stem from institutions that come into being and operate as the projection of individual citizens and their association with other citizens. I am aware that differently articulated concepts of democracy exist and influence the self-understanding and functioning of public authorities throughout the world. For instance, the idea of democracy applied in many contemporary states hinges on the self-government of one collective subject, be it the people or the nation. But the present discussion is about whether and how a specific political construct, which is different from a state and does not envisage a subject like "the people,"[4] conforms to democratic tenets. It is therefore essential to adopt an appropriate concept of democracy that remains true to its essence while proving applicable to the reality under examination. Otherwise, any theoretical and practical operation that sought to make a transnational entity (more) democratic would be doomed to failure.[5] Such a conclusion might certainly satisfy some observers, but it is not in agreement with the vision that inspired my research.

Against this backdrop, the chapter is structured as follows. First, it provides a systematic reading of the main legal provisions of EU law concerning democracy (Section 6.2), with a special focus on three defining aspects of European democracy: its lack of a demos (Section 6.2.1), its dual structure of legitimation (Section 6.2.2), and its multiple representation (Sections 6.2.3 and 6.2.4). After some brief intermediate conclusions (Section 6.3), the chapter proceeds with the core normative argument, namely that compromise is crucial to making the EU legislative process democratic (Section 6.4). The chapter concludes with an attempt to typologize the European democratic order, considering the importance that compromise-oriented activities have for its governance structure (Section 6.5).

[2] W. B. Gallie, "Essentially Contested Concepts" (1956) 56 *Proceedings of the Aristotelian Society* 167–198 at 169 and 183 ff.

[3] Manfred G. Schmidt, *Demokratietheorien: Eine Einführung*, 6th ed. (Springer, 2019), p. 2.

[4] Excluding the assimilation of the EU to a state, Avis 2/13 *Adhésion de l'Union à la CEDH* EU: C:2014:2454, paras. 156 and 193.

[5] This is, e.g., the case in Robert A. Dahl, "Can International Organizations Be Democratic? A Skeptic's View," in Ian Shapiro and Casiano Hacker-Cordón (eds.), *Democracy's Edges* (Cambridge University Press, 1999), p. 19.

6.2 The Principle of Democracy in EU Law

The European integration process and the principle of democracy did not really get off to a good start. So much so that a keen expert of the EU could maintain that the Community, in its original design, "was never intended to be a democratic organization."[6] Absent from the Founding Treaties, the principle of democracy made its first appearance in the case law of the Court of Justice in the late 1970s. The Court used it to advance and consolidate a novel interpretation of EU primary law. This interpretation allowed the European Parliament to defend in court its then limited legislative powers against encroachments by other institutions (read: the Council), although the Treaties did not expressly recognize that possibility. But the principle of democracy did not enjoy an autonomous existence. It derived its enforceability from another, more established principle of EU law, namely the principle of institutional balance.[7] The former was, so to speak, a normative reflection of the latter; and the Court used to mention them in the same breath, as in an almost symbiotic connection.[8]

The first codification of the principle of democracy into EU primary law came with the Treaty of Maastricht in 1993. Article F of that Treaty provided for the Union's obligation to "respect the national identities of its Member States, whose systems of government are founded on the principles of democracy." However, this provision did not say anything about democracy as an organizing and legitimizing principle of the European Union itself. According to democratic tenets, the provision was therefore incomplete. For if it is true that the EU can be democratic only if its Member States enjoy solid democratic credentials, it is equally true that Member States alone cannot ensure the democratic nature of the EU.

The situation changed with the Treaty of Amsterdam and, more remarkably, with the Treaty of Lisbon. Whereas the former Treaty amended Article F to provide that "[t]he Union is founded on the principles of liberty, democracy, respect for human rights and fundamental freedoms, and the rule of law, principles which are common to the

[6] G. F. Mancini, "Democracy and the European Court of Justice," in *Democracy and Constitutionalism in the European Union: Collected Essays* (Hart, 2000), p. 31.

[7] Stefania Ninatti, "How Do Our Judges Conceive of Democracy? The Democratic Nature of the Community Decision-Making Process under Scrutiny of the European Court of Justice" (2003) *Jean Monnet Working Paper* 4.

[8] See, e.g., Case C-138/79 *Roquette* v. *Council* EU:C:1980:249, para. 33.

Member States," the latter Treaty gave a totally new dimension to the idea of European democracy. EU primary law, as it now stands, not only includes democracy among its core values – those values that according to Article 2 TEU constitute the foundation of the Union – but it also comprises a brand-new title dedicated to the "Provisions on Democratic Principles." By so doing, the drafters of the Treaties endowed the Union with a rather demanding set of democratic requirements, making it one of the most promising and advanced experiments of democracy beyond the state.[9]

It bears noting that such momentous reforms of EU primary law have not yet been accompanied by changes of a similar scale in the CJEU's case law. European courts appear to favor a one-case-at-a-time approach, avoiding the formulation of an overarching doctrine of EU democracy. To be sure, there exists an ever-increasing body of judgments in the field of access to documents which puts transparency in seamless relation to the democratic nature of the European Union. In addition, the ECJ declared in a 2010 judgment that "[a]s one of the principles common to the Member States, [the principle of democracy] must be taken into consideration when interpreting acts of secondary law."[10] Nevertheless, these developments have led to only a very marginal increase in the use of the principle of democracy as an autonomous normative yardstick; the Court remains very cautious when it comes to integrating it in its findings. The principle stays in the background, even though cursory research on the Curia website seems to confirm that applicants refer to it with growing frequency in their pleas.[11]

Some changes may perhaps result from the ongoing operationalization of the values of Article 2 TEU. The CJEU has recently acknowledged that representative democracy "gives concrete expression to democracy as a value."[12] Such a development could suggest that the CJEU is gearing up for a bolder judicial employment of the principle of democracy, but it is too early to say – at the moment the leading role still belongs to the rule

[9] Armin von Bogdandy, "The European Lesson for International Democracy: The Significance of Articles 9–12 EU Treaty for International Organizations" (2012) 23 *European Journal of International Law* 315–334 at 319.

[10] Case C-518/07 *Commission* v. *Germany* EU:C:2010:125, para. 41.

[11] On the relationship between the principle of democracy and the case law of the CJEU, Koen Lenaerts, "The Principle of Democracy in the Case Law of the European Court of Justice" (2013) 62 *International and Comparative Law Quarterly* 271–315.

[12] Case C-418/18 P *Puppinck and Others* v. *Commission* EU:C:2019:1113, para. 64; Case T-754/14 *Efler and Others* v. *Commission* EU:T:2017:323, para. 37.

of law.[13] In any case, the "minimalist" approach followed by the Court is not per se to condemn. It could be argued that apex courts should avoid tying the development of a legal order to comprehensive and detailed doctrines, unless necessary. They should, instead, make an appropriate use of "silences."[14] This is no less true for the European Union, whose foundational texts are very difficult to amend. That said, those texts provide a clear outline of the supranational democratic order. In what follows, I will seek to reconstruct it.

6.2.1 A Democracy *without a* Demos

The EU is bound to be democratic, but it is also bound to be *demo*cratic without a *demos*. The Treaties do not embrace an understanding of democracy in terms of collective self-determination. The idea of a European collective subject, as in a sovereign people or a nation, is nowhere to be found. The term "people" always appears in the plural form save for a few unrelated exceptions, such as "young people" and "people applying for asylum." What is more, the establishment of a collective subject does not even belong to the broad ends of the Union. While the Preambles of the TEU and the TFEU as well as Article 1 TEU stipulate that the High Contracting Parties desire to establish "an ever closer union," they also explain that this "union" – in lowercase – is meant to be a union among "peoples." So, even in its most accomplished form, the EU will have to be organized in such a way as to preserve the distinct peoplehood of its component units.[15] Drawing on and updating an idea that goes back to nineteenth-century European republican thinkers,[16] the Treaties aim at bringing different peoples together in a polity that transcends and, at the same time, preserves their distinctiveness.

Such an understanding denotes a twofold evolution in the history of the forms of political organization; an evolution that, to my eyes, is in keeping with the "postnational constellation" in which we live.[17] As for

[13] Armin von Bogdandy, Piotr Bogdanowicz, Iris Canor, Maciej Taborowski, and Matthias Schmidt, "Guest Editorial: A Potential Constitutional Moment for the European Rule of Law – The Importance of Red Lines" (2018) 55 *Common Market Law Review* 983–995.

[14] Cass R. Sunstein, "Foreword: Leaving Things Undecided" (1996) 110 *Harvard Law Review* 4–101.

[15] J. H. H. Weiler, "In Defence of the Status Quo: Europe's Constitutional *Sonderweg*," in J. H. H. Weiler and Marlene Wind (eds.), *European Constitutionalism beyond the State* (Cambridge University Press, 2003), p. 10.

[16] Hans Gustav Keller, *Das "Junge Europa": 1834–1836* (Max Niehans Verlag, 1938).

[17] The concept of "postnational constellation" is inextricably associated with the German philosopher Jürgen Habermas. As regards the defining factual components of that

the first aspect of this evolution, the idea of a *demos* as "a pre-political community of shared destiny" does not correspond to the social reality of the vast majority of contemporary multicultural states.[18] It would therefore be odd to demand that the Union be what its Member States are not and cannot be, especially considering that the processes of exclusion, marginalization, and collective suffering on which many nation-states were built are today repudiated. Of course, it is not my intention to demonize the nation-state. Doing so would unjustifiably overlook the crucial, irreplaceable contribution that the statehood has made to ensuring the transition of large portions of humanity to more democratic political regimes and to a previously unknown welfare. It is however important to bear in mind that the birth of national *demoi* and statehood occurred under specific conditions – historical, political, legal, and social – and as a response to problems other than those that characterize the current stage of institutional and human development, notably in Europe (for example, interdependences and common risks).

The second and related aspect of the mentioned evolution concerns the very conditions for the exercise of democratically legitimate authority. Indeed, such conditions have changed profoundly. The exercise of public authority can no longer be only about creating equality through uniformity. It needs to prove sensitive to differences. In these circumstances, the importance of a collective subject appears if not altogether obsolete, at least significantly diminished. It is against this backdrop that the EU provides its distinctive democratic contribution, namely "a radical pluralization of the forms of legitimacy."[19] Such a pluralization occurs both vertically and horizontally. Whereas the vertical pluralization is a direct result of the European multi-level constitutionalism, the horizontal pluralization stems from the "mixed constitution" at the core of the EU institutional edifice. But to better understand what this pluralization entails, I will first provide an answer to the following question: if not a people, who is then standing at the center of the European democratic order?

constellation, Jürgen Habermas, "The Postnational Constellation and the Future of Democracy," in *The Postnational Constellation: Political Essays* (MIT Press, 2001), p. 58 ff.

[18] Ibid., p. 74. See also Martin Nettesheim, "Art. 10 EUV [Demokratische Grundsätze]," in Eberhard Grabitz, Meinhard Hilf, and Martin Nettesheim (eds.), *Das Recht der Europäischen Union* (C. H. Beck, 2015), vol. 1, para. 7.

[19] Pierre Rosanvallon, *Democratic Legitimacy: Impartiality, Reflexivity, Proximity* (Princeton University Press, 2011), p. 8.

6.2.2 The Relational Citizen as the Centerpiece of the European Democratic Order

According to the concept of democracy postulated at the beginning of this chapter, the EU's ultimate source of democratic legitimacy is the citizen.[20] The Treaties give expression to this concept in several provisions. It is indeed quite telling – and by no means accidental – that Title II of the TEU, which sets out the Provisions on democratic principles, begins with the principle of equality of European citizens.[21] Furthermore, the Treaties provide for the right of every citizen to participate in the democratic life of the Union, including through political parties or the European Citizens' Initiative,[22] and lay down the duty of the institutions to give their citizens "the opportunity to make known and publicly exchange their views in all areas of Union action."[23] All these provisions reflect the Union's commitment, as set out in the Preamble of the Charter of Fundamental Rights, to "place the individual at the heart of its activities." At this point, however, it is only reasonable to wonder: what about the Member States? Do the Treaties not expressly envisage them as a source of legitimacy?[24]

To answer this question, I shall begin from the "dual structure of democratic legitimation," as developed by Armin von Bogdandy, and enrich it with a further qualification. According to that notion, there are two "central elements which determine the Union's principle of democracy." On the one hand, there are the citizens as citizens of the Union, namely as members of a transnational aggregate. On the other hand, there are "the peoples in the European Union as organized by their respective Member States' constitutions."[25] As a consequence, the "dual

[20] Armin von Bogdandy, "Founding Principles," in Armin von Bogdandy and Jürgen Bast (eds.), *Principles of European Constitutional Law*, 2nd ed. (Hart/C. H. Beck/Nomos, 2011), p. 49.

[21] Art. 9 TEU.

[22] Art. 10(3) and (4) TEU and Art. 11(4) TEU, respectively. As for the impact of political parties at EU level, Peter Mair and Jacques Thomassen, "Political Representation and Government in the European Union" (2010) 17 *Journal of European Public Policy* 20–35 at 23 ff., arguing that, "[f]reed from the demands of governing, parties at the European level may be able to provide a more robust channel of representation than that currently on offer within the democratic polities of the member states."

[23] Art. 11(1) and (4) TEU.

[24] The importance of the Member States as a source of legitimacy of the European democratic order emerges clearly from EU primary law (for instance, Art. 10(2)(2) TEU) and from long-standing case law of the CJEU (for instance, Case C-621/18 *Wightman and Others* EU:C:2018:999, para. 44).

[25] von Bogdandy, "The European Lesson for International Democracy," 321 ff.

structure of democratic legitimation" posits that the citizens participate in the EU system of government in two ways: as citizens of the Union and as citizens of one of the European peoples. And since the EU system of government draws its legitimacy not only from the European elections but also from the national elections, it is not surprising that the Treaties require the members of the (European) Council to be "democratically accountable either to their national Parliaments, or to their citizens."[26]

This construction, however, needs another crucial qualification. The legitimacy of the EU is not only dual. It is enriched by the citizen's right to an equal participation in the democratic life of the Union, as provided for in Article 10(3) TEU. In this spirit, the Treaties do not understand individual citizens as insular but rather as relational subjects, who can influence the decision-making processes of the EU through those groups and associations in which the different facets of their identities find expression (for example, as an adherent of a certain religion, as a member of an ethnic group, as a member of a certain profession). Accordingly, Article 2 TEU defines the foundational values of the Union as "common to the Member States in a *society* in which pluralism, non-discrimination, tolerance, justice, solidarity and equality between women and men prevail."[27] By employing the concept of "society" and by stressing the relevance of eminently intersubjective values (such as pluralism, tolerance, and solidarity),[28] this provision not only recognizes the relational dimension of citizens but also requires the Union to protect the existence and furtherance of their interactions against the risk of an alienating self-reference.

Therefore, the view of an undifferentiated demos, an abstract sum of individuals, or a faceless people is foreign to the European constitutional order. Rather, the Treaties espouse what Martin Nettesheim calls a "*realistic* model of representation."[29] Realism in this sense embraces all the different forms in which the connection between institutions and citizens becomes lively and effective, especially that rich set of "democratic rights" that EU primary law recognizes with the purpose of facilitating the participation of the citizens in the management of public affairs.[30] This vision befits the ongoing "transformation of democracy," as observed

[26] Art. 10(2)(2) TEU. [27] Emphasis added.

[28] On the concept of European society, Armin von Bogdandy, *The Emergence of European Society through Public Law: A Hegelian and Anti-Schmittian Approach* (Oxford University Press, 2024). See also Alessandro Cavalli and Alberto Martinelli, *La società europea* (il Mulino, 2015).

[29] Nettesheim, "Art. 10 EUV," para. 62 (emphasis added).

[30] Case C-57/16 P *ClientEarth* v. *Commission* EU:C:2018:660, para. 84.

by Pierre Rosanvallon. As he put it, "present-day generality ... has to be understood as rooted in the partial parallelism of singularities" and "is intelligible only as the result of the aggregation and the overlapping of peculiarities."[31] As I will show, all this comes in handy when appraising the desirability of trilogues from a normative viewpoint.

The upshot of these considerations is that EU primary law does not provide for a collective subject that can stake a claim for self-determination. This dimension of democracy is not part of Europe's current setup or of its normative horizon. This, however, does not make the EU less democratic. In fact, this configuration fits in well with the essence of today's representative politics, which features an increasing urge for "pluralism, compassion, and proximity" as well as a growing unease with the "assimilation of the majority to the unanimous whole."[32] Near to elections, it is possible to witness the blossoming of communication and participation channels directed at narrowing the gap between citizens and institutions. These trends are consistent with a generalized disaffection towards political representation and elections, as evidenced by low voter turnouts.[33] In contemporary Western polities, elections are becoming just one instrument to make one's voice heard – one instrument among a plethora of others that may be perceived as more empowering, effective, and direct. At EU level, those instruments include petitions to the EP, applications to the Ombudsman, and European Citizens' Initiatives, to name but a few.

Be that as it may, the radical pluralization of the forms of legitimacy that the EU offers rests not only on the diversity inherent in its society but also on its system of representative institutions, especially the Parliament, the Council, and the Commission. Those institutions give rise to a mixed constitution – a constitution that aspires to give public recognition to different particularities and to recompose them into a general political will. In this context, trilogues play a key role. They not only make such a recomposition possible. They also embody the notion that "the reality of the general will is to be found not in the attempt to declare or stage it, but rather as the product of compromises, choices made among rival options, and preferences of a complex civil society."[34]

[31] Pierre Rosanvallon, "The Transformation of Democracy and the Future of Europe," in *Democracy Past and Future* (Columbia University Press, 2006), p. 222 f.

[32] Rosanvallon, *Democratic Legitimacy*, pp. 13 and 171 ff.

[33] In a similar vein, Philip Manow, *(Ent)demokratisierung der Demokratie: Ein Essay* (Suhrkamp, 2020), p. 13.

[34] Rosanvallon, "The Transformation of Democracy and the Future of Europe," p. 226.

6.2.3 *The Representative Nature of the European Democratic Order*

It is in line with the foregoing understanding that the other "Provisions on Democratic Principles" are to be construed, especially the provision stipulating that "the functioning of the Union shall be founded on representative democracy."[35] The drafters of the Treaty of Lisbon did not confine themselves to speaking of "democracy." They chose to underscore its "representative" nature, without providing a proper definition of that adjective. In my reading, this choice has at least four implications.

First, it implies the constitutionalization of a proper distance between the representatives and the represented. Such distance is not just a measure to make democracy in a large political system work. It is a precondition, a constitutive and thus indispensable element of any democratically organized entity. A polity that does not operationalize that distance is a polity where decisions neither lead to action nor give rise to political responsibility.[36] A proper distance becomes even more crucial when a polity is constitutionally committed to providing its citizens with extensive possibilities to participate in its decision-making processes, as stipulated in Article 11 TEU. Since there always are some who have greater resources than others and take better advantage of the opportunities that a political system affords, organizing a proper distance may be an effective way to keep the influence of affluent pressure groups in check. But there is more to it. Organizing a proper distance may also prevent an attitude of permanent campaigning from pervading all structures and processes of government. Political representation justifies the configuration of democratic institutions in such a way as to control the unfettered "ascendency of campaigning."[37] Ultimately, representative democracy – and the proper distance that ought to characterize it – provides the appropriate conditions for reformulating or redescribing disagreements and, in so doing, recomposing particularities into a political will. For instance, conservative political actors might be more inclined to support climate-change actions, as promoted by their

[35] Art. 10(1) TEU.

[36] Ernst-Wolfgang Böckenförde, "Demokratie und Repräsentation. Zur Kritik der heutigen Demokratiediskussion," in *Staat, Verfassung, Demokratie* (Suhrkamp, 1991), p. 379 ff.

[37] Amy Gutmann and Dennis Thompson, *The Spirit of Compromise: Why Governing Demands It and Campaigning Undermines It* (Princeton University Press, 2012), p. 90. See also Rosanvallon, *Democratic Legitimacy*, p. 220, arguing: "Rather than attempt to carry over the bond of identification from the electoral to the governmental sphere, it is better to recognize the functional necessity of distance in the latter and to give this new relationship its own specifically democratic form."

progressive colleagues, if those actions are devised in a way to reduce energy costs and keep the bureaucratic burden for businesses at a minimum.[38]

Secondly, the reference of Article 10 TEU to "representative democracy" is indicative of a precise understanding of the political process at EU level. Representation implies – although it is not coterminous with – responsiveness. It hinges on a *political* relation between representative institutions on the one hand, and a diverse and articulated universe of citizens on the other. Representation therefore calls for pluralism and the rejection of an indistinct mass public.[39] In this sense, Article 10 TEU not only enshrines an unequivocal, principled position against populist democracy, it also constitutionalizes the notion of a political process that strives for unity without postulating homogeneity. As repeatedly stated in these pages, EU primary law does away with the idea of a preexisting self-determining collective subject and espouses the idea of a legislative process that tends towards unity. This point is of great importance for my analysis since it provides trilogues with a strong legitimizing basis. Trilogues indeed are the instrument that helps political actors realize that unity. In doing so, they correspond to the idea of democracy envisaged in the Treaties.

Thirdly, by enshrining the principle of representative democracy immediately after that of equality, the Treaties assert the centrality of the concept of representation for the EU as a democratic project. European democracy is first and foremost a representative democracy. In this perspective, Article 11 TEU, which enshrines the idea of participatory democracy, gives expression to "participation as a means of government." This idea of participatory democracy is different from – and shares little with – the ideas of self-government and direct democracy. Rather, "it is more a matter of assisting the representative system, making it interactive, forcing it to become more transparent and open."[40] It is the way in which citizens seek to "take social possession" of their representative institutions. As recently affirmed by the Court of Justice,

[38] Frank R. Ankersmit, "Representational Democracy: An Aesthetic Approach to Conflict and Compromise" (2002) 8 *Common Knowledge* 24–46 at 36, arguing that the "politician must possess the essentially aesthetic talent of representing political reality in new and original ways."

[39] Nadia Urbinati, "Representative Democracy and Its Critics," in Sonia Alonso, John Keane, and Wolfgang Merkel (eds.), *The Future of Representative Democracy* (Cambridge University Press, 2018), p. 45.

[40] Rosanvallon, *Democratic Legitimacy*, p. 206.

the "system of representative democracy was *complemented*, with the Treaty of Lisbon, by instruments of participatory democracy … the objective of which is to *encourage* the participation of citizens in the democratic process and to *promote* dialogue between citizens and the EU institutions."[41] The message is thus clear: participatory democracy does not challenge the centrality of the representative institutions; their structures and prerogatives must remain untouched.[42]

Fourthly, by speaking of "representative democracy" and by referring to the functioning of the Union as a whole,[43] Article 10(1) TEU makes clear that being representative shall not be an exclusive feature of the Parliament and the Council, but it shall also concern the whole edifice of the Union, all its institutions. Now, considering that the EP and the (European) Council represent the citizens and the Member States respectively, which is the Commission representing? As known, the Treaties mandate the Commission to "promote the general interest of the Union and [to] take appropriate initiatives to that end."[44] But does this also mean that it *represents* that interest? Is it possible to understand the concept of representation as covering something other than the citizens and the Member States? The answer is yes, if one accepts a notion of representation that goes beyond the elections, as Article 10(1) TEU mandates. This notion corresponds to what some scholars call "multiple representation."[45]

6.2.4 *The Commission as a Representative Body*

The notion of multiple representation rests on the assumption that the distribution of government across different institutions can better reflect the existing diversity of preferences among citizens.[46] Following this

41 Case C-418/18 P *Puppinck*, para. 65 (emphasis added).

42 Floriana Sipala, "La vie démocratique de l'Union," in Giuliano Amato, Hervé Bribosia, and Bruno De Witte (eds.), *Genèse et destinée de la Constitution européenne/Genesis and Destiny of the European Constitution* (Bruylant, 2007), p. 370 f. Similarly, Joana Mendes, "Participation and the Role of Law after Lisbon: A Legal View on Article 11 TEU" (2011) 48 *Common Market Law Review* 1849–1877 at 1858 f.

43 Mair and Thomassen, "Political Representation and Government in the European Union," 23.

44 Art. 17(1) TEU.

45 This idea undergirds the whole book by Rosanvallon, *Democratic Legitimacy*. See also Daniel Innerarity, *Democracy in Europe: A Political Philosophy of the EU* (Palgrave Macmillan, 2018), ch. 6. On the representative nature of the Commission, Antoine Vauchez, *Democratizing Europe* (Palgrave Macmillan, 2016), pp. 53 and 57.

46 Innerarity, *Democracy in Europe*, p. 153.

notion, the Commission ought to be viewed as an institution that discharges its representative function by giving "meaning and voice to a social totality that cannot exist or express itself independently."[47] This totality should not be mistaken for a *demos*, which does not exist. Rather, it should be viewed as a "common weal," a general good that transcends the citizens and the Member States and needs to be striven for. To better understand the role of the Commission in relation to this "common weal," it is helpful to refer to the notion of "representation by impartiality," together with the related notion of "negative generality," as expounded by Rosanvallon.

According to the French historian and sociologist, the key feature of "representation by impartiality" – and of those institutions that embody such an idea – is:

> [The a]chievement of generality by way of detachment from particularity, through systematic rational construction of a point of view at some distance from any particular aspect of a given issue. This defines power in terms of *un lieu vide*, an empty place or vacuum. The generality of an institution is then reflected in the fact that no one can appropriate it. This is a negative generality. It is characterized by a structural variable (the fact of independence) and a behavioral variable (the maintenance of distance or equilibrium). This negative generality is what allows an institution to oversee or regulate the activities of others and what distinguishes the bearers of such authority from elective branches of government.[48]

Conceptualizing the representative role of the Commission in these terms is convincing for various reasons, both theoretical and practical. From a theoretical viewpoint, it places the Commission outside the elective dimension of representation, reconciling its constitutionally mandated independence with its constitutionally mandated representative nature. In this spirit, viewing the Commission as nonrepresentative because it is very hard to vote out of office is misleading. It fails to acknowledge the specific role of the Commission and, in more general terms, the variety of institutions that, at both national and European level, partake in the legitimate exercise of public authority without being inserted into the electoral cycle. "Throwing the scoundrels out," as Joseph Weiler famously put it, certainly makes sense in the context of electoral representation. The Commission, however, belongs to an altogether different constellation. Its representative nature as well as its legal and social legitimacy lie in its ability to present itself as an "impartial" actor,

[47] Rosanvallon, *Democratic Legitimacy*, p. 89.   [48] Ibid., p. 6.

capable of not prejudging a question and paying "attention to everyone's needs by treating all issues according to the dictates of law and reason."[49] While enjoying an independent *status* under the Treaties, the Commission must prove, through daily efforts, the impartial *quality* of its action. Unlike independence, which is guaranteed by legal provisions, impartiality "is something that needs to be perpetually constructed and validated."[50]

But the notion of representation I have just borrowed from Rosanvallon also makes sense from a practical viewpoint. The Commission not only enjoys a near monopoly over the legislative initiative, but it also has the power to adopt sanctions against legal persons, to launch infringement proceedings against the Member States, and, more recently, to police the respect for the EU's founding values of Article 2 TEU. In such a context, the transformation of the Commission into a genuine parliamentary government would inevitably weaken its legitimacy in the eyes of those actors that the Commission must regulate and control. To give meaning and voice to the general interest of the Union, the Commission must constantly cultivate and confirm its impartiality. Its legitimacy depends on its capacity for interceding among diverse, sometimes opposing interests. In the legislative domain, the Commission is faithful to its mandate insofar as it complies with two general criteria. First, it must elaborate legislative proposals that reflect, to the widest possible extent, the interest of the Union, as also emerges from the "open, transparent, and regular dialogue" and the "broad consultations" with representative associations, civil society, and parties concerned (Article 11 TEU). Secondly, it must protect those proposals in the different stages of the legislative procedure, while seeking to adjust them to the positions of the Parliament and the Council.

This view is far from being an "out of date functionalist view" of European democracy.[51] Arguably, it is not only the most consistent with the Treaties but also the most coherent with the normative aspirations of the EU as emergent democratic polity beyond the state. Upholding the independence and the legislative prerogatives of the Commission has at least two important consequences. First, it ensures an unfailing exposition of the interests represented by electoral institutions to those represented by an institution attentive to the interest of the Union as a

[49] Ibid., p. 98. [50] Ibid., p. 94 ff.
[51] For this criticism, Dominique Ritleng, "Does the European Court of Justice Take Democracy Seriously? Some Thoughts about the *Macro-Financial Assistance* Case" (2016) 53 *Common Market Law Review* 11–33 at 19.

whole.[52] Secondly, it may operate to the effect of ensuring that the scrutiny and the input of the national parliaments on newly proposed EU legislation do not become irrelevant as negotiations among the institutions progress. By withdrawing those proposals that the co-legislators want to amend in a manner contrary to their original objectives,[53] the Commission also guarantees that the negotiations do not produce an outcome that fundamentally deviates from the texts that the national parliaments evaluated and discussed at the beginning of the legislative process, in the eight-week period provided for in Protocol (No. 1).[54] In this sense, the prerogatives of the Commission are instrumental, albeit indirectly, in protecting the contribution of national parliaments to the legitimacy of European legislation.

The Commission is called upon to enrich the supranational legislative process through its distance from electoral dynamics, which are imbricated with particularity, and to "decide while the various contending parties express their own interests to the full."[55] Since the European legislative authority consists of the Parliament and the Council, the contribution of the Commission is not meant to take center stage – the Treaties indeed assign to the Commission important but less wide-ranging legislative prerogatives, as compared to those of the co-legislators. The intervention of the Commission is, however, crucial for the maintenance of a thriving democratic polity – a polity which takes pains, among other things, to ensure that the legislation integrates the interests expressed by electoral majorities with those of minorities and future generations.[56] In this sense, the mission of the Commission is to allay the short-sightedness that too often afflicts electoral institutions.

Note, however, that democratic impartiality is not equal to being apolitical. If there were still doubts about it until recently, the

[52] Therefore, the application of instruments of participatory democracy, such as the European Citizens' Initiative (Art. 11(4) TEU), cannot deprive the Commission of the power of legislative initiative. According to the ECJ, the Commission must enjoy broad discretion as to whether, and possibly how, to submit a legislative proposal to the Parliament and the Council as a follow-up to a European Citizens' Initiative. See Case C-418/18 P *Puppinck*, para. 60 ff.

[53] Case C-409/13 *Council* v. *Commission* EU:C:2015:217, para. 94 f.

[54] Art. 4 Protocol (No. 1) on the role of national parliaments in the European Union: "An eight-week period shall elapse between a draft legislative act being made available to national Parliaments in the official languages of the Union and the date when it is placed on a provisional agenda for the Council for its adoption or for adoption of a position under a legislative procedure."

[55] Rosanvallon, *Democratic Legitimacy*, p. 105.

[56] Innerarity, *Democracy in Europe*, p. 146.

European debt crisis has wiped those doubts away, once and for all.[57] As for the legislative role of the Commission, drafting a new piece of legislation, even when it is part of previously agreed annual interinstitutional programs, implies a great deal of discretion. It implies deciding among a variety of ideas and stimuli from the different departments, from representative associations, and from the civil society at large. It also implies setting the limits within which the co-legislators will be able to exercise their amending power – the Parliament and the Council cannot go as far as to alter the nature of the original proposal.[58] Furthermore, as acknowledged by the ECJ in a recent judgment, the Commission's prerogative of legislative initiative is subject to limited judicial review, precisely because of its eminently political nature.[59]

These considerations pose the question of how to ensure that the Commission is perceived as a public good. This lies at the heart of those proposals that seek to include independent institutions within a plural understanding of representative democracy.[60] One way is of course to make the Commission's structures and functions more transparent; to explain its activities in public documents; to foster public debate on its actions; to facilitate the access of citizens.[61] If the democratic character of the Commission depends on its impartiality, and if impartiality requires constant construction and validation, then the Commission has to make considerable efforts, as compared to the co-legislators, to gain the recognition of and inspire trust among the public. This is where Article 11 TEU, with its open-ended wording, comes into play.

In addition to a paragraph dedicated to the Commission,[62] Article 11 TEU enshrines a clear commitment to openness, transparency, and regular dialogue, while endowing the institutions with broad room for

57 On the fact that democratic impartiality is active, reparative, and, ultimately, political, Rosanvallon, *Democratic Legitimacy*, p. 104 ff. See also Vauchez, *Democratizing Europe*, p. 53 f.

58 See Chapter 2, Section 2.7.

59 Case C-418/18 P *Puppinck*, para. 89, where the ECJ endorsed the statement of the GC's judgment under appeal, according to which, "in exercising its powers of legislative initiative, the Commission must be allowed broad discretion, in so far as, through that exercise, it is called upon, pursuant to Article 17(1) TEU, to promote the general interest of the Union by carrying out, possibly, the difficult task of reconciling divergent interests."

60 Innerarity, *Democracy in Europe*, p. 143 ff.; Vauchez, *Democratizing Europe*, ch. 4.

61 Mendes, "Participation and the Role of Law after Lisbon," 1869 ff.

62 Under Art. 11(3) TEU, the European Commission "shall carry out broad consultations with parties concerned in order to ensure that the Union's actions are coherent and transparent."

maneuver when designing their participatory practices. Article 11 TEU therefore is a normative yardstick against which citizens and other institutions, especially the European Parliament, may appraise the quality of the practices put in place by the Commission.[63] To this end, the Parliament has an extensive variety of controlling tools and is generally very eager to use them. Furthermore, since the representative character of the Commission is more precarious than that of the co-legislators, Article 11 TEU might be construed as establishing more exacting standards vis-à-vis the former than the latter. Only effective participatory practices, together with enhanced transparency and timely reason-giving, may enable the Commission to start eroding the technocratic reputation that has long haunted it.

6.3 The European Union: Intermediate Conclusions on Multiple Representation in a Mixed Constitution

At this point, my analysis permits me to draw some intermediate conclusions. As the previous considerations highlight, the democratic nature of the European Union integrates at least three different modes of representation. First, the Parliament represents the European citizens *qua* transnational citizens. Contrary to the liberal understanding of parliamentary representation, each MEP represents the interests and needs of the European citizens – mostly of those who voted for them – rather than the interests and needs of an abstract unitary subject, which EU law does not mention anywhere. Secondly, the Council is the expression of a "corporative" representation. "Corporative" means that the Member States are represented as individual body politics (*corpora*) and operate in the Council in accordance with instructions, as in the *ancien régime*'s diets.[64] The Council is the projection of the Member States through the lens of their governments. Finally, there is the Commission, which articulates the interests and needs of a European "common weal" with its own mode of representation "by impartiality." Against this backdrop, it seems only reasonable to use the term "multiple" to describe this composite system of representative institutions.

Following this summary, I argue that the lack of a preexisting and self-determining collective subject and the presence of a system of multiple

[63] Mendes, "Participation and the Role of Law after Lisbon," 1859 ff.

[64] Filippo Pizzolato, "Rappresentanza politica e Unione europea" (2013) 23 *Rivista italiana di diritto pubblico comunitario* 371–400 at 373.

representation are evidence of the fact that the EU rests on a mixed constitution.[65] Despite persisting uncertainties about the precise contours of this concept, it is safe to maintain that mixed constitutions exist in the absence of a unitary legitimating subject (the people) and postulate the distribution of power among different institutions, each of which enjoys its own individual basis of legitimacy. Such institutions participate – possibly through different forms and degrees of involvement – in the exercise of single functions or tasks, which must be carried out *together*.[66] This collaboration serves to both generate and maintain the harmony necessary for civil coexistence. Mixed constitutions have often received praise as systems of government that provide stability, justice, and protection against abuse of power (for example, the constitution of Britain during the Victorian era).[67] But they have also received criticism as inherently conservative – they are said to be less quick at adjusting to societal needs and they are believed to generate legislative entrenchment.[68] It is not by chance that, in the famous 1863 booklet by Sir George Cornewall Lewis, *A Dialogue on the Best Form of Government*, which features a sort of Socratic discussion among three "ardent politicians" and their host, the defense of mixed constitutions is left in the hands of a character called Aristocraticus. He declares: "I am willing to make a compromise with democracy. I do not wish that democratic influence should be altogether excluded; but I cannot allow it the mastery."[69]

[65] The idea of the EU as a polity predicated on a mixed constitution is not uncommon in scholarly writings. See, e.g., Mario Telò, "Three European Constitutionalisms and Their Respective Legitimacy Requirements: Explaining the *longue durée* Stability of the EU Polity," in Sonia Lucarelli, Furio Cerutti, and Vivien A. Schmidt (eds.), *Debating Political Identity and Legitimacy in the European Union* (Routledge, 2011), p. 107 ff.; Neil MacCormick, *Questioning Sovereignty: Law, State, and Nation in the European Commonwealth* (Oxford University Press, 1999), ch. 9; P. P. Craig, "Democracy and Rule-Making within the EC: An Empirical and Normative Assessment" (1997) 3 *European Law Journal* 105–130 at 113 ff.

[66] This definition of "mixed constitution" is provided by Ernst-Wolfgang Böckenförde, "Sozialer Bundesstaat und parlamentarische Demokratie: Zum Verhältnis von Parlamentarismus und Föderalismus unter den Bedingungen des Sozialstaats," in *Staat, Nation, Europa* (Suhrkamp, 1999), p. 192 ff. The author uses the concept of "mixed constitution" to describe the nature of the German Federal Republic as resulting from those evolutions that go under the name of "unitary federal State" (*unitarischer Bundesstaat*), "cooperative federalism" (*kooperativer Föderalismus*), and "joint decision-making" (*Politikverflechtung*).

[67] Norberto Bobbio, "Governo misto," in Norberto Bobbio, Nicola Matteucci, and Gianfranco Pasquino (eds.), *Dizionario di politica*, 2nd ed. (Utet, 1983), p. 496.

[68] Schmidt, *Demokratietheorien*, p. 338 ff.

[69] George Cornewall Lewis, *A Dialogue on the Best Form of Government* (Parker Son and Bourn, 1863), p. 74.

Allow me to take advantage of this quotation to highlight another crucial point: mixed constitutions make compromise a necessary condition of political action.[70] Whereas no political system can do without compromise altogether, systems based on mixed constitutions show a structural – or even an elective – affinity to compromise.[71] This consideration certainly applies to the EU, given that such affinity is hardwired into the fabric of the European constitutional edifice. Since the Treaties – and the institutional balance enshrined therein – make legislation without compromise essentially impossible, the institutions gave birth to and consolidated the practice of trilogues, as bodies expressly devoted to the negotiation of compromises. It is thus possible to read that the EU is a "compromising Union";[72] or that the EU "is highly dependent on the legitimizing force of compromise";[73] or even that "the European way of life is a continuous negotiation."[74] However, even though the EU's structural affinity to compromise can be explained and legitimized in the light of its mixed constitution, the democratic character of such affinity is yet to be demonstrated. In other words, the question is whether there exist not only instrumental but also intrinsic democratic reasons to celebrate compromise and a decision-making process devoted to its attainment. Answering this question is what I set about doing in the next sections, taking trilogues as reference point.

6.4 Compromise, or How to Make the European Legislative Process Democratic

First, there needs to be an understanding of what "compromise" means. Etymologically, the word derives from the Latin "*compromissum*," which in turn results from the prefix "*cum*" (together) and the verb "*promittere*" (promise); so it means "promise together." The word originated as a Roman law concept, and it referred to the commitment of two conflicting parties to submit a difference to a third subject and to abide by the

[70] Böckenförde, "Sozialer Bundesstaat und parlamentarische Demokratie," p. 197.

[71] Marvin Rintala, "The Two Faces of Compromise" (1969) 22 *Western Political Quarterly* 326–332 at 326, affirming that "every political system can be classified … on the basis of its prevalent attitude towards compromise."

[72] Christopher J. Bickerton, *European Integration: From Nation-States to Member States* (Oxford University Press, 2012), p. 21 ff.

[73] Christine Reh, "European Integration as Compromise: Recognition, Concessions and the Limits of Cooperation" (2012) 47 *Government and Opposition* 414–440 at 416.

[74] Zygmunt Bauman, *Europe: An Unfinished Adventure* (Polity Press, 2004), p. 7.

resulting decision. After the 1215 Fourth Lateran Council, the word "*compromissum*" began to connote one of the procedures for the election of the Pope. In particular, "[c]ompromissum signified the delegation of final choice to a small commission whenever long sessions and repeated failures showed unanimous agreement to be unlikely." Furthermore, the English Parliament of the seventeenth century recognized "compromise as a formalized procedure (*Modi of Parliament*) whenever the Estates could not agree (or the greater part of the Knights, Proctors, Citizens, &c.) There, by consent of the whole Parliament, the *Matter might be compromised* to 25. chosen out of all Degrees, and to fewer, till at length it might come to 3. who might determine the case."[75] In all these examples, compromise implied delegating, to a person or a body, the authority to solve a pending dispute.

In contemporary Romance languages, especially in their legal lexica, the word "compromise" (in its Spanish, Portuguese, French, Italian, and Romanian variations) has retained this meaning, as it still designates agreements for the submission of specific disputes to a judicial or arbitral body – international law also employs the originally French term "*compromis*" to the same effect.[76] However, the word has also acquired another meaning, which is common not only to most Romance but also to most Germanic languages. It denotes a process whereby two or more parties settle a dispute by means of an agreement attained through mutual concessions.[77] As compared to the first meaning, this second meaning is both broader and stricter. The word has a broader meaning in that it does not suppose a delegation – the conflicting parties can themselves seek to solve the dispute at hand without necessarily resorting to third parties. It has a stricter meaning in that it specifies the way in which a dispute is to be solved, namely through mutual concessions. And although compromise can take many forms in the practice, scholarship usually differentiates between two basic typologies.

Before embarking on a brief explanation of those typologies, another remark is in order. Although compromise is a ubiquitous practice, its

[75] Both quotations are taken from Alin Fumurescu, *Compromise: A Political and Philosophical History* (Cambridge University Press, 2013), pp. 61 ff. and 88.

[76] Hugh Thirlway, "Compromis," in Rüdiger Wolfrum (ed.), *The Max Planck Encyclopedia of Public International Law* (Oxford University Press, 2012), vol. 2, p. 564.

[77] "compromise, n., sense 4.a," in *Oxford English Dictionary* (Oxford University Press, July 2023): "A coming to terms, or arrangement of a dispute, by concessions on both sides; partial surrender of one's position, for the sake of coming to terms; the concession or terms offered by either side."

meaning and value are context dependent. Compromise in the arts, for instance, might be seen as undesirable if its proliferation jeopardizes the existence of creativity and – some say – avant-gardism.[78] Compromise in physics, on the other hand, is simply unconceivable: could anyone really pretend to solve a difference between two divergent theories about a phenomenon in fluid dynamics by concocting a compromise theory that conflates elements of both?[79] When it comes to democratic politics, any appraisal of the practice of compromise needs to start from the assumption that that practice usually plays out against the backdrop of a constitution, which embodies a legally binding and enforceable agreement on the most fundamental values of a polity and provides for a set of inevitable constraints on the nature and scope of the concessions political actors can make to each other when negotiating policy arrangements.[80] Without this (perhaps) self-evident yet decisive qualification, there is the risk of overestimating the extent of what a compromise can accomplish or, vice versa, jeopardize.

6.4.1 *Inclusive versus Bartered Compromise: An Overstated Distinction*

Compromise may take two basic forms: inclusive compromise, based on generous concessions in a spirit of active cooperation, and bartered compromise, based on give-and-take and exchanges of promises through strategic and tactical practices. Both are compromises because both entail mutual concessions. Even when a seller and a potential buyer haggle over the price of a second-hand coat in a flea market, the final price is usually the result of mutual concessions, oftentimes in the form of splitting the difference. With terminological variances, this distinction is widely accepted among those who study the practice of compromise and must be illustrated, at least in general terms.[81]

First, a compromise may vary in relation to the "nature of the mutual concessions."[82] An inclusive compromise entails generous and costly

[78] This is the argument presented by Rachel Greenwald Smith, *On Compromise: Art, Politics, and the Fate of an American Ideal* (Graywolf Press, 2021). However, the lack of a sharper distinction between compromise in the arts and compromise in politics is the main shortcoming of this otherwise compelling and thought-provoking book.

[79] Véronique Zanetti, *Spielarten des Kompromisses* (Suhrkamp, 2022), p. 25.

[80] Avishai Margalit, *On Compromise and Rotten Compromises* (Princeton University Press, 2010), p. 89.

[81] Reh, "European Integration as Compromise," 422 ff.; Richard Bellamy, Markus Kornprobst, and Christine Reh, "Introduction: Meeting in the Middle" (2012) 47 *Government and Opposition* 275–295 at 275.

[82] Bellamy, Kornprobst, and Reh, "Introduction," 286 f.

concessions. A bartered compromise, on the other hand, is the result of rather minimal, tactical concessions. Secondly, a compromise may be distinguished in relation to the "degree of non-coercion" that underpins the negotiations.[83] An inclusive compromise comes into existence through other-regarding and cooperative behavior, inspired by the desire to accommodate each other's concerns to the greatest extent possible; while a bartered compromise is the result of a "competitive game," with the actors seeking to extract concessions and maximize gains. Thirdly, a compromise may vary in relation to its ability to transform the actors' perception of the "grounds for conflict."[84] An inclusive compromise usually stems from empathy and therefore brings about a better understanding of the opponent's concerns from the opponent's point of view.[85] Bartered compromise is accompanied by a low transformative impact, as negotiators remain incapable of comprehending each other's point of view, before and after negotiating the compromise.

This brief explanation might justify a normative preference for inclusive compromise,[86] as the product of cooperative, communicative, and other-regarding interactions. Bartered compromise is instrumental and dependent upon a contingent balance of forces, more akin to dealings among traders than to agreements among publicly accountable politicians, especially when they result from splitting the difference. For several reasons, however, bartered compromise is not as undignified as it is often said to be. First, tactical behaviors are not only part and parcel of politics but also normatively justifiable, for they may help political actors advance the interests of their constituencies and therefore provide better representation.[87] Secondly, bartered compromise can be the expression of a fair balance between inclusion and efficiency – for instance, when political actors discuss appropriations for funds or programs. Thirdly, even bartered compromise postulates elements of trust and reciprocity. It thus shares, as I will shortly show, the essential features that make compromise democratically valuable.[88] Finally, and on a different logical plane, distinguishing between inclusive and bartered

[83] Ibid., 286 f. [84] Ibid., 289 f. [85] Margalit, *On Compromise and Rotten Compromises*, p. 42.

[86] See, e.g., Reh, "European Integration as Compromise," 429, who argues that "only inclusive compromise has the potential to legitimize the EU as a divided, multilevel and functionally restricted polity."

[87] Gutmann and Thompson, *The Spirit of Compromise*, p. 52.

[88] Robert D. Putnam, *Making Democracy Work* (Princeton University Press, 1993), p. 170, quoting Kenneth Arrow as stating: "[v]irtually every commercial transaction has within itself an element of trust, certainly every transaction conducted over a period of time."

compromise is not always as immediate as it may seem, since it requires, among other things, the arduous task of gauging the real intentions of the negotiators. I will therefore avoid employing such a typological distinction when investigating the democratic value of compromise.[89]

6.4.2 *Explaining the Democratic Value of Compromise*

The democratic value of compromise has always occupied a significant role in academic reflections,[90] with an intriguing revival of interest over recent years – perhaps as an educated reaction to widespread populist ideology. Some of those reflections turn on the role of mutual concessions. For instance, one theory argues that mutual concessions generate democratic legitimacy because they are liable to benefit the citizens.[91] Whenever representatives of a constituency offer a concession to representatives of another constituency, it is as if the principals of the former were offering a concession to the principals of the latter. In graphic terms, that concession "is offered to you and me."[92] Others, instead, view compromise as a concretization of the principle of equality, which is "central to the normative justification of democracy."[93] For instance, one theory maintains that, unlike a lottery or a coin flip, compromise gives concrete expression to the norm of "respect for fellow citizens as co-rulers," thereby contributing to the foundation of a democratic process of mutual accommodation.[94]

[89] For other authors who believe that this distinction is overstated, see Zanetti, *Spielarten des Kompromisses*, p. 26; Élise Rouméas, "The Procedural Value of Compromise" (2021) 47 *Social Theory and Practice* 377–396 at 380.

[90] In addition to those studies already cited, a very partial list of works on the topic includes: Sandrine Baume and Yannis Papadopoulos, "Against Compromise in Democracy? A Plea for a Fine-Grained Assessment" (2022) 29 *Constellations* 1–17; Eric Beerbohm, "The Problem of Clean Hands: Negotiated Compromise in Lawmaking," in Jack Knight (ed.), *Compromise* (New York University Press, 2018), p. 1 ff.; Christian F. Rostbøll, "Democratic Respect and Compromise" (2017) 20 *Critical Review of International Social and Political Philosophy* 619–635; Daniel Weinstock, "Compromise, Pluralism, and Deliberation" (2017) 20 *Critical Review of International Social and Political Philosophy* 636–655; Richard Bellamy, "Democracy, Compromise and the Representation Paradox: Coalition Government and Policy Integrity" (2012) 47 *Government and Opposition* 441–465; Philippe Van Parijs, "What Makes a Good Compromise?" (2012) 47 *Government and Opposition* 466–480; Helmut Schulze-Fielitz, "Der politische Kompromiß als Chance und Gefahr für die Rationalität der Gesetzgebung," in Dieter Grimm and Werner Maihofer (eds.), *Gesetzgebungstheorie und Rechtspolitik* (Springer, 1988), p. 290 ff.; Hans Kelsen, *Vom Wesen und Wert der Demokratie* (J. C. B. Mohr, 1929), ch. 6.

[91] Beerbohm, "The Problem of Clean Hands," p. 30 ff.

[92] Ibid., p. 33.

[93] Rostbøll, "Democratic Respect and Compromise," 625 ff.

[94] Ibid., 629 f.

From a legal perspective, these theories have the advantage of emphasizing the procedural dimension of compromise, and "[l]egal scholarship cannot speak with the same authority about the factual conditions or outcomes of the law as it can with respect to its procedural and organizational issues."[95] The problem is that they either prove too much or show very limited attention to institutional reality. They largely disregard that compromise in legislative matters occurs among political actors, and they locate its positive effects too far beyond the realm of public institutions. Still, both theories point in the right direction. They demonstrate that compromise is an effective means to accommodate diversity and, therefore, an effective means to operationalize that "civilizing strategy of dealing with the 'other'" that Joseph Weiler views as the "normative hallmark of European federalism."[96] In addition, they attribute to compromise an intrinsic democratic character. I will therefore start from here and seek to clarify these two intuitions, with a special focus on trilogues. To this effect, three points are especially worth making.

Mutual Concessions as the Key to a Working System of Multiple Representation

As already argued, the EU's distinctive democratic contribution consists in a radical pluralization of the forms of representation and legitimacy. This pluralization occurs through the establishment and recognition of diverse levels of governance and diverse representative institutions – multi-level constitutionalism, a mixed constitution, and multiple representation are different manifestations of the same phenomenon. In this context, compromise is the means to "construct a collective good by bringing all sections of society together."[97] Exchanging concessions has an intrinsic democratic value because it postulates the willingness "to accommodate at least some aspects of the other person's views or … to discount one's aspirations in light of conflicting demands."[98] This perspective can be better appreciated when agreeing that representative politics is not about decision-makers abstaining "from drawing on their comprehensive conceptions of the good" in order to reach decisions that

[95] Christoph Möllers, *The Three Branches: A Comparative Model of Separation of Powers* (Oxford University Press, 2015), p. 5.

[96] Weiler, "In Defence of the Status Quo," p. 15 ff. For compromise as a practice that "by nature inculcates tolerance, trust and trustworthiness, respect of others and of their moral autonomy," Ankersmit, "Representational Democracy," 43.

[97] Bellamy, "Democracy, Compromise and the Representation Paradox," 458.

[98] Rouméas, "The Procedural Value of Compromise," 388.

persuade everyone (as is the case, for instance, in deliberative paradigms of democracy).[99] Rather, representative politics is about decision-makers articulating and supporting interests that draw on those conceptions of the good, in a process capable of conferring dignity upon them. Against this premise, I believe there hardly exists a practice as effective as compromise in ensuring the success of such an exercise.[100] If a polity systematically embraces compromise, it is probably less prone to neglect minority interests and values, thereby approximating to the ideas of dignity, equality, and pluralism.

Trilogues are the democratic secret of a political system that lives off the incremental construction of compromise. Their democratic value lies in the fact that they institutionalize a mechanism to allow for such a construction and that they place that mechanism at the heart of the European legislative process. And the effects of this institutionalization are tangible. Consider, for instance, the usual compliments and praises that negotiating teams address to each other in public after the successful conclusion of trilogues. Apart from a purely ritual meaning, those compliments and praises have an important strategic value, as they foster and maintain an institutional culture of compromise. A negotiating team that criticized the outcome of trilogues would not be seen as a reliable counterpart and would threaten not only the adoption of that specific dossier but the availability of the other institutions to future negotiations. However, more important for the current reasoning is the fact that those compliments and praises often reflect the genuine conviction that a draft legislative act emerging from trilogues is a better product than the original. Forging a compromise is a process that does change the perception of a proposal on the part of those who participate in the endeavor.[101] It gives rise to a sense of co-ownership that, in turn, makes the exchange of concessions politically attractive for all those involved – a breeding ground for the rise and consolidation of a "politics of recognition," as opposed to "identity politics." What is more, the normative structures underpinning the workings of trilogues can count on

[99] Weinstock, "Compromise, Pluralism, and Deliberation," 650.

[100] Ibid., 636, whose defense of compromise starts with the following words: "if we assume that contemporary liberal democracies are marked by the fact of pluralism ... then compromise should be the goal that political deliberation sets for itself."

[101] Beerbohm, "The Problem of Clean Hands," p. 31.

widespread acceptance among political actors,[102] and this fact further testifies to their democratic nature.[103]

That said, it is not uncommon to read that trilogues are the product of a predilection of EU political actors for efficiency, and that their proliferation comes at the expense of other important principles and values.[104] To my eyes, such a critique, which is common for systems of executive federalism,[105] does not consider that whereas trilogues certainly involve sacrifices in terms of openness, they also contribute to making the EU democratic. In fact, they are crucial to maintaining a political system characterized by the accommodation of – and respect for – diverse interests and priorities. And the democratic relevance of concepts such as accommodation and respect should be apparent, especially to those who agree that the legitimacy of governmental actions crucially depends on the ability of those actions to lead to forms of political interaction aimed at understanding.[106] Instead of devaluing the loyalty and responsiveness that the representatives owe to the represented, trilogues are – I argue – the means by which the representative system of the Union operationalizes the idea of multiple representation that lies at its core. They serve to meet the challenge of pluralism, which is a defining characteristic of the society envisioned in Article 2 TEU.

The Implications of the Normative Structures of Trilogues

Since reaching compromise implies self-inflicted losses, many authors raise the question as to why political actors should be interested in such an exercise in the first place.[107] In the case of trilogues, it is worth considering that they rely on normative structures, the purpose of which

102 As for some empirical evidence of the consensus surrounding trilogues, Christilla Roederer-Rynning and Justin Greenwood, "Black Boxes and Open Secrets: Trilogues as 'Politicised Diplomacy'" (2021) 44 *West European Politics* 485–509.

103 Möllers, *The Three Branches*, p. 76, who argues that the "democratic process depends on a consensus on the procedure."

104 Päivi Leino, "The Politics of Efficient Compromise in the Adoption of EU Legal Acts," in Marise Cremona and Claire Kilpatrick (eds.), *EU Legal Acts: Challenges and Transformations* (Oxford University Press, 2018), p. 30; Achim Hurrelmann, "Democracy beyond the State: Insights from the European Union" (2014) 129 *Political Science Quarterly* 87–105 at 99 ff.

105 Hueglin and Fenna, *Comparative Federalism*, p 240.

106 Innerarity, *Democracy in Europe*, p. 110.

107 Rouméas, "The Procedural Value of Compromise," 389. This is the criticism that Manin levels against Kelsen's theory of democracy. See Bernard Manin, *The Principles of Representative Government* (Cambridge University Press, 1997), p. 213, stating that "Kelsen makes the principle of compromise the keystone of his theory of democracy, though he fails to explain what motivates protagonists to reach compromises."

is to create favorable conditions for political actors to engage in compromise-oriented activities, such as turn-taking and agenda-setting.[108] In particular, these normative structures create clear incentives for the exchange of mutual concessions, leaving almost nothing to sheer goodwill. Political actors know only too well that if they want to participate in trilogues, they must also be able to make concessions. So much so that, if a piece of legislation does not enjoy a real chance of success owing to irreconcilable internal differences and divisions (mainly in the Council), the institutions do not go to trilogues. The failure to reform the EU's migration and asylum policy – perhaps the most conspicuous failure of the past legislature – is a case in point. Highly controversial among the Member States, the legislative package lay in the Council's lap for about five years without any trilogues ever taking place, until the Commission finally decided to withdraw the draft legislation. Fortunately, the 2020 Commission proposal of a "New Pact on Migration and Asylum" met a different fate, with the institutions reaching a political agreement in December 2023.[109]

Furthermore, institutionalized mechanisms for the negotiation of compromise, such as trilogues, may cause a nonnegligible level of certainty and predictability in the political process, as compared to political systems dominated by party politics. If correctly engineered, those mechanisms may not only prod political actors into favoring inclusive over bartered compromise, but they may also contribute to improving the overall accountability of the legislative process. In terms of institutional topography, trilogues concentrate the most influential political decisions in one specific place, thereby countering an excessive dispersion of legislative power – trilogues make power more traceable.[110] However, accountability can be ensured only to the extent that the European public is made aware of who participates in trilogues. To this effect, the institutions do not need to make trilogues public, since publicity might lead

[108] Weinstock, "Compromise, Pluralism, and Deliberation," 650. See also Chapter 3, Section 3.6 and Chapter 4.

[109] European Commission, "Communication from the Commission to the European Parliament, the Council, the European Economic and Social Committee and the Committee of the Regions on a New Pact on Migration and Asylum," COM(2020) 609 final, 23 September 2020.

[110] It is also possible to argue that trilogues embody the symbolic focal point of the European legislative power, where politics and law meet. On the notion of "symbolical focal point" (*symbolische Mitte*), Armin von Bogdandy, "Parlamentarismus in Europa: eine Verfalls- oder Erfolgsgeschichte?" (2005) 130 *Archiv des öffentlichen Rechts* 445–464 at 462.

to political actors engaging in venue-shifting. Rather, and more prosaically, they should start publishing, on a regular basis, the lists of participants and the agendas ahead of a scheduled meeting. The introduction of this measure has been subject to discussions for many years. The time is now ripe to act on those discussions.

It would be possible to take this line of reasoning a little further and imagine the construction of a collegial responsibility for trilogue negotiators. Indeed, they are in a better position to influence legislation than those who intervene "downstream," at a stage when the ability to change things is limited. They should therefore bear the largest share of responsibility for the final output. As argued by Eric Beerbohm, making offers and having them incorporated into a compromise text is a responsibility-accruing activity.[111] Although the idea of a collegial responsibility might appear problematic, as a cooperative activity does not always imply an equal influence of everyone on the outcome, its design and implementation simply seek to offer a practical accountability criterion for trilogues, which work behind closed doors and enjoy significant latitude in determining the content of EU legislation. The creation of a collegial responsibility would probably fundamentally change trilogues, as it would make them full-blown joint constitutional committees. However, a serious public discussion about this topic might have the beneficial side effect of motivating negotiating teams to take their report-back obligations more seriously than they currently do, if only to explain their positions in relation to emerging deals.

The Overestimation of Political Conflict

Finally, I would like to counter a widespread strand of thought that celebrates competitive politics as the quintessence of democracy and views integration- and compromise-oriented political processes as antidemocratic. Not only are the adherents to this strand of thought remarkably silent when it comes to determining when and why compromise and integration are indeed excessive. They also present a reductive understanding of democracy, based exclusively on conflicts and majority voting. Without denying the democratic validity of these two elements,[112] I believe this understanding fails to acknowledge that democracy is as much about conflict as it is about will-formation.[113] In particular, a

[111] Beerbohm, "The Problem of Clean Hands," p. 35.

[112] Jeremy Waldron, *The Dignity of Legislation* (Cambridge University Press, 1999).

[113] LB and JHR, "Editorial: Talking about European Democracy" (2017) 13 *European Constitutional Law Review* 207–220 at 212.

democratic polity is supposed to create policies out of intricate masses of divergent interests and ideas. To this end, it relies heavily on compromise, be it in a party, within a coalition, or between branches of the legislative authority. The search for a majority is usually also the search for compromise.[114] Whereas the democratic vibrancy of a society rests on the existence and persistence of conflicts and competition among interests and ideas, the democratic nature of a representative system is crucially dependent on its ability to bring those interests and ideas into a constructive synthesis. Agonist theories of democracy are much more dependent on compromise than they like to admit.[115] Let me be a little more specific.

When political conflicts reach the institutional realm, the legislative institutions cannot limit themselves to restaging those conflicts and letting majority voting do the rest. They must also mobilize their members and generate sufficient support around specific policy proposals. Otherwise, no piece of legislation would ever see the light of day. This responsibility is the flipside of the distance between representatives and represented that, as argued, inheres in the concept of representative democracy. Representation finds part of its normative justification precisely in that distance, which puts political actors in a condition to "transcend the fragmentation of political reality."[116] It is here that the practice of compromise turns out to be not only factually indispensable but also normatively desirable. It is factually indispensable because it is a prerequisite of majority voting.[117] It is normatively desirable because it allows two different dimensions – of conflict and cooperation – to meet and coexist.[118] It presupposes the former, while allowing for the latter. More importantly still, it does not lead to the obliteration of conflict, as any compromise expresses an underlying and continuing conflict, which can form the basis for further political competition.[119] In other words, the practice of compromise feeds on the tension between competition and cooperation, "between the recognition of the legitimacy of conflict and the aspiration to consensus."[120]

[114] Schulze-Fielitz, "Der politische Kompromiß," p. 307.

[115] For a critique that effectively highlights this point, George Vasilev, "The Uneasy Alliance between Consensus and Democracy" (2015) 77 *Review of Politics* 73–98.

[116] Ankersmit, "Representational Democracy," 39.

[117] Schulze-Fielitz, "Der politische Kompromiß," p. 307 and 316.

[118] Margalit, *On Compromise and Rotten Compromises*, p. 38.

[119] Gutmann and Thompson, *The Spirit of Compromise*, p. 12. See also Chapter 4, Section 4.4.3.

[120] Rosanvallon, *Democratic Legitimacy*, p. 12.

I believe that if the practice of compromise is accompanied by a robust practice of reason-giving, it is unlikely to have de-democratizing effects. At the same time, it is worth remembering that it is precisely the existence and credible threat of majority voting that induces political actors to engage in compromise-seeking activities. And the greater the majority required, the wider the scope of those activities. In the case of the EU, the practice of compromise has an important legitimizing function as well: "Majority decisions alone would not lead to decisions that are generally accepted as legitimate in a multinational confederation like the EU. Federal systems like the European Union, which must attempt to integrate an enormous amount of societal diversity, cannot avoid incorporating strong elements of a consociational system into their arrangement of political decision-making."[121] Moreover, an overblown appreciation of political conflict cannot account for the existence of a broad group of polities whose functioning is crucially dependent on compromise-oriented decision-making processes and that, those processes notwithstanding, fare pretty well in democratic terms. These polities go under the name of "negotiation democracies" and will be part of the next section. I will highlight the strong structural closeness of the EU to those polities, hinting at a possible future direction for European comparative democracy studies.

6.5 The EU *qua* Negotiation Democracy: A Typological Clarification and a Research Agenda

The mechanisms to resolve political conflicts differ significantly from polity to polity. Depending on a variety of factors, democracy theorists have long distinguished between Westminster and consensus models of democracy. And, according to one of the most influential comparativists, the EU is remarkably close to the latter.[122] However, for reasons that I will provide shortly, I believe that the most suitable model for the EU is the germane – yet not coterminous – model of "negotiation democracy" (*Verhandlungsdemokratie*).[123] Although by no means new, this model has

[121] Stefan Oeter, "Federalism and Democracy," in Armin von Bogdandy and Jürgen Bast (eds.), *Principles of European Constitutional Law*, 2nd ed. (Hart/C. H. Beck/Nomos, 2011), p. 74.

[122] Arend Lijphart, *Patterns of Democracy: Government Forms and Performance in Thirty-Six Countries*, 2nd ed. (Yale University Press, 2012), p. 33.

[123] Gerhard Lehmbruch, "Einleitung: Von der Konkurrenzdemokratie zur Verhandlungsdemokratie – zur Entwicklung eines typologischen Konzepts," in

not thus far been applied to the study of the European Union – in fact, it has received very little attention outside German-speaking academia. Developed through a set of qualitative case studies, the model of negotiation democracy probably owes its limited success to the current predilection of comparatists for quantitative methods.[124] With this in mind, the following considerations should also be regarded as the outline of a future research agenda.

As the name suggests, "negotiation democracy" designates collective decision-making systems in which decisions do not primarily result from hierarchical-majority structures and competitive processes, but rather from structures and processes which demand that political actors negotiate and compromise, in a spirit of diffuse cooperation.[125] The model originates from a series of studies carried out by political scientist Gerhard Lehmbruch, starting from the 1960s. In fact, the model of negotiation democracy could be viewed as one of Lehmbruch's main legacies to political theory and comparative politics. In his intellectual trajectory, Lehmbruch not only studied the functioning of the Austrian and Swiss political systems, in order to show that they were both examples of what he then called "*Proporzdemokratie*" – later to be renamed "*Verhandlungsdemokratie.*"[126] But he also reconstructed the preconditions that favored the birth and consolidation of negotiation democracies, highlighting the important role of institutional traditions, political culture, federal arrangements, elites, and corporatism (another of Lehmbruch's main research interests and legacies).[127] Furthermore, he

Verhandlungsdemokratie: Beiträge zur vergleichenden Regierungslehre (Westdeutscher Verlag, 2003), p. 7 ff.

124 Arthur Benz, "Lehmbruch versus Lijphart: Comparing Democratic Governments as Multidimensional Regimes," in Volker Schneider and Burkard Eberlein (eds.), *Complex Democracy: Varieties, Crises, and Transformations* (Springer, 2015), p. 73 f.

125 Roland Czada, "Demokratietypen, institutionelle Dynamik und Interessenvermittlung: Das Konzept der Verhandlungsdemokratie," in Hans-Joachim Lauth (ed.), *Vergleichende Regierungslehre: Eine Einführung*, 3rd ed. (VS Verlag, 2010), p. 285, arguing that the concept of negotiation democracy "is based on the realistic idea, often neglected in both normative democratic theory and classical government theory, that voter and voting majorities are only one of many different resources for action in the political process" (my translation).

126 Gerhard Lehmbruch, "Proporzdemokratie: Politisches System und politische Kultur in der Schweiz und in Österreich (1967)," in *Verhandlungsdemokratie: Beiträge zur vergleichenden Regierungslehre* (Westdeutscher Verlag, 2003), p. 16 ff.

127 Gerhard Lehmbruch, "Die korporative Verhandlungsdemokratie in Westmitteleuropa (1996)," in *Verhandlungsdemokratie: Beiträge zur vergleichenden Regierungslehre* (Westdeutscher Verlag, 2003), p. 154 ff.

challenged the so-called small state hypothesis, which posited that the requisites for the thriving of negotiation democracies could be found only in small polities.

In this way, Lehmbruch laid the groundwork for including the Federal Republic of Germany in the group of negotiation democracies, alongside Switzerland and Austria. To substantiate his position, he showed that Germany has historically exhibited a lesser degree of hierarchy in its structures and processes than was usually believed – here Lehmbruch took issue with accounts of influential scholars of the German statehood, such as Otto Hintze and Max Weber.[128] He also showed that since the Peace of Westphalia – especially the establishment of confessional parity in imperial collegial institutions and the replacement of majority rule with the so-called *amicabilis compositio* in the Reichstag – "negotiating systems have become an integral part of the institutional repertoire of German politics."[129] Finally, he showed that the particular structure of German executive federalism has given birth to a thick network of bodies designed to provide space for negotiations and to facilitate cooperation at both vertical and horizontal levels.

I believe that Lehmbruch's negotiation democracy provides a more fruitful basis for comparative research and a better foundation for understanding the EU than Lijphart's "consensus democracy." To begin with, the designation "negotiation democracy" is more straightforward, as it spells out in clear terms the type of processes and structures from which the EU seeks to draw its legitimacy, namely compromise-oriented negotiations. Secondly, the model of negotiation democracy stems from a set of studies that illustrate a continuity – almost a path dependence – between negotiation systems in past polities (late Holy Roman Empire) and in contemporary democracies (Germany, Switzerland, and Austria). And this circumstance is of great value when studying the EU, as it shows that negotiation systems are compatible with robust democratic developments – all the foregoing states rank very high in the Economist Intelligence Unit's Democracy Index 2023.[130] Furthermore, negotiation democracies are a subset of mainland European (con)federal countries,

128 Ibid., p. 156 ff.

129 Gerhard Lehmbruch, "Verhandlungsdemokratie, Entscheidungsblockaden und Arenenverflechtung," in Wolfgang Merkel and Andreas Busch (eds.), *Demokratie in Ost und West: Für Klaus von Beyme* (Suhrkamp, 1999), p. 408.

130 Economist Intelligence Unit, "Democracy Index 2023: Age of Conflict," February 2024. On a total of 167 indexed countries and territories, Switzerland ranks eighth, the Netherlands ninth, Germany twelfth, and Austria eighteenth. They all belong to the

and by employing the model of negotiation democracy I am also embedding the EU in a precise historical and cultural tradition.[131]

Thirdly, Lehmbruch's model of negotiation democracy is more sensitive to the procedural aspects of democracy, as compared to Lijphart's typological distinction. It is based on three dimensions (party competition, joint decision-making, and neo-corporatism) and focuses on those institutionalized processes and structures whereby political actors manage interdimensional tensions. Lehmbruch, for instance, showed that the German political system, characterized by a tight coupling between party competition and joint decision-making, could overcome interdimensional tensions through informality.[132] I therefore believe that the model of negotiation democracy is more suitable for integrating a defining aspect of decision-making in the EU, namely the multiplicity of informal mechanisms that build bridges between the different institutions and actors that animate the European mixed constitution. The interest here is in trilogues, but the model of negotiation democracy could be used to make democratic sense of other informal mechanisms, such as the Euro Group and the Informal Council meetings.

Finally, the model of negotiation democracy places the EU next to another interesting field of research, which goes under the name of "complex democracy." Indeed, the model of negotiation democracy and the theory of complex democracy have had a long, mutually enriching bond. The theory was sketched out in 1970 as a research agenda by political scientist Fritz W. Scharpf,[133] and it has been recently revived, updated, and fleshed out by political philosopher Daniel Innerarity. On the one hand, Lehmbruch's studies on *Proporzdemokratie* influenced Scharpf's initial idea;[134] on the other hand, Scharpf's notion of "joint decision-making" made a decisive contribution to the construction of negotiation democracy as a model for comparative research.[135] The core intuition underlying the theory of complex democracy is that the major threat to democracy comes not from violence, corruption, or inefficiency, but from simplicity. The theory therefore posits that a successful renewal

group of "full democracies," which comprises twenty-four countries and accounts for 7.8 percent of the world population.

131 Lehmbruch, "Die korporative Verhandlungsdemokratie," p. 156 f.

132 Benz, "Lehmbruch versus Lijphart," p. 73.

133 Schmidt, *Demokratietheorien*, p. 245 ff.

134 Ibid., p. 248.

135 See, e.g., Fritz W. Scharpf, "Einführung: Zur Theorie von Verhandlungssystemen," in Arthur Benz, Fritz W. Scharpf, and Reinhard Zintl (eds.), *Horizontale Politikverflechtung: Zur Theorie von Verhandlungssystemen* (Campus Verlag, 1992), p. 11 ff.

of contemporary democracies warrants, in conceptual terms, overcoming the supposed incompatibility between democracy and complexity and, in operational terms, making institutional frameworks and processes more diverse and articulate rather than simpler.[136] With this in mind, a complex democracy is one capable of orchestrating all its dimensions in a balanced manner.[137] And trilogues epitomize the attempt to manage complexity through the institutionalization of negotiation channels (the exchange of mutual concessions) between the different representative dimensions of the EU.

In sum, the model of negotiation democracy and the theory of complex democracy are in a virtuous bond, and this bond might help us regard the complexity of the EU's institutional system not necessarily as an unfortunate accident but rather as a valuable resource. Whereas not all negotiation democracies are per se "kinder" and "gentler,"[138] they certainly offer conditions suitable for a democratic coexistence. They are widely believed to be better equipped to integrate different segments of society, to protect minorities, to resolve deeply rooted conflicts between social groups, and to mediate interests.[139] Be that as it may, the European Union has chosen a path towards democracy that relies on the multiplicity of representative institutions and participatory channels. This choice is meant to make the institutions more responsive to the pluralism that characterizes European society. Granted, this path may imply a less clear and efficient translation of individual preferences into collective decisions and, sometimes, a less clear attribution of responsibility. But what might appear as a weakness could actually be a strength.

As regards the relationship between democracy and the attribution of responsibility, Daniel Innerarity interestingly argued that "the more advanced a system is and the more democratic its political culture, the more indeterminate is the ultimate definition of power and the identification of responsibility."[140] Therefore, the complexity of a system can be either a symptom of structural flaws or a sign of its efforts to adjust to complex surroundings. The European Union, it seems to me, falls into the second category. If only because recent data show that 54 percent of Europeans are satisfied with the way democracy works in the EU; 70 percent are satisfied

136 Daniel Innerarity, *Una teoría de la democracia compleja: Gobernar en el siglo XXI*, 3rd ed. (Galaxia Gutenberg, 2020), p. 11 ff.

137 Ibid., p. 25.

138 Lijphart, *Patterns of Democracy*, p. 274 ff.

139 Schmidt, *Demokratietheorien*, p. 323.

140 Innerarity, *Una teoría de la democracia compleja*, p. 140.

with free and fair elections; 70 percent are satisfied with freedom of speech; 66 percent are satisfied with the level of respect for fundamental rights; 61 percent are satisfied with the possibility for individual citizens to participate in political life.[141] Furthermore, according to Eurobarometer, European citizens tend to trust the EU (47 percent) more than their national parliaments (33 percent) or governments (32 percent).[142] The European Union is not a showcase of democracy and these figures are not watertight. But they certainly warn us against writing too premature an epitaph to European democracy.[143]

[141] European Parliament, "EP Spring 2023 Survey: Democracy in Action – One Year before the European Elections – Report," EB 99.1, Spring 2023, at 62 ff.

[142] European Commission, "Standard Eurobarometer 99 – Spring 2023 – First Results: Public Opinion in the European Union," May–June 2023, at 9.

[143] J. H. H. Weiler, "The Crumbling of European Democracy," in Mark A. Graber, Sanford Levinson, and Mark Tushnet (eds.), *Constitutional Democracy in Crisis?* (Oxford University Press, 2018), p. 629.

Conclusions

This book has investigated trilogues as the democratic secret of European legislation. To this end, it has proceeded in two steps. The first step has been analytical in nature, in that it has described and reconstructed the law and practice of European legislation through a close engagement with the relevant normative sources (Chapters 1–3). The second step has been partly doctrinal and partly theoretical (Chapters 4–6). It has been doctrinal to the extent that it has sought to capture and give distinctive meaning to "informality" as both a key concept of EU law and an essential feature of trilogues. It has been theoretical to the extent that it has discussed, appraised, and legitimized trilogues in the light of theories of public authority and democracy beyond the nation-state. In this second step, the line of reasoning has also benefitted from a comparative chapter, which has thrown into sharper relief the advantages of a legislative process based on trilogues.

Without repeating the content of each chapter, I confine myself to highlighting two main takeaways of this book. The first relates to the informal nature of trilogues. In this regard, the book has shown that informality implies the creation of a space in which the penetration of legal normativity is significantly limited. This, however, does not entail that trilogues operate in a normative vacuum, as informality relies on a thick body of norms, which rest on effective political and social enforcement mechanisms. The second takeaway concerns the relationship between trilogues and democracy. Crucial for a plausible theorization of this relationship have been the two concepts of multiple representation (Article 10 TEU) and compromise. Since the democratic legitimacy of the European legislative process and trilogues hinges on the combined effects of those concepts, the book argued in Chapter 6 that European democracy studies stand to benefit greatly from a stronger engagement with the model of "negotiation democracy" and the theory of complex democracy. By offering a more articulate narrative of these takeaways, this book has aimed at enriching the public and scientific debates about the European legislative process in general, and trilogues in particular.

That said, trilogues can – and should – be improved, while preserving their informal nature. As regards the issue of transparency, I believe that the proceedings of trilogues should remain confidential. Confidentiality ensures that political actors keep regarding trilogues as an attractive venue for negotiations. However, confidentiality can be maintained only on condition that trilogues are publicly announced in advance and agendas and lists of participants are made accessible online. Another important element is to strengthen the effectiveness of the report-back obligations in public settings (for example, parliamentary committees), so that the public can gather information about the state of negotiations as appropriate. Although the pro-transparency policies of the EP might put that institution at a tactical disadvantage vis-à-vis the Council, such a disadvantage might partly be offset through regular oral reports in committee meetings that expose not only the EP's positions and priorities but also those of the Council and the Commission. This might motivate the Council to adopt a set of reforms to its modes and mechanics of decision-making with a view to making them more public, as demanded by the Treaties and other institutional actors.[1]

Following the suggestions of those Member States that are most actively engaging in creating a greater culture of transparency in the Council, I believe it would be important to ensure both "[a] more uniform recording of the main political lines of discussion within the Council and national statements" and a "systematic publication of legislative milestone documents of the Council."[2] By so doing, national parliaments would be in a better position to follow their governments at EU level and to hold them to account, thereby actively contributing to the democratic legitimacy of European legislation. The introduction of enough time between trilogues to facilitate their scrutiny function might also be beneficial for the national parliaments.

[1] European Ombudsman, "Special Report of the European Ombudsman in Strategic Inquiry OI/2/2017/TE on the Transparency of the Council Legislative Process," OI/2/2017/TE, 16 May 2018.

[2] See, e.g., "Increasing Transparency & Accountability: The Key to a Better Functioning of the EU – Joint Non Paper by Belgium, Denmark, Estonia, Finland, Ireland, Latvia, Luxembourg, Slovenia, Sweden and the Netherlands," January 2020.

The objective of future changes should in addition concern the representation of the Council in trilogue negotiations. Whereas the EP has achieved a fair representation of its political forces, with all parliamentary groups having the right to send their shadow rapporteurs,[3] the Council participates only through representatives of the incumbent Presidency. Such a situation creates two main problems. First, since the negotiations of legislative files often straddle several Presidency terms, the negotiating teams of the Council change while those of the EP and the Commission remain the same. The Parliament and the Commission therefore have a significant advantage in terms of knowledge of the file and negotiations dynamics. Secondly, the brevity of the six-month Presidency has negative effects on the overall quality of EU legislation, which often takes shape during rushed trilogues and technical meetings in the last days of each semester. To my eyes, this situation could be improved by allowing representatives from the Presidency trios a more active participation in the negotiations. Such a change would reduce the risk of agency slack on the part of the negotiating teams and provide the work of the Council with more continuity, enabling a better implementation of the long-term goals and common agendas that the trios set for themselves.

One point is worth emphasizing again. I believe that trilogues should, by and large, remain a space for the spontaneous emergence of social norms and of a powerful social framework. Against this backdrop, an important role is to be played by the European civil servants. Obliged by Article 11(1) of the Staff Regulations to carry out their duties and conduct themselves "solely with the interests of the Union in mind,"[4] they can crucially contribute not only to the transmission and consolidation of those norms and the creation of that framework but also to drawing the attention of political actors to their correct implementation, if the situation demands it.

[3] A critical point might be the limited involvement of Eurosceptic MEPs, as evidenced by Ariadna Ripoll Servent and Lara Panning, "Eurosceptics in Trilogue Settings: Interest Formation and Contestation in the European Parliament" (2019) 42 *West European Politics* 755–775.

[4] Regulation No. 31 (EEC), 11 (EAEC), laying down the Staff Regulations of Officials and the Conditions of Employment of Other Servants of the European Economic Community and the European Atomic Energy Community, OJ 1962 No. 45/135.

Bibliography

Abbott, Kenneth W., Keohane, Robert O., Moravcsik, Andrew, Slaughter, Anne-Marie and Snidal, Duncan, "The Concept of Legalization" (2000) 54 *International Organization* 401.

Alemanno, Alberto and Pech, Laurent, "Thinking Justice Outside the Docket: A Critical Assessment of the Reform of the EU's Court System" (2017) 54 *Common Market Law Review* 129.

American Political Science Association, "Toward a More Responsible Two-Party System: A Report of the Committee on Political Parties" (1950) 44 *American Political Science Review*.

Andreas, Holger, "Theoretical Terms in Science," in Edward N. Zalta (ed.), *The Stanford Encyclopedia of Philosophy* (2021).

Ankersmit, Frank R., "Representational Democracy: An Aesthetic Approach to Conflict and Compromise" (2002) 8 *Common Knowledge* 24.

Bagehot, Walter, *The English Constitution* (first published 1867, Cambridge University Press, 2004).

Bagehot, Walter, *Physics and Politics: Or Thoughts on the Application of the Principles of Natural Selection and Inheritance to Political Society* (first published 1873, Cambridge University Press, 2010).

Baldwin, Robert and Houghton, John, "Circular Arguments: The Status and Legitimacy of Administrative Rules" (1986) *Public Law* 239.

Baratta, Roberto, "Notes sur les fonctions et limites des accords interinstitutionnels," in Antonio Tizzano (ed.), *Verso i 60 anni dai Trattati di Roma: stato e prospettive dell'Unione europea* (Giappichelli, 2016).

Baratta, Roberto, "Diritto e prassi evolutiva dell'Eurogruppo" (2015) *Il Diritto dell'Unione Europea* 493.

Barber, Michael and McCarty, Nolan, "Causes and Consequences of Polarization," in Jane Mansbridge and Cathie Jo Martin (eds.), *Negotiating Agreement in Politics: Report of the Task Force on Negotiating Agreement in Politics* (American Political Science Association, 2013).

Barón Crespo, Enrique, "El desarrollo de la codecisión como procedimiento legislativo de la UE" (2012) *Cuadernos Europeos de Deusto* 19.

Bassi, Franco, "Circolari amministrative," in *Digesto delle Discipline Pubblicistiche* (Utet, 1989).
Bauman, Zigmunt, *Europe: An Unfinished Adventure* (Polity Press, 2004).
Baume, Sandrine and Novak, Stéphanie, "Compromise and Publicity in Democracy: An Ambiguous Relationship," in Sandrine Baume and Stéphanie Novak (eds.), *Compromises in Democracy* (Palgrave Macmillan, 2020).
Baume, Sandrine and Papadopoulos, Yannis, "Against Compromise in Democracy? A Plea for a Fine-Grained Assessment" (2022) 29 *Constellations* 1.
Beerbohm, Eric, "The Problem of Clean Hands: Negotiated Compromise in Lawmaking," in Jack Knight (ed.), *Compromise* (New York University Press, 2018).
Bellamy, Richard, "Democracy, Compromise and the Representation Paradox: Coalition Government and Policy Integrity" (2012) 47 *Government and Opposition* 441.
Bellamy, Richard, Kornprobst, Markus and Reh, Christine, "Introduction: Meeting in the Middle" (2012) 47 *Government and Opposition* 275.
Benz, Arthur, "Lehmbruch Versus Lijphart: Comparing Democratic Governments as Multidimensional Regimes," in Volker Schneider and Burkard Eberlein (eds.), *Complex Democracy: Varieties, Crises, and Transformations* (Springer, 2015).
Berti, Giorgio, "Stato di diritto informale" (1992) 42 *Rivista trimestrale di diritto pubblico* 3.
Bicchieri, Cristina, Muldoon, Ryan and Sontuoso, Alessandro, "Social Norms," in Edward N. Zalta (ed.), *The Stanford Encyclopedia of Philosophy* (2011).
Bickerton, Christopher J., *European Integration: From Nation-States to Member States* (Oxford University Press, 2012).
Bieber, Roland, "Rechtswirkung und gerichtliche Kontrolle des EG-Haushalts. Zugleich Anmerkung zur Entscheidung des EuGH vom 3. Juli 1986, Rs. 34/86 (Rat gegen Europäisches Parlament)" (1986) 101 *Deutsches Verwaltungsblatt* 961.
Bieber, Roland, "Das Gesetzgebungsverfahren der Zusammenarbeit gemäß Art. 149 EWGV" (1989) 22 *Neue Juristische Wochenschrift* 1395.
Bieber, Roland, "Artikel 232 (ex-Artikel 199 EGV) [Geschäftsordnung; Verhandlungsniederschriften]," in Hans von der Groeben, Jürgen Schwarze and Armin Hatje (eds.), *Europäisches Unionsrecht*, 7th ed. (Nomos, 2015).
Blom-Hansen, Jens and Senninger, Roman, "The Commission in EU Policy Preparation" (2021) 59 *Journal of Common Market Studies* 625.
Bobbio, Norberto, "Governo misto," in Norberto Bobbio, Nicola Matteucci and Gianfranco Pasquino (eds.), *Dizionario di politica*, 2nd ed. (Utet, 1983).
Böckenförde, Ernst-Wolfgang, "Sozialer Bundesstaat und parlamentarische Demokratie: Zum Verhältnis von Parlamentarismus und Föderalismus unter den Bedingungen des Sozialstaats," in *Staat, Nation, Europa: Studien zur Staatslehre, Verfassungstheorie und Rechtsphilosophie* (Suhrkamp, 1999).
Boyron, Sophie, "Maastricht and the Codecision Procedure: A Success Story" (1996) 45 *International and Comparative Law Quarterly* 293.
Bradley, Kieran St. Clair, "Legal Developments in the European Parliament" (1989) 9 *Yearbook of European Law* 235.

Brandsma, Gijs Jan, "Transparency of EU Informal Trilogues through Public Feedback in the European Parliament: Promise Unfulfilled" (2019) 26 *Journal of European Public Policy* 1464.

Brandsma, Gijs Jan, Dionigi, Maja K., Greenwood, Justin and Roederer-Rynning, Christilla, "Trilogues in Council: Disrupting the Diplomatic Culture?" (2021) 28 *Journal of European Public Policy* 10.

Brandsma, Gijs Jan and Meijer, Albert, "Transparency and Efficiency of Multi-actor Decision-Making Processes: An Empirical Analysis of 244 Decisions in the European Union" (2022) 88 *International Review of Administrative Sciences* 626.

Brunkhorst, Hauke, "Democracy under Siege: The Decay of Constitutionalization and the Crisis of Public Law and Public Opinion," in Poul F. Kjaer and Niklas Olsen (eds.), *Critical Theories of Crisis in Europe: From Weimar to the Euro* (Rowman & Littlefield International, 2016).

Bultena, Anita, "Negotiations in the Ordinary Legislative Procedure: The Perspective of the European Parliament," in Flora A. N. J. Goudappel and Ernst M. H. Hirsch Ballin (eds.), *Democracy and Rule of Law in the European Union: Essays in Honour of Jaap W. de Zwaan* (Asser Press/Springer, 2016).

Burchardt, Dana and Putzer, Max, "Kompetenzgrenzen im deutschen und europäischen Vermittlungsverfahren" (2011) 26 *Zeitschrift für Gesetzgebung* 68.

Bürgin, Alexander, "Intra- and Inter-Institutional Leadership of the European Commission President: An Assessment of Juncker's Organizational Reforms" (2018) 56 *Journal of Common Market Studies* 837.

Calliess, Christian, *Die neue Europäische Union nach dem Vertrag von Lissabon* (Mohr Siebeck, 2010).

Canetti, Elias, *Crowds and Power* (Continuum, 1981).

Carrau, Javier Guillem, "Los trílogos en el procedimiento legislativo de la UE: *el informal law making* en la nueva agenda legislativa europea" (2014) 92–93 *Revista de las Cortes Generales* 45.

Cavalli, Alessandro and Martinelli, Alberto, *La società europea* (il Mulino, 2015).

Chambers, Simone, "Behind Closed Doors: Publicity, Secrecy and the Quality of Deliberation" (2004) 12 *Journal of Political Philosophy* 389.

Chamon, Merijn, "Upholding the 'Community Method': Limits to the Commission's Power to Withdraw Legislative Proposals – *Council v Commission* (C-409/13)" (2015) 40 *European Law Review* 895.

Charlemagne, "Changing Parliamentary Perspectives," *The Economist*, 18 May 2019.

Charlemagne, "Giving Faces to 'Faceless Eurocrats,'" *The Economist*, 21 May 2022.

Chisholm, Donald, *Coordination without Hierarchy: Informal Structures in Multiorganizational Systems* (University of California Press, 1989).

Clapp, James E., Thornburg, Elizabeth G., Galanter, Marc and Shapiro, Fred R., *Lawtalk: The Unknown Stories behind Familiar Legal Expressions* (Yale University Press, 2011).

Cooper, Harry, "Where European Democracy Goes to Die," *Politico*, 12 July 2016.

Corbett, Richard, Jacobs, Francis and Neville, Darren, *The European Parliament*, 9th ed. (John Harper, 2016).

Cornewall Lewis, George, *A Dialogue on the Best Form of Government* (Parker Son and Bourn, 1863).

Costa, Olivier, Dehousse, Renaud and Trakalová, Aneta, "Codecision and 'Early Agreements': An Improvement or a Subversion of the Legislative Procedure?" (2011) *Notre Europe*.

Costello, Rory and Thomson, Robert, "The Distribution of Power among EU Institutions: Who Wins under Codecision and Why?" (2013) 20 *Journal of European Public Policy* 1025.

Craig, Paul, "Democracy and Rule-Making within the EC: An Empirical and Normative Assessment" (1997) 3 *European Law Journal* 105.

Craig, Paul, "The Eurogroup, Power and Accountability" (2017) 23 *European Law Journal* 234.

Crowe, Richard, "The European Budgetary Galaxy" (2017) 13 *European Constitutional Law Review* 428.

Curtin, Deirdre, "The Constitutional Structure of the Union: A Europe of Bits and Pieces" (1993) 30 *Common Market Law Review* 17.

Curtin, Deirdre and Leino, Päivi, "In Search of Transparency for EU Law-Making: Trilogues on the Cusp of Dawn" (2017) 54 *Common Market Law Review* 1673.

Czada, Roland, "Demokratietypen, institutionelle Dynamik und Interessenvermittlung: Das Konzept der Verhandlungsdemokratie," in Hans-Joachim Lauth (ed.), *Vergleichende Regierungslehre: Eine Einführung*, 3rd ed. (VS Verlag, 2010).

Dahl, Robert A., "Can International Organizations Be Democratic? A Skeptic's View," in Ian Shapiro and Casiano Hacker-Cordón (eds.), *Democracy's Edges* (Cambridge University Press, 1999).

Dani, Marco, "Rehabilitating Social Conflicts in European Public Law" (2012) 18 *European Law Journal* 621.

Dankert, Pieter, "The Joint Declaration by the Community Institutions of 30 June 1982 on the Community Budgetary Procedure" (1983) 20 *Common Market Law Review* 701.

Dann, Philipp, "The Political Institutions," in Armin von Bogdandy and Jürgen Bast (eds.), *Principles of European Constitutional Law*, 2nd ed. (Hart/C. H. Beck/Nomos, 2011).

Dann, Philipp, "The Council," in Robert Schütze and Takis Tridimas (eds.), *Oxford Principles of European Union Law: The European Union Legal Order* (Oxford University Press, 2018).

David, René, "Sources of Law," in *International Encyclopedia of Comparative Law* (J. C. B. Mohr (Paul Siebeck)-Martinus Nijhoff Publishers, 1984).

De Ruiter, Rik and Neuhold, Christine, "Why Is Fast Track the Way to Go? Justifications for Early Agreement in the Co-decision Procedure and Their Effects" (2012) 18 *European Law Journal* 536.

De Ruiter, Rik and Neuhold, Christine, "Subsidiarity Watchdogs and the Kennel of Trilogues: When Do They Bark? The Role of National Parliaments in Trilogue Negotiations" (2021) 28 *Journal of European Public Policy* 93.

De Ruyt, Jean, *L'Acte unique européen: commentaire* (Editions de l'Université de Bruxelles, 1987).

Decker, Frank, "Das Scheitern des Spitzenkandidatensystems und andere populäre Irrtümer über die Demokratisierung der Europäischen Union" (2019) 50 *Zeitschrift für Parlamentsfragen* 870.

Dehousse, Renaud, "Constitutional Reform in the European Community: Are There Alternatives to the Majoritarian Avenue?" (1995) 18 *West European Politics* 118.

Dell, Edmund, "The Report of the Three Wise Men" (1993) 2 *Contemporary European History* 35.

Delreux, Tom and Laloux, Thomas, "Concluding Early Agreements in the EU: A Double Principal–Agent Analysis of Trilogue Negotiations" (2018) 56 *Journal of Common Market Studies* 300.

Desilver, Drew, "The Polarization in Today's Congress Has Roots That Go Back Decades," *Pew Research Center*, 10 March 2022.

Dewost, Jean-Louis and Lepoivre, Marc, "La déclaration commune du Parlement européen, du Conseil et de la Commission relative à différentes mesures visant à assurer un meilleur déroulement de la procédure budgétaire, signée le 30 juin 1982" (1982) 25 *Revue du Marché Commun* 514.

Duverger, Maurice, *Introduction à la politique* (Gallimard, 1964).

Ehlermann, Claus-Dieter, "Die Einheitliche Europäische Akte: Die Reform der Organe" (1986) 9 *Integration* 101.

Elazar, Daniel J., "Federalism and Consociational Regimes" (1985) 15 *Publius: The Journal of Federalism* 17.

Elazar, Daniel J., *Exploring Federalism* (University of Alabama Press, 1987).

Farina, Cynthia R., "Congressional Polarization: Terminal Constitutional Dysfunction?" (2015) 115 *Columbia Law Review* 1689.

Farrel, Henry and Héritier, Adrienne, "The Invisible Transformation of Codecision: Problems of Democratic Legitimacy" (2003) *Sieps*.

Fehling, Michael, "Informelles Verwaltungshandeln," in Wolfgang Hoffmann-Riem, Eberhard Schmidt-Aßmann and Andreas Voßkuhle (eds.), *Grundlagen des Verwaltungsrechts*, 2nd ed. (C. H. Beck, 2012).

Forman, John, "The Conciliation Procedure" (1979) 16 *Common Market Law Review* 77.

Foster, Nigel G., "The New Conciliation Committee under Article 189b EC" (1994) 19 *European Law Review* 185.

Frankenberg, Günter, "Critical Comparisons: Re-thinking Comparative Law" (1985) 26 *Harvard International Law Journal* 411.

Fromage, Diane, "How to Ensure That National Parliaments (Truly) 'Contribute Actively to the Good Functioning of (Tomorrow's) EU'?" (2020) 26 *European Law Journal* 472.

Frowein, Jochen Abr., "Die rechtliche Bedeutung des Verfassungsprinzips der parlamentarischen Demokratie für den europäischen Integrationsprozeß" (1983) 18 *Europarecht* 301.

Frowein, Jochen Abr., "Erinnerungen an die 'Groupe Vedel,'" in Ulrich Becker, Armin Hatje, Michael Potacs, and Nina Wunderlich (eds.), *Verfassung und Verwaltung in Europa: Festschrift für Jürgen Schwarze zum 70. Geburtstag* (Nomos, 2014).

Fumurescu, Alin, *Compromise: A Political and Philosophical History* (Cambridge University Press, 2013).

Gallie, W. B., "Essentially Contested Concepts" (1955) 56 *Proceedings of the Aristotelian Society* 167.

Galligan, Denis J., *Law in Modern Society* (Oxford University Press, 2007).
Garman, Julie and Hilditch, Louise, "Behind the Scenes: An Examination of the Importance of the Informal Processes at Work in Conciliation" (1998) 5 *Journal of European Public Policy* 271.
Giannini, Massimo Severo, "Circolare," in *Enciclopedia del Diritto* (Giuffrè, 1960).
Giersdorf, Fabian, *Der informelle Trilog: Das Schattengesetzgebungsverfahren der Europäischen Union* (Duncker & Humblot, 2019).
Ginsburg, Tom and Stephanopoulos, Nicholas, "The Concepts of Law" (2017) 84 *University of Chicago Law Review* 147.
Gómez-Leal Pérez, María, "El procedimiento legislativo ordinario en la práctica: los acuerdos en primera lectura" (2015) *Cuadernos Europeos de Deusto* 101.
Greenwald Smith, Rachel, *On Compromise: Art, Politics, and the Fate of an American Ideal* (Graywolf Press, 2021).
Greenwood, Justin and Roederer-Rynning, Christilla, "Taming Trilogues: The EU's Law-Making Process in a Comparative Perspective," in Olivier Costa (ed.), *The European Parliament in Times of EU Crisis: Dynamics and Transformations* (Palgrave Macmillan, 2019).
Grunden, Timo, "Informelle Machtarchitekturen im parlamentarischen Regierungssystem – Zur Analyse der Entstehung, Funktion und Veränderung informeller Institutionen," in Stephan Bröchler and Timo Grunden (eds.), *Informelle Politik: Konzepte, Akteure und Prozesse* (Springer, 2014).
Guiot, François-Vivien, "La 'Commission politique', une 'commission impossible'? Construction d'un paradoxe" (2021) 57 *Cahiers de droit européen* 419.
Gutmann, Amy and Thompson, Dennis, *The Spirit of Compromise: Why Governing Demands It and Campaigning Undermines It* (Princeton University Press, 2012).
Habermas, Jürgen, "The Postnational Constellation and the Future of Democracy," in *The Postnational Constellation: Political Essays* (MIT Press, 2001).
Habermas, Jürgen, *Zur Verfassung Europas: Ein Essay*, 5th ed. (Suhrkamp, 2014).
Häge, Frank M. and Naurin, Daniel, "The Effect of Codecision on Council Decision-Making: Informalization, Politicization and Power" (2013) 20 *Journal of European Public Policy* 953.
Han, Byung-Chul, *The Transparency Society* (Stanford University Press, 2015).
Hanke, Christian, "Informale Regeln als Substrat des parlamentarischen Verhandlungssystems. Zur Begründung einer zentralen Kategorie der Parlamentarismusforschung" (1994) 25 *Zeitschrift für Parlamentsfragen* 410.
Hartmann, Martin, *Vertrauen: Die unsichtbare Macht* (S. Fischer, 2020).
Hatch, Marie Jo, *Organization Theory: Modern, Symbolic, and Postmodern Perspectives*, 3rd ed. (Oxford University Press, 2013).
Hatje, Armin and Schwarze, Jürgen, "Der Zusammenhalt der Europäischen Union" (2019) 54 *Europarecht* 153.
Hayes-Renshaw, Fiona and Wallace, Helen, *The Council of Ministers*, 2nd ed. (Palgrave Macmillan, 2006).
Heller, Hermann, *Staatslehre* (A. W. Sijthoff's Uitgeversmij N.V., 1934).
Heller, Hermann, "The Nature and Structure of the State" (1996) 18 *Cardozo Law Review* 1139.

Hibbing, John R. and Theiss-Morse, Elizabeth, *Congress as Public Enemy: Public Attitudes toward American Political Institutions* (Cambridge University Press, 1995).

Hillebrandt, Maarten and Leino-Sandberg, Päivi, "Administrative and Judicial Oversight of Trilogues" (2021) 28 *Journal of European Public Policy* 53.

Horst, Patrick, "Das Management der dritten Großen Koalition in Deutschland 2013 bis 2015: unangefochtene Dominanz der drei Parteivorsitzenden" (2015) 46 *Zeitschrift für Parlamentsfragen* 852.

Huber, Katrin and Shackleton, Michael, "Codecision: A Practitioner's View from Inside the Parliament" (2013) 20 *Journal of European Public Policy* 1040.

Hueglin, Thomas O. and Fenna, Alan, *Comparative Federalism: A Systematic Inquiry*, 2nd ed. (University of Toronto Press, 2015).

Hurrelmann, Achim, "Democracy beyond the State: Insights from the European Union" (2014) 129 *Political Science Quarterly* 87.

Innerarity, Daniel, *Democracy in Europe: A Political Philosophy of the EU* (Palgrave Macmillan, 2018).

Innerarity, Daniel, *Una teoría de la democracia compleja: Gobernar en el siglo XXI*, 3rd ed. (Galaxia Gutenberg, 2020).

Isensee, Josef, "Verfassungsrecht als 'politisches Recht,'" in Josef Isensee and Paul Kirchhof (eds.), *Handbuch des Staatsrechts*, 3rd ed. (C. F. Müller, 2014).

Jacobs, Sir Francis, "Comparative Law and European Union Law," in Mathias Reimann and Reinhard Zimmermann (eds.), *The Oxford Handbook of Comparative Law*, 2nd ed. (Oxford University Press, 2019).

Jacqué, Jean-Paul, "La pratique des institutions communautaires et le développement de la structure institutionnelle communautaire," in Roland Bieber and Georg Ress (eds.), *Die Dynamik des Europäischen Gemeinschaftsrechts / The Dynamics of EC-Law: Die Auslegung des Europäischen Gemeinschaftsrechts im Lichte nachfolgender Praxis der Mitgliedstaaten und der EG-Organe* (Nomos, 1987).

Jacqué, Jean-Paul, "Une vision réaliste de la procédure de codécision," in Aline De Walsche and Laure Levi (eds.), *Mélanges en hommage à Georges Vandersanden: promenades au sein du droit européen* (Bruylant, 2008).

Jacqué, Jean-Paul, "Lost in Transition: The European Commission between Intergovernmentalism and Integration," in Dominique Ritleng (ed.), *Independence and Legitimacy in the Institutional System of the European Union* (Oxford University Press, 2016).

JHR and LB, "Editorial: *Spitzenkandidaten* and the European Union's System of Government" (2019) 15 *European Constitutional Law Review* 609.

Kaiser, Robert G., *Act of Congress: How America's Essential Institution Works, and How It Doesn't* (Vintage, 2014).

Kardasheva, Raya, "Package Deals in EU Legislative Politics" (2013) 57 *American Journal of Political Science* 858.

Keller, Hans Gustav, *Das "Junge Europa": 1834–1836* (Max Niehans Verlag, 1938).

Kelsen, Hans, *Vom Wesen und Wert der Demokratie* (J. C. B. Mohr (Paul Siebeck), 1929).

Kersten, Jens, "Art. 77 GG," in Theodor Maunz and Günter Dürig (eds.), *Grundgesetz: Kommentar* (C. H. Beck, 2012).

Kirchhof, Paul, "Mittel staatlichen Handelns," in Josef Isensee and Paul Kirchhof (eds.), *Handbuch des Staatsrechts*, 3rd ed. (C. F. Müller, 2007).

Klabbers, Jan, "Informal Instruments before the European Court of Justice" (1994) 31 *Common Market Law Review* 997.

Klabbers, Jan, "Institutional Ambivalence by Design: Soft Organizations in International Law" (2001) 70 *Nordic Journal of International Law* 403.

Kluth, Winfried, "Der Vermittlungsausschuß," in Josef Isensee and Paul Kirchhof (eds.), *Handbuch des Staatsrechts*, 3rd ed. (C. F. Müller, 2005).

Kommers, Donald P. and Miller, Russell A., *The Constitutional Jurisprudence of the Federal Republic of Germany*, 3rd ed. (Duke University Press, 2012).

Krajewski, Markus and Rösslein, Ulrich, "Art. 15 AEUV [Grundsatz der Offenheit]," in Eberhard Grabitz, Meinhard Hilf and Martin Nettesheim (eds.), *Das Recht der Europäischen Union* (C. H. Beck, 2013).

Kreppel, Amie, "Typologies and Classifications," in Shane Martin, Thomas Saalfeld and Kaare W. Strøm (eds.), *The Oxford Handbook of Legislative Studies* (Oxford University Press, 2014).

Krick, Eva, "The Myth of Effective Veto Power under the Rule of Consensus. Dynamics and Democratic Legitimacy of Collective Decision-Making by 'Tacit Consent'" (2017) *Négociations* 109.

LB and JHR, "Editorial: Talking about European Democracy" (2017) 13 *European Constitutional Law Review* 207.

Lee, Frances E., "Bicameral Representation," in George C. Edwards III, Frances E. Lee and Eric Schickler (eds.), *The Oxford Handbook of the American Congress* (Oxford University Press, 2011).

Lehmbruch, Gerhard, "Verhandlungsdemokratie, Entscheidungsblockaden und Arenenverflechtung," in Wolfgang Merkel and Andreas Busch (eds.), *Demokratie in Ost und West: Für Klaus von Beyme* (Suhrkamp, 1999).

Lehmbruch, Gerhard, "Einleitung: Von der Konkurrenzdemokratie zur Verhandlungsdemokratie – zur Entwicklung eines typologischen Konzepts," in *Verhandlungsdemokratie: Beiträge zur vergleichenden Regierungslehre* (Westdeutscher Verlag, 2003).

Lehmbruch, Gerhard, "Die korporative Verhandlungsdemokratie in Westmitteleuropa," in *Verhandlungsdemokratie: Beiträge zur vergleichenden Regierungslehre* (Westdeutscher Verlag, 2003).

Lehmbruch, Gerhard, "Proporzdemokratie: Politisches System und politische Kultur in der Schweiz und in Österreich," in *Verhandlungsdemokratie: Beiträge zur vergleichenden Regierungslehre* (Westdeutscher Verlag, 2003).

Lehnert, Matthias, "Der Einfluss der Parteipolitik auf das Vermittlungsverfahren: Eine Analyse der Einigungsvorschläge (1949–2005)," in Helmar Schöne and Julia von Blumenthal (eds.), *Parlamentarismusforschung in Deutschland: Ergebnisse und Perspektiven 40 Jahre nach Erscheinen von Gerhard Loewenbergs Standardwerk zum Deutschen Bundestag* (Nomos, 2009).

Leino, Päivi, "The Politics of Efficient Compromise in the Adoption of EU Legal Acts," in Marise Cremona and Claire Kilpatrick (eds.), *EU Legal Acts: Challenges and Transformations* (Oxford University Press, 2018).

Lenaerts, Koen, "The Principle of Democracy in the Case Law of the European Court of Justice" (2013) 62 *International and Comparative Law Quarterly* 271.

Lenaerts, Koen, Maselis, Ignace and Gutman, Kathleen, *EU Procedural Law* (Oxford University Press, 2014).

Levitsky, Steven and Ziblatt, Daniel, *How Democracies Die* (Viking, 2018).

Lewis, Jeffrey, "Council of Ministers and European Council," in Erik Jones, Anand Menon and Stephen Weatherill (eds.), *The Oxford Handbook of the European Union* (Oxford University Press, 2012).

Lijphart, Arend, *Patterns of Democracy: Government Forms and Performance in Thirty-Six Countries*, 2nd ed. (Yale University Press, 2012).

Lo Bianco, Santino, "Informal Decision-Making in the EU: Assessing Trialogues in the Light of Deliberative Democracy," in Jaap de Zwaan, Martijn Lak, Abiola Makinwa and Piet Willems (eds.), *Governance and Security Issues of the European Union: Challenges Ahead* (Asser Press/Springer, 2016).

Longley, Lawrence D. and Oleszek, Walter J., *Bicameral Politics: Conference Committees in Congress* (Yale University Press, 1989).

Lord, Christopher, "The Democratic Legitimacy of Codecision" (2013) 20 *Journal of European Public Policy* 1056.

Lord Plumb, "Building a Democratic Community: The Role of the European Parliament" (1989) 45 *The World Today* 112.

Loughlin, Martin, "The Silences of Constitutions" (2018) 16 *International Journal of Constitutional Law* 922.

Luhmann, Niklas, *Legitimation durch Verfahren*, 9th ed. (Suhrkamp, 2013).

Luhmann, Niklas, *Soziale Systeme: Grundriß einer allgemeinen Theorie*, 16th ed. (Suhrkamp, 2015).

Lupo, Nicola, "The Commission's Power to Withdraw Legislative Proposals and its 'Parliamentarisation', between Technical and Political Grounds" (2018) 14 *European Constitutional Law Review* 311.

Lynch, Suzanne and Gridneff, Ilya, "Europe's American President: The Paradox of Ursula von der Leyen," *Politico*, 6 October 2022.

MacCormick, Neil, *Questioning Sovereignty: Law, State, and Nation in the European Commonwealth* (Oxford University Press, 1999).

MacCormick, Neil, *Institutions of Law: An Essay in Legal Theory* (Oxford University Press, 2007).

Mair, Peter and Thomassen, Jacques, "Political Representation and Government in the European Union" (2010) 17 *Journal of European Public Policy* 20.

Malhotra, Deepak, *Negotiating the Impossible* (Berrett-Koehler Publishers, 2016).

Mancini, G. F., "Democracy and the European Court of Justice," in *Democracy and Constitutionalism in the European Union: Collected Essays* (Hart, 2000).

Manin, Bernard, *The Principles of Representative Government* (Cambridge University Press, 1997).

Mann, Thomas, "Art. 77 [Verfahren bei Gesetzesbeschlüssen]," in Michael Sachs (ed.), *Grundgesetz: Kommentar*, 8th ed. (C. H. Beck, 2018).

Mann, Thomas E. and Ornstein, Norman J., *The Broken Branch: How Congress Is Failing America and How to Get It Back on Track* (Oxford University Press, 2006).

Manow, Philip, *In the King's Shadow: The Political Anatomy of Democratic Representation* (Polity Press, 2010).

Manow, Philip, *(Ent)demokratisierung der Demokratie: Ein Essay* (Suhrkamp, 2020).

Manzella, Andrea, "Legislation and Legislative Procedures between the Parliament, the Council and the Commission," in Giuliano Amato, Enzo Moavero-Milanesi, Gianfranco Paquino, and Lucrezia Reichlin (eds.), *The History of the European Union: Constructing Utopia* (Bloomsbury, 2019).

March, James G. and Olsen, Johan P., "Elaborating the 'New Institutionalism,'" in Sarah A. Binder, R. A. W. Rhodes and Bert A. Rockman (eds.), *The Oxford Handbook of Political Institutions* (Oxford University Press, 2008).

Margalit, Avishai, *On Compromise and Rotten Compromises* (Princeton University Press, 2010).

Marquand, David, *Parliament for Europe* (Jonathan Cape, 1979).

Martin, Cathie Jo, "Negotiating Political Agreements," in Jane Mansbridge and Cathie Jo Martin (eds.), *Negotiating Agreement in Politics: Report of the Task Force on Negotiating Agreement in Politics* (American Political Science Association, 2013).

Martin, Cathie Jo, "Conditions for Successful Negotiation: Lessons from Europe," in Jane Mansbridge and Cathie Jo Martin (eds.), *Negotiating Agreement in Politics: Report of the Task Force on Negotiating Agreement in Politics* (American Political Science Association, 2013).

Martines, Francesca, "I triloghi alla luce dei principi di democrazia, equilibrio istituzionale, efficienza e trasparenza" (2018) *Diritto pubblico comparato ed europeo* 311.

Martínez Iglesias, María José, "The Accidental Democracy: A European Model," in Sacha Garben, Inge Govaere and Paul Nemitz (eds.), *Critical Reflections on Constitutional Democracy in the European Union* (Hart, 2019).

Martínez Iglesias, María José, "Better Law-Making and the Interinstitutional (Dis)agreements: Some Comments" (2020) 26 *European Law Journal* 108.

Maurer, Andreas, "(Co-)Governing after Maastricht: The European Parliament's Institutional Performance 1994–1999: Lessons for the Implementation of the Treaty of Amsterdam," POLI 104/rev., October 1999.

McCown, Ada C., *The Congressional Conference Committee* (Columbia University Press, 1927).

Mead, Rebecca, "In Brexit Britain, the Parliament Choir Is in Purgatory: In a Thirteenth-Century Chapel Deep inside Westminster, a Choral Society Crosses Party Lines," *The New Yorker*, 4 November 2019.

"Mechanisms of Secrecy" (2008) 121 *Harvard Law Review* 1556.

Meinel, Florian, *Selbstorganisation des parlamentarischen Regierungssystems: Vergleichende Studien zu einem Verfassungsproblem der Bundesrepublik Deutschland* (Mohr Siebeck, 2019).

Meinel, Florian, *Vertrauensfrage: Zur Krise des heutigen Parlamentarismus* (C. H. Beck, 2019).

Mendes, Joana, "Participation and the Role of Law after Lisbon: A Legal View on Article 11 TEU" (2011) 48 *Common Market Law Review* 1849.

Menkel-Meadow, Carrie, *Negotiation: A Very Short Introduction* (Oxford University Press, 2022).

Merati-Kashani, Jasmin, "Vermitteln im Vermittlungsausschuss – Mediation in der Bundesgesetzgebung?" (2011) 30 *Neue Zeitschrift für Verwaltungsrecht – Extra* 1.

Michels, Robert, *Zur Soziologie des Parteiwesens in der modernen Demokratie*, 2nd ed. (Alfred Kröner Verlag, 1925).

Mill, John Stuart, "Considerations on Representative Government," in *On Liberty, Utilitarianism, and Other Essays* (first published 1861, Oxford University Press, 2015).

Miller, Bernhard, *Der Koalitionsausschuss: Existenz, Einsatz und Effekte einer informellen Arena des Koalitionsmanagements* (Nomos, 2011).

Misztal, Barbara A., *Informality: Social Theory and Contemporary Practice* (Routledge, 2000).

Möllers, Christoph, "European Governance: Meaning and Value of a Concept" (2006) 43 *Common Market Law Review* 313.

Möllers, Christoph, "Vermittlungsausschuss und Vermittlungsverfahren" (2010) 32 *JURA – Juristische Ausbildung* 401.

Möllers, Christoph, *Die Möglichkeit der Normen: Über eine Praxis jenseits von Moralität und Kausalität* (Suhrkamp, 2015).

Möllers, Christoph, *The Three Branches: A Comparative Model of Separation of Powers* (Oxford University Press, 2015).

Morlok, Martin, "Informalisierung und Entparlamentarisierung politischer Entscheidungen als Gefährdungen der Verfassung?" (2003) 62 *Veröffentlichungen der Vereinigung der Deutschen Staatsrechtslehrer* 37.

Mourlon-Druol, Emmanuel, "How Informality Can Play Out in European Integration," in Lennaert van Heumen and Mechthild Roos (eds.), *The Informal Construction of Europe* (Routledge, 2019).

Müller-Terpitz, Ralf, "Art. 50 GG," in Theodor Maunz and Günter Dürig (eds.), *Grundgesetz: Kommentar* (C. H. Beck 2017).

Nettesheim, Martin, "Art. 10 EUV [Demokratische Grundsätze]," in Eberhard Grabitz, Meinhard Hilf and Martin Nettesheim (eds.), *Das Recht der Europäischen Union* (C. H. Beck, 2015).

Nettesheim, Martin, "Art. 13 EUV [Organe der Union]," in Eberhard Grabitz, Meinhard Hilf and Martin Nettesheim (eds.), *Das Recht der Europäischen Union* (C. H. Beck, 2015).

Neunreither, Karlheinz, "Governance without Opposition: The Case of the European Union" (1998) 33 *Government and Opposition* 419.

Neustadt, Richard E., *Presidential Power and the Modern Presidents: The Politics of Leadership from Roosevelt to Reagan* (The Free Press, 1991).

Neyer, Jürgen, *The Justification of Europe: A Political Theory of Supranational Integration* (Oxford University Press, 2012).

Nicoll, William, "EEC Budgetary Strains and Constraints" (1987) 64 *International Affairs* 27.

Ninatti, Stefania, "How Do Our Judges Conceive of Democracy? The Democratic Nature of the Community Decision-Making Process under Scrutiny of the European Court of Justice" (2003) *Jean Monnet Working Paper*.

Nocilla, Damiano, "Autonomia, coordinamento e leale collaborazione tra i due rami di un parlamento bicamerale" (1998) 48 *Rivista trimestrale di diritto pubblico* 935.

Nohlen, Dieter, "Parlamentarisierung," in Dieter Nohlen and Rainer-Olaf Schultze (eds.), *Lexikon der Politikwissenschaft: Theorien, Methoden, Begriffe* (C. H. Beck, 2002).

Norton, Philip, "Power behind the Scenes: The Importance of Informal Space in Legislatures" (2019) 72 *Parliamentary Affairs* 245.

Novak, Stéphanie, "The Silence of Ministers: Consensus and Blame Avoidance in the Council of the European Union" (2013) 51 *Journal of Common Market Studies* 1091.

Novak, Stéphanie, Rozenberg, Olivier and Bendjaballah, Selma, "Enduring Consensus: Why the EU Legislative Process Stays the Same" (2021) 43 *Journal of European Integration* 475.

Nugent, Neill and Rhinard, Mark, *The European Commission*, 2nd ed. (Palgrave Macmillan, 2015).

Nugent, Neill and Rhinard, Mark, "Is the European Commission *Really* in Decline?" (2016) 54 *Journal of Common Market Studies* 1199.

Nugent, Neill and Rhinard, Mark, "The 'Political' Roles of the European Commission" (2019) 41 *Journal of European Integration* 203.

O'Dwyer, Una, "La dynamique historique des relations interinstitutionnelles. Le point de vue d'un praticien sur l'évolution de la procédure de codécision" (2010) *Revue du Droit de l'Union Européenne* 487.

Oeter, Stefan, "Federalism and Democracy," in Armin von Bogdandy and Jürgen Bast (eds.), *Principles of European Constitutional Law*, 2nd ed. (Hart/C. H. Beck/Nomos, 2011).

Oleszek, Walter J., Oleszek, Mark J., Rybicki, Elizabeth and Heniff Jr., Bill, *Congressional Procedures and the Policy Process*, 11th ed. (Sage/CQ Press, 2019).

Palermo, Francesco and Kössler, Karl, *Comparative Federalism: Constitutional Arrangements and Case Law* (Hart, 2017).

Palmeri, Tara, "The Most Exclusive Dining Club in Brussels: *Inside the G5 Where* 'the Best Jokes Are Told' and Major EU Policies are Pre-cooked," *Politico*, 18 June 2015.

Panning, Lara, "Building and Managing the European Commission's Position for Trilogue Negotiations" (2021) 28 *Journal of European Public Policy* 32.

Pannes, Anna-Tina, *Informalität: Theoretische und empirische Dimensionen informeller Entscheidungsprozesse in Regierungsformationen: Ein Analyseansatz* (Springer, 2015).

Pasetti-Bombardella, Francesco, "La controversia fra il Consiglio e il Parlamento europeo sul bilancio generale 1986" (1986) *Rivista di diritto europeo* 207.

Pasetti-Bombardella, Francesco, "Le Parlement face au Conseil," in Jean-Victor Louis and Denis Waelbroeck (eds.), *Le Parlement européen dans l'évolution institutionnelle*, 2nd ed. (Editions de l'Université de Bruxelles, 1989).

Patrin, Maria, *Collegiality in the European Commission: Legal Substance and Institutional Practice* (Oxford University Press, 2023).

Patzelt, Werner J., "Minderheitsregierung? Warum eigentlich nicht!," *Frankfurter Allgemeine Zeitung*, 9 December 2019.

Pauwelyn, Joost, Wessel, Ramses A. and Wouters, Jan, "Informal International Lawmaking: An Assessment and Template to Keep It both Effective and Accountable," in Joost Pauwelyn, Ramses A. Wessel and Jan Wouters (eds.), *Informal International Lawmaking* (Oxford University Press, 2012).

Pennera, Christian and Schoo, Johann, "La Codécision – Dix ans d'application" (2004) 40 *Cahiers de droit européen* 531.

Persily, Nathaniel, "Stronger Parties as a Solution to Polarization," in Nathaniel Persily (ed.), *Solutions to Political Polarization in America* (Cambridge University Press, 2015).

Pescatore, Pierre, "Some Critical Remarks on the 'Single European Act'" (1987) 24 *Common Market Law Review* 9.

Peters, B. Guy, "Coordination in the EU," in Erik Jones, Anand Menon and Stephen Weatherill (eds.), *The Oxford Handbook of the European Union* (Oxford University Press, 2012).

Pierson, Paul, *Politics in Time: History, Institutions, and Social Analysis* (Princeton University Press, 2004).

Pircher, Brigitte and Farjam, Mike, "Oppositional Voting in the Council of the EU between 2010 and 2019: Evidence for Differentiated Politicisation" (2021) 22 *European Union Politics* 472.

Pizzolato, Filippo, "Rappresentenza politica e Unione europea" (2013) 23 *Rivista italiana di diritto pubblico comunitario* 371.

P.K., "On Transparency – but Do Not Mention Brexit!" (2019) 44 *European Law Review* 587.

Ponzano, Paolo, "Il voto nel Consiglio: il compromesso di Ioannina alla luce del Trattato di Lisbona" (2009) *Il Diritto dell'Unione Europea* 77.

Pozen, David E., "Transparency's Ideological Drift" (2018) 128 *Yale Law Journal* 100.

Puetter, Uwe, *The European Council and the Council: New Intergovernmentalism and Institutional Change* (Oxford University Press, 2014).

Putnam, Robert D., "Diplomacy and Domestic Politics: The Logic of Two-Level Games" (1988) 42 *International Organization* 427.

Putnam, Robert D., *Making Democracy Work: Civic Traditions in Modern Italy* (Princeton University Press, 1993).

Rasmussen, Anne, "Early Conclusion in Bicameral Bargaining: Evidence from the Co-decision Legislative Procedure of the European Union" (2010) 12 *European Union Politics* 41.

Rebasti, Emanuele, "The Legal Regime Applicable to the Council Presidency: Competing Conceptual Approaches and Pragmatic Solutions," in Ramona Coman and Vivien Sierens (eds.), *EU Council Presidencies in Times of Crises* (Palgrave Macmillan, 2024).

Reh, Christine, "European Integration as Compromise: Recognition, Concessions and the Limits of Cooperation" (2012) 47 *Government and Opposition* 414.

Reh, Christine, "Is Informal Politics Undemocratic? Trilogues, Early Agreements and the Selection Model of Representation" (2014) 21 *Journal of European Public Policy* 822.

Reh, Christine, Héritier, Adrienne, Bressanelli, Edoardo and Koop, Christel, "The Informal Politics of Legislation: Explaining Secluded Decision Making in the European Union" (2011) 49 *Comparative Political Studies* 1112.

Renzsch, Wolfgang, "Deutschland, einig Bundesstaat?," *Frankfurter Allgemeine Zeitung*, 9 March 2020.

Rintala, Marvin, "The Two Faces of Compromise" (1969) 22 *Western Political Quarterly* 326.

Ripoll Servent, Ariadna and Panning, Lara, "Eurosceptics in Trilogue Settings: Interest Formation and Contestation in the European Parliament" (2019) 42 *West European Poltics* 755.

Ritleng, Dominique, "Does the European Court of Justice Take Democracy Seriously? Some Thoughts about the *Macro-Financial Assistance* Case" (2016) 53 *Common Market Law Review* 11.

Robinson, Mary T. W., "The Political Implications of the Vedel Report" (1972) 7 *Government and Opposition* 426.

Roederer-Rynning, Christilla and Greenwood, Justin, "Black Boxes and Open Secrets: Trilogues as 'Politicised Diplomacy'" (2021) 44 *West European Politics* 485.

Roger, Charles B., *The Origins of Informality: Why the Legal Foundations of Global Governance Are Shifting, and Why It Matters* (Oxford University Press, 2020).

Roger, Léa, *Voice(s) in the European Parliament: Deliberation and Negotiation in EP Committees* (Nomos, 2016).

Romano, Santi, "Diritto e corretta costituzionale," in *Scritti minori* (Giuffrè, 1950).

Romano, Santi, "Lo Stato moderno e la sua crisi," in *Scritti minori* (Giuffrè, 1950).

Romano, Santi, *L'ordinamento giuridico*, 2nd ed. (Sansoni, 1951).

Romano, Santi, *The Legal Order* (Routledge, 2017).

Roos, Mechthild and Neuhold, Christine, "Studying the Informal in European Integration: A Research Guide," in Lennaert van Heumen and Mechthild Roos (eds.), *The Informal Construction of Europe* (Routledge, 2019).

Roos, Mechthild and van Heumen, Lennaert, "Introduction," in Lennaert van Heumen and Mechthild Roos (eds.), *The Informal Construction of Europe* (Routledge, 2019).

Rosanvallon, Pierre, "The Transformation of Democracy and the Future of Europe," in *Democracy Past and Future* (Columbia University Press, 2006).

Rosanvallon, Pierre, *Democratic Legitimacy: Impartiality, Reflexivity, Proximity* (Princeton University Press, 2011).

Rossi, Lucia Serena, "The Principle of Equality among Member States of the European Union," in Lucia Serena Rossi and Federico Casolari (eds.), *The Principle of Equality in EU Law* (Springer, 2017).

Rostbøll, Christian F., "Democratic Respect and Compromise" (2017) 20 *Critical Review of International Social and Political Philosophy* 619.

Rouméas, Élise, "The Procedural Value of Compromise" (2021) 47 *Social Theory and Practice* 377.

Rozenberg, Olivier, "The Council of the EU: from the Congress of Ambassadors to a genuine Parliamentary Chamber?," PE 608.855, January 2019.

Rudzio, Wolfgang, *Das politische System der Bundesrepublik Deutschland*, 9th ed. (Springer, 2015).

Ruffert, Matthias, "Entformalisierung und Entparlamentarisierung politischer Entscheidungen als Gefährdungen der Verfassung?" (2002) 117 *Deutsches Verwaltungsblatt* 1145.

Ruffert, Matthias, "The Many Faces of Rule-Making in the EU," in Elaine Fahey (ed.), *The Actors of Postnational Rule-Making: Contemporary Challenges of European and International Law* (Routledge, 2016).

Rugge, Giacomo, "Trilogues and Access to Documents: *De Capitani* v. *Parliament*" (2019) 56 *Common Market Law Review* 237.

Rugge, Giacomo, "The Euro Group's Informality and *locus standi* before the European Court of Justice: *Council v. K. Chrysostomides & Co. and Others*" (2021) 81 *Heidelberg Journal of International Law* 917.

Rybicki, Elizabeth, "Amendments between the Houses: Procedural Options and Effects," CRS Report R41003, 14 March 2022.

Saalfeld, Thomas, "Germany: Stable Parties, Chancellor Democracy, and the Art of Informal Settlement," in Wolfgang C. Müller and Kaare Strøm (eds.), *Coalition Governments in Western Europe* (Oxford University Press, 2000).

Sadurski, Wojciech, "Legitimacy, Political Equality, and Majority Rule" (2008) 21 *Ratio Juris* 39.

Sandulli, Aldo, *Il ruolo del diritto in Europa: L'integrazione europea dalla prospettiva del diritto amministrativo* (FrancoAngeli, 2018).

Sartori, Giovanni, "Will Democracy Kill Democracy? Decision-Making by Majorities and by Committees" (1975) 10 *Government and Opposition* 131.

Schaffner, Brian F., "Party Polarization," in George C. Edwards III, Frances E. Lee and Eric Schickler (eds.), *The Oxford Handbook of the American Congress* (Oxford University Press, 2011).

Scharpf, Fritz W., "The Joint-Decision Trap: Lessons from German Federalism and European Integration" (1988) 66 *Public Administration* 323.

Scharpf, Fritz W., "Einführung: Zur Theorie von Verhandlungssystemen," in Arthur Benz, Fritz W. Scharpf and Reinhard Zintl (eds.), *Horizontale Politikverflechtung: Zur Theorie von Verhandlungssystemen* (Campus Verlag, 1992).

Schmidt, Manfred G., *Political Institutions in the Federal Republic of Germany* (Oxford University Press, 2003).

Schmidt, Manfred G., *Demokratietheorien: Eine Einführung*, 6th ed. (Springer, 2019).

Schmidt, Vivien A., "Democracy and Legitimacy in the European Union Revisited: Input, Output and 'Throughput'" (2013) 61 *Political Studies* 2.

Schmidt, Vivien A., "Politicization in the EU: Between National Politics and EU Political Dynamics" (2019) 26 *Journal of European Public Policy* 1018.

Schoch, Friederich, "Entformalisierung staatlichen Handelns," in Josef Isensee and Paul Kirchhof (eds.), *Handbuch des Staatsrechts*, 3rd ed. (C. F. Müller, 2005).

Schönberger, Christoph, "Das Parlament: Geschichte einer europäischen Erfindung," in Martin Morlok, Ute Schliesky and Dieter Wiefelspütz (eds.), *Parlamentsrecht: Handbuch* (Nomos, 2016).

Schoo, Johann and Görlitz, Niklas, "Artikel 15 AEUV [Grundsatz der Offenheit]," in Jürgen Schwarze (ed.), *EU-Kommentar*, 3rd ed. (Nomos, 2012).

Schoo, Johann and Görlitz, Niklas, "Artikel 295 AEUV [Interinstitutionelle Vereinbarungen]," in Jürgen Schwarze (ed.), *EU-Kommentar*, 3rd ed. (Nomos, 2012).

Schuett-Wetschky, Eberhard, "Auswanderung der Politik aus den Institutionen: Schwächung der Demokratie? Zur Legitimation der Parteiendemokratie" (2001) 11 *Zeitschrift für Politikwissenschaft* 3.

Schuett-Wetschky, Eberhard, "Regierung, Parlament oder Parteien: Wer entscheidet, wer beschließt?" (2005) 36 *Zeitschrift für Parlamentsfragen* 489.

Schulze-Fielitz, Helmut, "Der politische Kompromiß als Chance und Gefahr für die Rationalität der Gesetzgebung," in Dieter Grimm and Werner Maihofer (eds.), *Gesetzgebungstheorie und Rechtspolitik* (Springer, 1988).

Schulze-Fielitz, Helmut, "Das Verhältnis von formaler und informaler Verfassung," in Alex Görlitz and Hans-Peter Burth (eds.), *Informale Verfassung* (Nomos, 1998).

Schulze-Fielitz, Helmut, "Konstitutionalisierung der Informalität? Nutzen und Grenzen einer Nachführung des Verfassungsrechts an informale Prozesse der Entscheidungsfindung," in Julian Krüper, Heike Merten and Martin Morlok (eds.), *An den Grenzen der Rechtsdogmatik* (Mohr Siebeck, 2010).

Schürmann, Thomas, "Plenardebatte," in Martin Morlok, Ute Schliesky and Dieter Wiefelspütz (eds.), *Parlamentsrecht: Handbuch* (Nomos, 2016).

Scott, W. Richard, *Institutions and Organizations: Ideas, Interests, and Identities*, 4th ed. (Sage, 2014).

Shackleton, Michael, "The Politics of Codecision" (2000) 38 *Journal of Common Market Studies* 325.

Shlaim, Avi, "The Vedel Report and the Reform of the European Parliament" (1973) 27 *Parliamentary Affairs* 159.

Siefken, Sven T., "Regierungsbildung 'wider Willen' – der mühsame Weg zur Koalition nach der Bundestagswahl 2017" (2018) 49 *Zeitschrift für Parlamentsfragen* 407.

Simmel, Georg, *Soziologie* (Duncker & Humblot, 1908).

Sipala, Floriana, "La vie démocratique de l'Union," in Giuliano Amato, Hervé Bribosia and Bruno De Witte (eds.), *Genèse et destinée de la Constitution européenne/Genesis and destiny of the European Constitution* (Bruylant, 2007).

Smith, Steven S., Roberts, Jason M. and Vander Wielen, Ryan J., *The American Congress*, 9th ed. (Cambridge University Press, 2015).

Stacey, Jeffrey, *Integrating Europe: Informal Politics and Institutional Change* (Oxford University Press, 2010).

Starski, Paulina, "Die 'Große Koalition' als Problem des Verfassungsrechts: Recht auf effektive Opposition vs. Gleichheit der Abgeordneten" (2016) 69 *Die Öffentliche Verwaltung* 750.

Stasavage, David, "Open-Door or Closed-Door? Transparency in Domestic and International Bargaining" (2004) 58 *International Organization* 667.

Steffani, Winfried, *Parlamentarische und präsidentielle Demokratie: Strukturelle Aspekte westlicher Demokratien* (Springer, 1979).

Strahan, Randall W., "Party Leadership," in George C. Edwards III, Frances E. Lee and Eric Schickler (eds.), *The Oxford Handbook of the American Congress* (Oxford University Press, 2011).

Stüwe, Klaus, "Der Bundesrat in Zeiten Großer Koalitionen" (2008) *Aus Politik und Zeitgeschichte* 24.

Sunstein, Cass R., "Foreword: Leaving Things Undecided" (1996) 110 *Harvard Law Review* 4.

Tanenhaus, Sam, "The Power of Congress: Before L.B.J., Progressives Saw Bipartisanship as a Blight. What Happened?," *The New Yorker*, 12 January 2015.

Taylor, Miles, "Introduction," in Walter Bagehot, *The English Constitution* (Oxford University Press, 2009).

Telò, Mario, "Three European Constitutionalisms and Their Respective Legitimacy Requirements: Explaining the *longue durée* Stability of the EU Polity," in Sonia Lucarelli, Furio Cerutti and Vivien A. Schmidt (eds.), *Debating Political Identity and Legitimacy in the European Union* (Routledge, 2011).

Thirlway, Hugh, "Compromis," in Rüdiger Wolfrum (ed.), *The Max Planck Encyclopedia of Public International Law* (Oxford University Press, 2012).

Toope, Stephen J., "Formality and Informality," in Daniel Bodansky, Jutta Brunnée and Ellen Hey (eds.), *The Oxford Handbook of International Environmental Law* (Oxford University Press, 2008).

Tsebelis, George, *Veto Players: How Political Institutions Work* (Sage/Princeton University Press, 2002).

Urbinati, Nadia, "Representative Democracy and Its Critics," in Sonia Alonso, John Keane and Wolfgang Merkel (eds.), *The Future of Representative Democracy* (Cambridge University Press, 2018).

Urfalino, Philippe, "La décision par consensus apparent. Nature et propriétés" (2007) 45 *Revue européenne des sciences sociales* 47.

van Middelaar, Luuk, *Alarums & Excursions: Improvising Politics on the European Stage* (Agenda Publishing, 2019).

Van Parijs, Philippe, "What Makes a Good Compromise?" (2012) 47 *Government and Opposition* 466.

van Tatenhove, Jan, Mak, Jeannette and Liefferink, Duncan, "The Inter-play between Formal and Informal Practices" (2006) 7 *Perspectives on European Politics and Society* 8.

Vasilev, George, "The Uneasy Alliance between Consensus and Democracy" (2015) 77 *Review of Politics* 73.

Vauchez, Antoine, *Brokering Europe: Euro-Lawyers and the Making of a Transnational Polity* (Cambridge University Press, 2015).

Vauchez, Antoine, *Democratizing Europe* (Palgrave Macmillan, 2016).

Vermeule, Adrian, *Mechanisms of Democracy: Institutional Design Writ Small* (Oxford University Press, 2007).

von Achenbach, Jelena, *Demokratische Gesetzgebung in der Europäischen Union: Theorie und Praxis der dualen Legitimationsstruktur europäischer Hoheitsgewalt* (Springer, 2014).

von Achenbach, Jelena, "Verfassungswandel durch Selbstorganisation: Triloge im europäischen Gesetzgebungsverfahren" (2016) 55 *Der Staat* 1.

von Achenbach, Jelena, "Transparenz statt Öffentlichkeit und demokratischer Repräsentation: Aktuelle Entwicklungen des Verhandelns in Trilogen im EU-Gesetzgebungsverfahren" (2018) *Die Öffentliche Verwaltung* 1025.

von Alemann, Florian, *Die Handlungsform der interinstitutionellen Vereinbarung: Eine Untersuchung des Interorgansverhältnisses der europäischen Verfassung* (Springer, 2006).

von Beyme, Klaus, *Der Gesetzgeber: Der Bundestag als Entscheidungszentrum* (Westdeutscher Verlag, 1997).

von Bogdandy, Armin, *Gubernative Rechtsetzung: Eine Neubestimmung der Rechtsetzung und des Regierungssystems unter dem Grundgesetz in der Perspektive gemeineuropäischer Dogmatik* (Mohr Siebeck, 2000).

von Bogdandy, Armin, "Parlamentarismus in Europa: eine Verfalls- oder Erfolgsgeschichte?" (2005) 130 *Archiv des öffentlichen Rechts* 445.

von Bogdandy, Armin, "Founding Principles," in Armin von Bogdandy and Jürgen Bast (eds.), *Principles of European Constitutional Law*, 2nd ed. (Hart/C. H. Beck/ Nomos, 2011).

von Bogdandy, Armin, "The European Lesson for International Democracy: The Significance of Articles 9–12 EU Treaty for International Organizations" (2012) 23 *European Journal of International Law* 315.

von Bogdandy, Armin, *The Emergence of European Society through Public Law: A Hegelian and Anti-Schmittian Approach* (Oxford University Press, 2024).

von Bogdandy, Armin, Bogdanowicz, Piotr, Canor, Iris, Taborowski, Maciej and Schmidt, Matthias, "Guest Editorial: A Potential Constitutional Moment for the European Rule of Law – The Importance of Red Lines" (2018) 55 *Common Market Law Review* 983.

von Münch, Ingo, "Anmerkungen zur Koalitionsdemokratie und ein Plädoyer für die Beendigung des Lagerdenkens" (2015) 46 *Zeitschrift für Parlamentsfragen* 874.

Voßkuhle, Andreas, "Opposition im Europäischen Parlament," in Ulrich Becker and others (eds.), *Verfassung und Verwaltung in Europa: Festschrift für Jürgen Schwarze zum 70. Geburtstag* (Nomos, 2014).

Waldron, Jeremy, *The Dignity of Legislation* (Cambridge University Press, 1999).

Waldron, Jeremy, *Law and Disagreement* (Oxford University Press, 1999).

Weiler, J. H. H., "Parlement européen, integration européenne, démocratie et légitimité," in Jean-Victor Louis and Denis Waelbroeck (eds.), *Le Parlement européen dans l'évolution institutionnelle*, 2nd ed. (Editions de l'Université de Bruxelles, 1989).

Weiler, J. H. H., "European Democracy and Its Critics: Polity and System," in *The Constitution of Europe: "Do the New Clothes Have an Emperor?" and Other Essays on European Integration* (Cambridge University Press, 1999).

Weiler, J. H. H., "In defence of the Status Quo: Europe's Constitutional *Sonderweg*," in J. H. H. Weiler and Marlene Wind (eds.), *European Constitutionalism Beyond the State* (Cambridge University Press, 2003).

Weiler, J. H. H., "The Crumbling of European Democracy," in Mark A. Graber, Sanford Levinson and Mark Tushnet (eds.), *Constitutional Democracy in Crisis?* (Oxford University Press, 2018).

Weinstock, Daniel, "Compromise, Pluralism, and Deliberation" (2017) 20 *Critical Review of International Social and Political Philosophy* 636.

Westlake, Martin, "The Community Express Service: The Rapid Passage of Emergency Legislation on German Unification" (1991) 28 *Common Market Law Review* 599.

Wheare, K. C., "Walter Bagehot" (1974) 40 *Proceedings of the British Academy* 173.

Wieduwilt, Hendrik, "Viele heimliche Gesetzgeber: Für die Flut der Vorschriften sorgt längst nicht mehr nur der Bundestag," *Frankfurter Allgemeine Zeitung*, 28 November 2018.

Wille, Emilio, "The Conciliation Procedure and the European Parliament's Pursuit of Legislation Power" (1984) 49 *Il Politico* 489.

Willemsen, Roger, *Das Hohe Haus: Ein Jahr im Parlament*, 6th ed. (Fischer, 2016).

Williamson, David, "Conciliation Procedure in the European Law-Making Process" (2006) 12 *Journal of Legislative Studies* 1.

Wolak, Jennifer, *Compromise in an Age of Party Polarization* (Oxford University Press, 2020).

Yardley, Jim, "Has Europe Reached the Breaking Point?," *The New York Times Magazine*, 15 December 2015.

Zanetti, Véronique, *Spielarten des Kompromisses* (Suhrkamp, 2022).

Ziller, Jacques, "Sdoppiamento funzionale e trappola della decisione congiunta nell'Unione europea," in Elisabetta Colombo (ed.), *Le istituzioni e le idee. Studi indisciplinati offerti a Fabio Rugge per il suo settantesimo compleanno* (Giuffrè, 2022).

Ziller, Jacques, *Advanced Introduction to European Union Law* (Edward Elgar, 2020).

Zürn, Michael, "Democratic Governance beyond the Nation-State: The EU and Other International Institutions" (2000) 6 *European Journal of International Relations* 183.

Index

Books in the Series

The European Union, Emerging Global Business and Human Rights
Aleydis Nissen

The European Central Bank and the European Macroeconomic Constitution
Klaus Tuori

The Procedural and Organisational Law of the European Court of Justice: An Incomplete Transformation
Christoph Krenn

The New Economic Governance of the Eurozone: A Rule of Law Analysis
Paul Dermine

Digital Constitutionalism in Europe: Reframing Rights and Powers in the Algorithmic Society
Giovanni De Gregorio

Can the European Court of Human Rights Shape European Public Order?
Kanstantsin Dzehtsiarou

The Constitutional Boundaries of European Fiscal Federalism
Brady Gordon

Private Selves: Legal Personhood in European Privacy Protection
Susanna Lindroos-Hovinheimo

Fissures in EU Citizenship: The Deconstruction and Reconstruction of the Legal Evolution of EU Citizenship
Martin Steinfeld

The Boundaries of the EU Internal Market: Participation without Membership
Marja-Liisa Öberg

The Currency of Solidarity: Constitutional Transformation during the Euro Crisis
Vestert Borger

Empire of Law: Nazi Germany, Exile Scholars and the Battle for the Future of Europe
Kaius Tuori

In the Court We Trust: Cooperation, Coordination and Collaboration between the ECJ and Supreme Administrative Courts
Rob van Gestel and Jurgen de Poorter

Beyond Minimum Harmonisation: Gold-Plating and Green-Plating of European Environmental Law
Lorenzo Squintani

The Court of Justice of the European Union as an Institutional Actor: Judicial Lawmaking and its Limits
Thomas Horsley

The Politics of Justice in European Private Law: Social Justice, Access Justice, Societal Justice
Hans-W Micklitz

The Transformation of EU Treaty Making: The Rise of Parliaments, Referendums and Courts Since 1950
Dermot Hodson and Imelda Maher

Redefining European Economic Integration
Dariusz Adamski

Human Rights in the Council of Europe and the European Union: Achievements, Trends and Challenges
Steven Greer, Janneke Gerards and Rosie Slowe

Core Socio-Economic Rights and the European Court of Human Rights
Ingrid Leijten

Green Trade and Fair Trade in and with the EU: Process-based Measures within the EU Legal Order
Laurens Ankersmit

New Labour Laws in Old Member States: Trade Union Responses to European Enlargement
Rebecca Zahn

The Governance of EU Fundamental Rights
Mark Dawson

The International Responsibility of the European Union: From Competence to Normative Control
Andrés Delgado Casteleiro

Frontex and Non-Refoulement: The International Responsibility of the EU
Roberta Mungianu

Gendering European Working Time Regimes: The Working Time Directive and the Case of Poland
Ania Zbyszewska

EU Renewable Electricity Law and Policy: From National Targets to a Common Market
Tim Maxian Rusche

European Constitutionalism
Kaarlo Tuori

Brokering Europe: Euro-Lawyers and the Making of a Transnational Polity
Antoine Vauchez

Services Liberalization in the EU and the WTO: Concepts, Standards and Regulatory Approaches
Marcus Klamert

Referendums and the European Union: A Comparative Enquiry
Fernando Mendez, Mario Mendez and Vasiliki Triga

The Allocation of Regulatory Competence in the EU Emissions Trading Scheme
Jospehine van Zeben

The Eurozone Crisis: A Constitutional Analysis
Kaarlo Tuori and Klaus Tuori

International Trade Disputes and EU Liability
Anne Thies

The Limits of Legal Reasoning and the European Court of Justice
Gerard Conway

New Governance and the Transformation of European Law: Coordinating EU Social Law and Policy
Mark Dawson

The Lisbon Treaty: A Legal and Political Analysis
Jean-Claude Piris

The European Union's Fight Against Corruption: The Evolving Policy Towards Member States and Candidate Countries
Patrycja Szarek-Mason

The Ethos of Europe: Values, Law and Justice in the EU
Andrew Williams

State and Market in European Union Law: The Public and Private Spheres of the Internal Market before the EU Courts
Wolf Sauter and Harm Schepel

The European Civil Code: The Way Forward
Hugh Collins

Ethical Dimensions of the Foreign Policy of the European Union: A Legal Appraisal
Urfan Khaliq

Implementing EU Pollution Control: Law and Integration
Bettina Lange

European Broadcasting Law and Policy
Jackie Harrison and Lorna Woods

The Transformation of Citizenship in the European Union: Electoral Rights and the Restructuring of Political Space
Jo Shaw

The Constitution for Europe: A Legal Analysis
Jean-Claude Piris

The European Convention on Human Rights: Achievements, Problems and Prospects
Steven Greer

Social Rights and Market Freedom in the European Constitution: A Labour Law Perspective
Stefano Giubboni

EU Enlargement and the Constitutions of Central and Eastern Europe
Anneli Albi

For EU product safety concerns, contact us at Calle de José Abascal, 56–1°, 28003 Madrid, Spain or eugpsr@cambridge.org.

www.ingramcontent.com/pod-product-compliance
Lightning Source LLC
LaVergne TN
LVHW011812200926
848484LV00005B/1160
* 9 7 8 1 0 0 9 4 4 5 2 0 7 *